Gender, Art and Death

Gender, Art and Death

Janet Todd

CONTINUUM • NEW YORK

1993
The Continuum Publishing Company
370 Lexington Avenue
New York, NY 10017

Printed in Great Britain

Library of Congress Cataloging-in-Publication Data

Todd, Janet M., 1942–
    Gender, art and death / Janet Todd.
        p.   cm.
    Includes bibliographical references.
    ISBN 0–8264–0598–3
    1. English literature—Women authors—History and criticism.
2. Women and literature—Great Britain.   3. Sex role in literature.
4. Death in literature.   I. Title.
PR119.T63   1993
820.9′9287—dc20   93–7944
                                                                CIP

Contents

Acknowledgements

I should like to thank the *British Journal of Eighteenth Century Studies* for permission to reprint '*Pamela*: or the bliss of servitude'; *Studies on Voltaire and the Eighteenth Century* for 'Marketing the self: Mary Carleton, Miss F and Susannah Gunning'; and Harvester-Wheatsheaf for 'Jane Austen, politics and sensibility', from *Feminist Criticism: theory and practice*, ed. Susan Sellers. 'Who's afraid of Jane Austen?' originally appeared in *Jane Austen: new perspectives (Women and Literature*, new series, vol. 3), ed. Janet Todd (New York: Holmes & Meier, 1983), pp. 107–27, and is reprinted by permission of the publisher.

Introduction: memory and women's studies

In 1971 when teaching in Florida I began the *Mary Wollstonecraft Newsletter* to write about women of the 1970s. It was a time when Wollstonecraft was hardly known and when many considered such female and polemical figures unacceptable as topics of serious research. Outside the confines of counter-academic newsletters it was still difficult to make comment on Helen Maria Williams except as a footnote to Wordsworth or on Mary Hays beyond a 'thing ugly and petticoated'. Alistair Cooke, the presenter of heritage Britain to America through the series 'Masterpiece Theatre', could not tell the Marys Shelley and Wollstonecraft apart, and both were known mainly for helping Percy create *Frankenstein*. It would be some time before women scholars had to worry about constructing a prescriptive alternative canon or establishing totalizing laws for the interpretation of female authors.

It was not mere prejudice that prevented literary criticism. Before the 'death' of the author and his or her 'evacuation' from the text, comment required a certain familiarity with the writer in the reader of the criticism. Hence inevitably those few interested in the work of early women were forced into some biography. This biographical interest differed from traditional biographical-literary interest since the latter was usually dependent on an already existing literary reputation of an author; the new feminist biography desired to make reputation and present a subject both as an achiever in a conventional way and as a voice of an alternative message. There was a good deal of identification and much searching for parallels as a generation sought validation for the present through turning the past into its predecessor. Inevitably Mary Wollstonecraft, who had the marketing awareness to call her work *A Vindication of the Rights of Woman* instead of *Letters on Education*, was rediscovered.

I have recently been to a museum of labour in my present home town of Norwich, where I noted many of the items familiar to me from a kitchen I inhabited as a child in Wales. What do I see when I look at them in the museum? What does a person of twenty or thirty see, one who is unlikely ever to have cleaned the range or turned the mangle? There is, I suspect, sentimentality for both groups inherent in the uncontextualizing of the item – the one with the now overlaid memory risks the indulgence of heritage, momentarily licensed to bore others with a newly sanctioned, untheorized reminiscence; the other can be triggered to speak generally, with the security of a prepackaged and inexperienced opinion, of the place of woman in an alien economy of an alien household. Both responses are oddly embarrassing: distant cultural memory irritates those who have placed it; the condescending generalization irritates those for whom memory appears if not truth, then at least the truth effect. It is impossible to look at the 1970s biographies of Mary Wollstonecraft without the embarrassment of past use or present abuse.

By 1976, my own *Mary Wollstonecraft Newsletter* had metamorphosed into *Women & Literature* and was much overshadowed by a new generation of more academically acceptable and sponsored periodicals. So for volume 1 of the new *Signs* I was asked to write a review article of the biographies of Mary Wollstonecraft, the clustering of which had been a phenomenon of the early 1970s. I could not yet assume knowledge of her now utterly familiar life and I told it with the enthusiasm and seriousness that marked the not-so-new convert. I took my information mainly from Godwin's *Memoirs of the Author of A Vindication of the Rights of Woman*, the extraordinary inappropriateness of which in 1798 I was certainly not prepared to admit when the popular psychology of the 1970s urged self-expression and a burning of physical or rhetorical masks; nor was I briefed to see the gender appropriation in the work when subterfuges and strategies had not yet become the clichés of criticism.

It is easy to look back and see the fashioning of image. In the 1970s I could regard with some amusement Emma Rauschenbusch-Clough summarizing the subject of her 1898 biography: 'The vindicator of the rights of her sex is not known to have betrayed a woman during the whole course of her sad, eventful life. She disdained to tamper with the affections of any man' – clearly this is not a biography needing reprinting in a 'post-feminist' decade. I was equally amused at G. R. Stirling Taylor's 1911 image: 'Mary Wollstonecraft plunged deeply into that sea of primeval emotion and desire which flows and rages for ever at the base of every one of the little lighthouses of passing social theory.' But now the 1970 biographies also clearly reveal their stylistic date; in America Eleanor Flexner's *Mary Woll-stonecraft*, for example, was typical in its lack of interest in intellectual trends in the formation of its subject's ideas, in its seriousness, and in its approval of its subject; in Britain Claire Tomalin's *Life and Death of Mary Wollstonecraft* was more flippant but equally sure of singular identity and peculiar female subjectivity. Rooted at the time in America, I was clearly irritated not by Tomalin's discursive and metaphysical naïvety but with her failure of tact when she described her subject as a woman of 'imperfect heroism' in language I labelled excessive and crass. I took her to task for various errors which she would not have fallen into had she been reading the little feminist magazines in which we fans of Mary Wollstonecraft were placing our supportive and empirical scholarship.

But, despite what I saw as factual errors and lapses of taste, I appreciated Tomalin's biography and was affronted to read the review of the Oxford historian Richard Cobb in the *Times Literary Supplement* for 6 September 1974, in which he called Wollstonecraft silly, egotistical, envious, rancorous and meddlesome and her works mediocre and ill written. Having just completed the first full-length bibliography of Mary Wollstonecraft, I was peculiarly familiar with the tradition of abuse stemming from the Reverend Richard Pol-whele's *The Unsex'd Females* in 1798 (which lubriciously associated Wollstonecraft with the new botany and a vision of young girls dissecting vegetable 'organ[s] of unhallow'd lust'), travelling through the *Anti-Jacobin* review (which had the hopelessly monogamous Wollstonecraft lending herself 'to half the town'), to Ferdinand Lundberg and Marynia L. Farnham's *Modern Woman: The Lost Sex* (which reduced Wollstonecraft and her oeuvre to a case of penis envy over which lay 'the shadow of the phallus . . . darkly, threat-eningly' and her reputation to the poisoned source of later feminism). Full of righteous information, I wrote an answer to Cobb called 'The Polwhelean Tradition and Richard Cobb'.

In an American context of spirited feminism, I had assumed by 1974 that the overt defamatory tradition was extinct: so, as I wrote, 'it was with something akin to a naturalist's wonder before a live dodo' that I reviewed Cobb's opinion. Now that a couple of decades have gone by and I too find myself irked at being corrected out of a lifelong 'Fanny Burney' into 'Frances' or out of providing their titles to aristocratic women such as the Duchess of Newcastle and the Countess of Winchilsea, I am a little more sympathetic to older critics who cannot avoid calling women authors by their first names, however sternly I took the habit to task in the 1970s: 'Mary was always silly' wrote Cobb in that sophisticated-familiar-coterie tone I did not then associate with the *Times Literary Supplement* – though even at that distant time I did note the existence of Cobb in Tomalin's acknowledgements. My review was overkill; a more subtle English reader answered the jauntiness by pointing out that on the night of her attempted suicide Wollstonecraft did *not* follow the course of the boat race, as Cobb had declared.

A decade on and Mary Wollstonecraft was widely known; many of her early enthusiasts had either moved sideways into 'French' feminism or versions of feminist theory privileging discourse, or they had shifted into opposing the academic intellectual process in its entirety. The first group inevitably found biographical scholarship of the undeconstructed sort hopelessly old-fashioned, while the opposers tended to sneer at any academic feminism: I remember giving lectures on Wollstonecraft in the late 1970s and early 1980s that were on the one hand blamed for any criticism of a figure who had become an icon and on the other for not discussing the gendered pen and constructed authority rather than the woman author, omitting proper articulation of the newly fashionable dichotomy: public and private. By now Wollstonecraft was well enough known for specific and detailed comment to be made on her most famous works. Biographies trailed off.

At this point a figure who let far less dangle out in a 1970s way and was far more secretive came into partial view: Aphra Behn. Despite her reputation for having led a licentious life, she could not easily be brought into the libertarian philosophies of the 1960s since even a cursory glance at her work revealed a support for royalist absolutism and a commitment to social hierarchy. Consequently she did not inspire the early feminist biographical enthusiasm which Mary Wollstonecraft had received. Her work, not falling into the autobiographical and polemical pattern of Wollstonecraft's, was also against her and only when race became a far more important issue for general critics in the late 1980s, so catapulting her short political fiction *Oroonoko* to fame, did she inspire much critical comment.

As women writers changed from being women authors into producers of discursive strategies, and as writing turned from being self-expression into performative act, it was clear that Behn was poised to make it into feminist fashion, to become the star (in the rarefied firmament of early modern women's scholarship) of the 1980s, as Wollstonecraft of the 1970s. By now even vulgar feminists were wise to strategies and the involuntary investment of the critic's self in criticism. Construction had been followed by reconstruction

and deconstruction; psychoanalysis of the text followed psychologiz-
ing of the author, and the discursive took over from the textual which
had annihilated the literary.

But Aphra Behn had a slow start. Exactly a decade after my
founding the *Mary Wollstonecraft Newsletter* I was asked to review
Reconstructing Aphra, which came out in 1980. Clearly I was aware of
change, but not more than was proper in suburban New Jersey
where I then lived; so I faced the flamboyant packaging of Angeline
Goreau's book with the uneasiness of a devotee of the historical
footnote. As a reviewer, I received from the publisher a card listing
Behn's accomplishments, a picture of the buxom Aphra, seductively
complemented by the larger coquettish picture of the author herself.
Though censorious I managed to find 'the narcissism . . . overt and
appealing', it seems, and I looked forward to the reconstruction of
Aphra and the deconstruction of Angeline, as more or less promised.
The performance as usual was duller than the promise, but at this
distance what amuses me is my own bemused reaction to the
marketing of an image: what I was seeing was of course the future –
a feminist message packaged by post-feminism.

Nonetheless the substance was of its age. Aphra Behn was the
everywoman for our time: 'Her autobiography is ours', wrote
Goreau. Inevitably, since little is clear in the life of Behn, much of
what Goreau wrote was in the subjunctive, the treatment was high
romance.

Yet Behn's strength in critical fashion lay not in her apititude for
biography but in her apparent refusal. At the moment biography
(except in the mythical financial rewards it is said occasionally to
achieve) is not well respected in fashionable academic circles. It may
próvide material for a study of genre but it itself is rarely practised by
the ambitious young Cultural Materialist or New Historicist intending
to make a mark on the academy. Indeed a thoroughgoing New
Historicist biography would be an extraordinary thing, encoding the
subject within the totalizing strategies of its meta-discourse. How
would it be written or articulated? How would a life of negotiated
speaking be constructed? How tell the story of theatrical role and
masquerade? How represent the self in the language of the modern?
Why, when there is disjunction between the speaking voice and
representation of the self, try to represent the self self-identically at
all? If female signature does not represent female consciousness and
certainly not unconsciousness in the text, then why search for female
signature and why write its life and times? If female univocality is
merely a strategy and there is no identity of authorial voice, what

shall the biographer listen to? If all is reduced to referentiality, exchange commodities and the female body, how tell one reference and one body from another, one biography from another? Does this wonderfully repetitive language avoid the embarrassment a reader would feel if I called Mary Wollstonecraft a sister or reminisced about a mangle? Can one hold to these unimaginative epistemological niceties or will the biographer and the reader, playing of course with the possible fictitiousness of selves, be jointly seduced back by story itself? I suppose one should never worry about narrative losing out. How then if one wished to straddle the historical and New Historical fence might that old-fashioned enterprise of producing a historical continuum of identity be changed? How might one comment on single texts and avoid that now maligned enterprise of making early texts enabling pretexts for a production of modern feminism?

And even if one wished to compromise, to write biographical and historical criticism using the useful insights of New Historicism, one has the problems of one's own rhetoric. What language should be chosen? In an article published in 1983, part of which I used in a book finished in the late 1980s called *The Sign of Angellica*, I wrote that Mary Carleton's texts offered mixed self-projections 'in keeping with other Restoration images created by women, with men in mind'. I used that phraseology because I then (too optimistically) hoped to appeal to a general reader as well as a specialized scholar and because I was signalling my awareness that this was twentieth-century commentary on seventeenth-century material by quoting and reversing a popular, quite obviously sexist advertisement of a few years before. In a recent article, a much younger scholar quoted me and went on to claim that the texts in fact present 'a mutually destabilizing conjunction of distinct personae'. Now is this transformative discourse figuring a new representational regime in criticism? If it is adopted, does the adopter add to the critique of the regime of modernity or extend the regime backwards? In other New Historicist instances is the use of economic and sociological, the terminology of exchange and circulation, a hopeless involvement in a market economy or a proper understanding of present ideology? Are there any cooperations and compromises possible?

Without having the desire or competence to discuss the history of New Historicism or its definitions in detail, as an old critic within literary history in a feminist mode I do, I think, need to consider its uses, knowing that such a statement lays me open to the charge of misunderstanding it entirely. But I do not see that New Historicism need be a total strategy, nor do I think that it threatens the 'quasi-monastic order' of conventional scholars, as H. Aram Veeser argues in the introduction to his volume of essays *The New Historicism*. A monastery is a guardian of discourse and this is surely what New Historicism is likewise; as ism it will take its historical place among other would-be revolutionary systems and can be picked over and fragmented as all have been. Can it then illuminate my interest in the mutual imitation of life and writing about life and the complexity of the intended and unintended allusion? Will it help me avoid the slur of being a mere archivist foolishly grazing in the Public Record Office instead of in the latest collections of coterie academic essays (once the initial anecdote is discovered)? It is back to the mangle, either caught in my memory with its duplicities and inexpressible fullness or contextualized according to an anachronistic aesthetic or, further, juxtaposed with the spinning jenny to destabilize its discourse.

New Historicism is damaging to literary study in its insistence on reading for subversion, its refusal to read for assumed authorial intention and its assumption that a writer's subversiveness consists in a refusal of determined reading. Both Wollstonecraft and Behn write what are not initially and supremely Bakhtinian texts allowing no fixed meaning, whatever we now feel free to do with them; in many of their works they wish to change minds and reinforce opinion, for the idea of politics both imply is less the play of signifiers than the desire to dominate. New Historicism is dangerous when it tends to award ideological gold stars only to that which unsettles what we disapprove, so that Behn has low marks in the category of political indeterminacy and high ones for unsettling gender. It is sometimes irritating in its overuse of its wonderful verbs (my favourite is 'gesturing', which has something of the languid power of the 'motioning' done by sentimental ladies in eighteenth-century novels, but 'evacuate' comes a close second). It is downright offputting when it uses its jargon and sheer difficulty to divide high-flying critics in large lecture halls from hewers of wood and drawers of water in the stacks, and from its frequent assumption that it can live on the hewers' labour. The great trinity of gender, race and class that now so splendidly illuminates texts can also dazzle the reader into seeing no shades and shadows and may become as dogmatically dominating as 'moral seriousness' and 'taste' in the academic church of the 1950s and 1960s.

A reconstruction of the past after some archival study and wide reading over a long period of time has, I like to think, some authority. It is as partial as memory is, but its authority has to be asserted if one is not to be caught entirely in what Aphra Behn called the 'Gingle' of the time.

Yet, inevitably the reconstruction is not disinterested from a present perspective and, if New Historicism helps one to hold a scepticism about goals and to remember that there is no absolute referentiality or objectivity, it is no bad thing.

After a talk on suicide and Mary Wollstonecraft some years ago I was asked if I really thought she had tried to kill herself with such thoughts as I had given her in my paper; the questioner went on to accuse me of having little understanding of real suicide since, if I had, I would have seen the absurdity of my speculations. In the terms of the language I used – of culture's influence on a person or the living of life of and through art – obviously my notion of her construction of herself and her note sounded rather absurd, but not invalid for all that. A language which included 'negotiation', 'erasure', 'discursive scenes' and 'representation' would perhaps avoid this absurd appearance since it would not be so clear that an embarrassing movement had taken place from the construction of literature to the woman who supposedly did jump on a particular night. The question would not have been asked or, I suppose, 'staged' if I had either employed this vocabulary or stayed with my own and used it for criticism only of the fictional Elinor in *The Wanderer*.

Yet of course the questioner is partially right; the 'real' Mary Wollstonecraft no doubt jumped because of hormones, lack of vitamins, the weather, any number of things, and it is true that I do not know what these are and that I cannot know. But they may include the sense of herself as an admiring spectator, some self-dramatizing that makes an unpleasant act possible in the way Godwin and Hume did not consider when they spoke of rational suicide. It is possible, also, to become experiential in anticipation and state that, if I did jump into the Thames, literature would be partly implicated and that there would be some literary self-dramatization in my note.

So New Historicism, mingled as it usually is with Cultural Materialism, is exhilarating in its refusal to allow the description of a single identity in the biographical subject, the creation of the sort of images that the early biographies of both Behn and Wollstonecraft provided, and, when it emphasizes 'negotiation', the reciprocities and exchanges between discourses which empower and change them. When it manages to avoid the overuse of a vocabulary that takes all significance from choice, it draws attention to the choice of events for narration and it insists on the linguistic basis of reality and the cultural production of knowledge – as it seems to me many in the seventeenth and eighteenth centuries did, albeit in different languages. It draws attention again to the fact that material conditions affect representation, although, as with previous isms, it never quite shows how. It has allowed culture and politics to come back together in its obsession with power, and it has suggested the ability of power to absorb its opposition, although this can be too strenuously stated. The contradictions in discourse it stresses initially suggest the difficulty of social change but may possibly enable it a little, improvement being quite difficult to come by through any theory. So perhaps some amount of New Historicism will provide an answer to the problem of how to avoid making one's criticism ahistorically expressive of 1970s sexual politics alone without abandoning them altogether.

But are these the reasons for interest? Perhaps it is really uneasiness, not interest – an uneasiness which in the end simply masks a desire to try to be in fashion. I fear, though, that I will not go beyond everyone's mother in accessorizing my old habits with a few new words. Perhaps it is a replay of that ghastly 1950s femininity that Behn so robustly ignored 300 years earlier and Wollstonecraft so strenuously combatted 150 years ago, a

> permanent exertion and straining of thoughts toward whatever it is these others . . . can be seen to be doing, and will do; a ceaseless straining of antennae toward the signals they broadcast . . . anticipatory intervening, engaging, entering presciently into stifling alliances. . . .[1]

Or is this, too, but the trope of confessional modesty?

For still with all the modernity and post-modernity I fear a residual Leavisism, a concept, however dented, of the Literary, as well as an early 1970s tendency to admire a literary heroine. In both of these Behn and Wollstonecraft are involved. For towards the end of her life Behn saw herself as a serious and, she hoped, long-lasting artist, though in a context in which the arts remained material and political without their post-romantic autonomous world, and she and her age had a tendency to admiration. Wollstonecraft was not so sure of herself as artist, despite seeing value in her own imprecise and self-expressing writing, and she held a curious sense of the aesthetic beyond the political and personal, though shocked to find sublimity 'absolutely immoral' (*The French Revolution*) and artists, 'generally speaking, licentious'. This sense of Art is perhaps a last feminine delusion, an absurd belief in an aspect of essentially masculine culture which should long ago have been abandoned. But gender is flexible and in flux. Perhaps it is still not necessary to collapse the achievements of some, especially newly discovered, women writers into the culture of the many. The author is not necessarily lost in her discursive fields.

The remarks on New Historicism have little to do with what I have done in the following pieces, but any collecting of the past leads to some assessment of that past which in turn affects intentions. Beyond these remarks, this introduction is intended to contextualize my brief, primarily biographical speculations and to explain their different tones through hinting at the various stylistic desires they incorporate.

Janet Todd
Norwich, 1992

Notes

1 Christina Thurmer-Rohr, *Vagabonding*, trans. Lise Weil (Cambridge: Polity Press, 1992), p. 26.

1 Aphra Behn: the 'lewd Widow' and her 'Masculine Part'

Public female writers of the Restoration were obliged to excite and interest an audience with their images. In order to write a woman had to gender the artistic subject and engender art as more 'feminine' wiles than 'masculine' skill and wit. The association of sex and text for a woman problematized art as a form of authority and as a means of creating a culturally privileged artistic self.

Mediated and facilitated by both male and female expectations, the images of women writers ranged from the elaborate and orchestrated secrecy of the poet and playwright Katherine Philips, 'the matchless Orinda', to the display of 'Female Sweetness and a Manly Grace' of the 'ingenious Aphra Behn'.[1] But the most current public image for the female author was created by men: that of whore or slattern. This image came primarily from seventeenth-century satirists, including Robert Gould, the probable composer of the phrase 'lewd Widow' for a character in a play by Aphra Behn; he insisted on pulling the playwright down to the level of the actress and the actress to the prone position of the whore. The image has interestingly reappeared more eulogistically in late twentieth-century New Historical feminist criticism.

I

In June 1669 Dryden put on *Tyrannic Love*, a tragedy with parts in it for every celebrity of the theatre, including Nell Gwyn, Pepys's 'bold merry slut'. At the end of the play she enacted her suicide to the copious tears of the audience. After this fatal fall she was picked up and carried off on a bier. As the bier arrived at the wings, however, she suddenly leapt off it, crying:

Hold, are you mad? you damn'd confounded Dog,
I am to rise, to speak the Epilogue.

After this resurrection she walked to the front of the stage, where
she announced, 'I'le come dance about your Beds at nights.' Here
she alluded to her public reputation as a notorious whore, which the
coterie playhouse audience knew well; the reputation contrasted with
her role in the play as the virtuous Valeria. Nell Gwyn was usually
associated with *comedy* and the audience was aware of this when she
went on to speak these lines:

> . . . I walk because I dye
> Out of my Calling in a Tragedy.
> O Poet, damn'd dull Poet, who could prove
> So senseless! to make *Nelly* dye for Love;
> Nay, what's yet worse, to kill me in the prime
> Of *Easter*-Term, in Tart and Cheese-cake time! . . .[2]

In Aphra Behn's *The City Heiress, or Sir Timothy Treat-all* (1682) the
actress Charlotte Butler, much satirized for lewdness and greed,
acted the role of a virginal heroine who was given her own name,
Charlot; like Nell Gwyn's, Butler's epilogue draws attention to the
woman behind the part and the incongruity of her dramatic role and
personal reputation. In both sets of concluding lines, then, there is
almost no input from the acted character and much from the
glamorous personality acted offstage. As Pepys revealingly remarked
of another work, Shirley's *Hyde Park*, '[It] is but a very moderate play;
only, an excellent Epilogue spoke by Becke Marshall.'[3]

In the epilogues spoken by actresses the tone of tragedy or comedy
might be broken, the poet mocked – even if self-mocked for the
speakers had not usually written the words – the *theatrical* role
declared and the sensual character of the woman acting offstage
suggested. Epilogues thus became a winking at the audience, excluding the playwright from an audience–actor compact. At these
moments the actress was refusing to be content with the playwright's
play to keep disbelief suspended.

Beyond epilogues, both actresses and playwrights kept the line
between stage and street blurred, though they used different means
to do so. In their texts playwrights might describe the actual physical
attributes of the actress they knew would play the role, while
actresses often provided parts of their theatrical costumes themselves
– sometimes these were known to have been received from admirers

and keepers. Men could and did go to the tiring-room to watch actresses dressing, though the King, who had other opportunities of voyeurism, tried to stop the practice for his subjects. In his diatribe against the theatre, *The Play-House. A Satyr* (1689), Robert Gould imagines entry into the tiring-room where the actress who has just inflamed desire by denial – that is by acting on stage rather than in bed – inflames the amorous watcher still further by getting 'wantonly' into her shift. For Gould the actress is the whore and the stage her place of pimping. This simultaneous controlling of the sexuality of the actress's body and the advertising of her physical wares, this self-consciousness of display, meant that, as far as the actress was concerned, a sort of theatrical pornography was of the madam as well as of the whore.

The writer of the first prologue to a play after the Restoration known to include a professional actress on the public stage assumed that men would titter and have some difficulty separating the woman not only from the role she played but also from the basic public-professional role for women: that of prostitute. When the King had broken with the prewar public stage by allowing women habitually to replace the earlier boys, he had followed his act with a royal warrant of 1662 which *insisted* that women play female roles, thus suggesting the ambiguously sexual titillation that moralists had earlier deplored in the male playing of women's parts. He also drew attention to the lewd possibilities of the new mixed companies when he caused his warrant to demand that female roles be 'harmless delights' avoiding the 'prophane, obscene and scurrilous' – a comic demand in the light of Charles's future patronage of the theatres and the use of its ladies for royal service. The assumption that actresses were working whores is caught some years later by the satirist Tom Brown, when he declared

'Tis as hard a matter for a pretty Woman to keep herself honest in a Theatre, as 'tis for an Apothecary to keep his Treacle from the Flies in Hot Weather; for every Libertine in the Audience will be buzzing about her Honey-Pot.

The imagery is characteristic of this sort of comment.[4]

The initial result of woman's arrival was, then, an elaborate resexualizing of the feminine body and its objectification on- and offstage, as well as a fictionalizing of the self presumed to inhabit that body. Much play was made of parts and acts. Clearly the audience was aware of the actress's public personal life and had come to watch a play, an actress and a social celebrity; it had thus come prepared to take some enjoyment from outside the fictional text of the play. In such circumstances the personality of the actor could only intermittently be submerged in the part. It becomes fitting then that in epilogues such as those spoken by Nell Gwyn and Charlotte Butler the actress should spoil one type of pleasure – of representation – to create another – of presentation of her 'self'. When later Jeremy Collier came to attack the wicked Restoration stage, it was the blurring of real and pretended in the use of women in epilogues that he found most disquieting:

> . . . the *Prologues* and *Epilogues* are sometimes Scandalous to the last Degree . . . Now here properly speaking, the *Actors* quit the *Stage*, and remove from Fiction into Life. Here they converse with the *Boxes*, and *Pit*, and address directly to the Audience. . . . Upon such Occasion one would imagine if ever, the Ladies should be used with Respect, and the Measures of Decency observ'd. But here we have Lewdness without Shame or Example: Here the *Poet* exceeds himself. Here are such strains as would turn the Stomach of an ordinardy [*sic*] Debauchee, and be almost nauseous in the *Stews*. And to make it the more agreeable, Women are commonly pick'd out for this service.[5]

If the actress was often assumed to be the prostitute, analogy could be made between the masked actress on stage and the masked woman off, whether whore plying her trade in the galleries and pit or lady in her box – though social lines were not as drawn as this implies.[6] Occasionally a subtle connection may be made, one which may even include the playwright. In Aphra Behn's first performed play, *The Forc'd Marriage* (staged in 1670), the actor speaking the prologue creates the playwright or 'Poetess' as a kind of actress and, pointing to offstage spectator-whores and masked ladies, suggests both as spies or secret agents for the female playwright (and inevitably too for the actress). So a sense of slightly threatening feminine collectivity is created: 'The Poetess too, they say, has Spies abroad.' But the actress who follows the actor to conclude the prologue denies this collectivity and the stratagems it implies; she firmly separates the actress from the whore, the 'Vizard' in the audience, and she reduces women from agents and manipulators to sexualized bodies with amorous power but no threat since these bodies exist only 'to pleasure you'.

Usually, however, the on- and offstage analogy is entirely abusive. Both male and female playwrights accused the audience of imitating the supposed lewd conduct of the actresses, but hypocritically denying it, then blaming the playwright for showing them a mirror of themselves. In fact the verbal bawdry denigrated on the stage in the illuminated theatre, ostensibly by women in the audience, served together with seductive 'modesty' as foreplay to activity in the darkened inns of Paddington – or so playwrights like Behn and Wycherley charged.[7] In *The Play-House. A Satyr*, after a lewd description of the audience as diseased and drunken punks and their customers as voyeurs of the 'proud Mimicks' on the stage, Gould imagines life and theatre coalescing in 'a Play-House Punk in Drink':

> Inspir'd by Lust's Enthusiastick rage,
> She'd prostitute her self ev'n on the Stage,
> Strip naked, and, without a thought of shame,
> Do things Hell's blackest Fiend wou'd blush to name.[8]

Insistently Gould brings the playhouse and the world offstage together, so that the lewd horror allowed in the theatre becomes possible in the larger world of society and the court: "tis the *Stage/* That makes these *Insects* gain upon the Age.'[9] In imagination the final copulation, which in the end makes the lewdness on the stage frustrating and unsatisfying and to which both playwrights and actresses playfully allude, is hideously performed by the punk in public profanation of a private act. Life corrupts art and art corrupts life.

In 'act', whether scandalous or not, it is clear that the actor/actress had the upper hand in the playhouse and that often the playwright was demoted to the level of the butt in the audience. It seemed evident to Gould, therefore, that there should be some bad feeling between playwright and actor, and he charged that the actor kept the playwright poor although the playwright had in fact made the actor rich. He concluded that power had especially shifted towards the actor when the two theatrical companies united in 1682. Characteristically he makes his point by taking his now impotent playwright 'behind the Scenes' into the actors' and actresses' private room to revolt him into judging them 'by the Lump' as 'idle, pimping, spunging Slaves'.[10] When the playwright was female, the comic antagonism of playwright and audience, caught in the epilogue convention of betraying the playwright and in the economic antagonism suggested by Gould, inevitably became part of the sexual antagonism of men and women, in which some of 'the sex' took the treacherous part.

There are elements in Aphra Behn's plays that suggest the female playwright – the placing of an opening exposition in the mouths of women or the frequent reversed scene of the female gaze on the male body. There are also signs of her admiration of particular actresses both as actresses and as seductive and mirroring forms with whom her own stance of feminine adoration, especially of the royal brothers, James and Charles, inevitably link her. She is one of the few writers to dedicate a work to Nell Gwyn, while Elizabeth Barry, the most famous actress of the day, once mistress and acting pupil of the libertine courtier Earl of Rochester, took part in a large number of Behn's plays and is praised by her in the poem 'Our Cabal'. Nonetheless, since the actress is made so often to obliterate the author and the image of the actress as whore is so potent, it seems likely that a female playwright such as Behn would wish for some means of retaliation in the seemingly unequal struggle, as well as having some need of it if she aimed to avoid reduction from 'poetess' to 'punk'. If the actress can disturb representation, so, after all, can the playwright, who can at one time underline, at another undermine, the acting body's inability or readiness to become a vehicle of representation.

Much in Behn's plays concerns theatre, much serving as a kind of meta-criticism and commenting on theatrical business and performance. Occasionally Behn goes further, referring to particular acting moments and dramatizing the actress as actress or as contingent woman. In these cases the actress is presented as immanent and acting in the present, having no claim to the status that lasting and privileged art might convey. In *The Rover*, the verbal and physical wit of the young girl certainly triumphs – though the audience does not stop to wonder at a triumph that means giving her virginal self and her considerable dowry to a much prostituted and penniless man; in other plays, however, the woman might get her man while showing little wit and skill. Sympathetic men such as the Rover himself are also presented with wit, but the sexual difference assures that no man is presented in a play as desirable *without* wit where a woman played by a pretty actress can be so. In such presentations women are reduced to the power of the sexual body; the reduction can be imaged in the bad acting that, in the theatre, conventionally denotes lack of wit and useful self-knowledge.

In her overtly political play the farcial *The Roundheads* (1682), Behn presents a Roundhead wife, Lady Lambert, smitten by one of the sexy cavaliers. She believes that she has enormous social status appreciated by all: 'I thought I'd been so elevated above the common

Crowd, it had been visible to all Eyes who I was.' The man, however, like some of the audience of a sexually alluring actress, sees simply a sexualized body, in this case of an upstart wife. 'A thing just like a Woman', he calls her, and comment is made on her 'ill acted Greatness'.[11] Lady Lambert's notion of the royalty to which she aspires is entirely theatrical; she frequently talks a species of blank verse and gives vent to Shakespearean sentiments on Royalty. She draws attention to acting all the time, either through her assumption of social status, to which she has no right by birth and breeding, or through her pretence of religious piety, of which she has none. That she decides to 'act' publicly suggests already a licentiousness in the sexualized schemes of the theatre and prostitution into which she has entered; that she cannot act credibly and is yet lusted after suggests the real attraction of the lady onstage.

In what is possibly Behn's last play, *The Widow Ranter*, the chaotic state of the mismanaged colony of Virginia where the play is set is symbolized partly in the American women who, like Lady Lambert, put on airs and dress to which they have no social claim. Mrs Flirt declares herself the daughter of a royalist gentleman, when the others know her father to have been a puritan tailor. In the end she captures a pretend parson not through status but copulation, the act itself. There remains no difference between her and the punk in the audience except that her act is not enacted.

II

If the Restoration is the first period in which English women commonly acted on the public stage, it is also the first period in which they entered culture as public women of letters. Clearly the female playwright did not construct herself in a vacuum, since there was, as for the actress, already an outside image of her as whore or slattern. As the puritan William Prynne had attacked the idea of the actress in 1633 as a 'notorious whore', seventy years later the critic Chagrin in the *Comparison between the Two Stages* can exclaim of women writers

> What a Pox have Women to do with the Muses? I grant you the Poets call the Nine Muses by the names of Women, but why so? not because the Sex has anything to do with Poetry, but because in that Sex they're much fitter for prostitutes.[12]

Gould described women writers who

> . . . when their verse did fail
> To get 'em Brandy, Bread and Chease and Ale,
> Their wants by Prostitution were supply'd,
> Shew but a Tester, you might up and ride:
> For *punk* and *Poetess* agree so Pat,
> You cannot well be *This* and not be *That*.[13]

In the 'Description of a Poetess', also probably by Gould, the female author is a tart, by day plying the upper galleries and by night 'ranging to the common stews/ Where she as freely buggers with the Jews.'[14] In *A Journal from Parnassas* a woman playwright has no claim to poetic status since she is basing her claim on her freedom 'of the Pitt', in which, the writer declares, 'each Orange-Wench has an equal right'. The Earl of Rochester calls his fictional authoress a 'tottering barke' in the literary tempests who firmly addresses herself

> Dear Artemiza, poetry's a snare:
> Bedlam has many Mansions: have a Care.
> Your Muse diverts you, makes the Reader sad;
> You Fancy you'r inspir'd, he thinkes you mad . . .
> . . . Whore is scarce a more reproachfull name,
> Then Poetesse.[15]

A woman dramatist might wish to capitalize on this insistent identi- fication and take up the sexual image of poetess-punk. So she might describe herself as a mistress trying to seduce her audience; play- writing would then become part of the repertoire of female charms, a part with staying power since, by refusing fulfilment of desire, it could keep it raised. In this self-imaging, the assocation of whore and actress would inevitably be relevant, for the female playwright was after all a manipulator of whores.

Aphra Behn clearly defined herself as a professional writer and it is fitting that her main identification in her life was as dramatist, since it underscored the theatrical self-displaying aspect of the professional woman writing and negotiating with the paying world. Inevitably perhaps – especially at the start of her career and within the commercial theatre – she *did* need to create a sexualized reputa- tion as playwright, playing with the trope of the usually male love poet aiming at sexual conquest of an audience and using the connection of female playwright and sexualized actress. The part of the prologue of *The Forc'd Marriage* spoken by the actress rather than the actor suggests that feminine cleverness or wit is essential only when sexual attractiveness or beauty fails or becomes too cheap a commodity. The epilogue of *Sir Patient Fancy* subsumes feminine linguistic skill into an overall seductiveness of women whether this is acting or writing: 'Quickest in finding all the subtlest ways/ To make your joys: why not to make you plays?'[16] Feminine writing skill, equivalent to the actress's acting skill, is here part of the raising and manipulating of male desire which is the ultimate source of money for the woman.

Certainly the image of the woman writer as whore was not one that the seventeenth century would easily let Aphra Behn escape. In a poem probably from the early 1680s and almost certainly referring to Behn, 'To the Sappho of the Age. Suppos'd to Ly-In of a Love-Distemper, or a Play', Wycherley cleverly exploits the conventional puns of parts, acts and claps, letting coalesce in the common manner of male satirists the whore and authoress, and providing an extended analogy of whoring and writing, of literary production and procreation. He takes up the invitation of the female writer's prologue: to accept the pleasure of the body as of the text.

If read literally and as description of a chronological sequence, this poem of Wycherley's seems to suggest an early history of whoredom for Behn, combined with a later one of authorship:

> Once, to your Shame, your Parts to all were shown,
> But now, (tho' a more Public Woman grown,)
> You gain more Reputation in the Town;
> Grow Public, to your Honour, not your Shame,
> As more Men now you please, gain much more Fame;
> Who, for your Parts, got much more Praise before,
> But, as your Pains, in bringing forth, were more;
> But now, more credit you from all Men gain,
> As you bring forth, in Public, with less Pain,
> Your easiest Off-springs of your Wanton Brain . . .[17]

Yet, if this poem is useful as commentary on the authorial apprehension of the female writer, it has limited use for specific and individual biography. At that level it needs to be remembered that Sappho is a generic name for women writers, being used also in this period for Katherine Philips and Ann Bradstreet, and, had he wanted to be more pointed, Wycherley could easily have indicated Behn's name through employing the usual dashes or, if he had aimed at making real biographical hits, by referring to particular titles of Behn's work

in the manner of Gould in *The Play-House. A Satyr* or the authors of
The Rehearsal. Incidentally, if Wycherley's poem is taken as proof of
prostitution, it will also have to be taken as proof of childbearing, of
which there is no evidence for Behn.

It is therefore disturbing to see Wycherley (with Gould) taking his
place in constructions of Behn's biography and interacting with the
increasingly fixed image of playwright as playful courtesan. This
image, in which the playwright certainly colluded at defined
moments, has become one dear to the heart of modern New Historical criticism, which seems at times as eager to sexualize female
activity as contemporary satirists. Despite the discursive playfulness
of the mode, keeping most points on the level of representation and
verbal play, it does sometimes allow a sudden drop from high
metaphor to reality, from frolicsome comment to serious biography.
In other words there is a tendency to literalize metaphor and in the
process anachronize the self. Consequently the imaging and self-
imaging expand to become the self-identification of the woman writer
in her writing moment and quotidian living, and in this construction
the whore-punk may obliterate the powerful political historian, the
anxious prophet or the commerical playwright, all of which identities
Aphra Behn might have owned. The result of the process is that no
public space can easily be taken by the seventeenth-century woman
without our seeing her seducing the modern reader with her
approved shame.

In an entertaining example of this kind of criticism, 'Who was that
masked woman? The prostitute and the playwright in the comedies
of Aphra Behn', Cathy Gallagher argues that Behn 'purposely'
constructs her 'scandal' out of 'overlapping discourses of commercial,
sexual, and linguistic exchange' and that she introduces to the world
of English letters the professional woman writer as 'a new-fangled
whore'. Behn, Gallagher asserts, makes a persona that 'titillates,
scandalizes, arouses pity, and indicates the vicissitudes of authorship
and identity'. The author-whore persona is not simply an instrumen-
tal trope here but, rather, the basis of self-identification, making of
'female authorship per se a dark comedy'. This comedy in Gallagher's
version explores the bond between the unaccustomed liberty which
the stage for the first time offered women and at the same time
describes women's 'confinement behind both literal and metaphorical
vizard masks'.[18]

With such analyses it is hard for the reader of criticism to avoid
seeing the modern critic as the author of Aphra Behn, the playwright-
actress-whore, making a theatrical version of the playwright fit for

the stage of modern criticism. Indeed the playful, stimulating tone is not unlike that of the actress speaking her prologue before the audience must settle down to view the play; in this case the play is the playwright herself and all her works. Although verbally as entertaining as the actress on her stage, these sorts of readings have the disadvantage that they foreclose on any historical reconstruction of the playwright as professional producer by positing only 'unseeable selfhood', the 'necessary obscurity of the "public woman"', and alienated production.[19]

While Gallagher wants to find Behn as masked woman and whore a 'symbolic figure of authorship for the Restoration' (something of a tendency among biographical as well as textual critics of Behn, the most flamboyant of whom, Germaine Greer, also frequently encodes Behn as whore), in fact women writers after Behn either dissociated themselves from her life or praised her for her mental qualities and verbal skills. None used her image to embrace the whorish role here ascribed to her. In addition, within her writings Behn herself rarely makes the whore a figure of power, though she may show unscrupulous women using a promise of sexuality to manipulate men.

III

In the preface to *The Rover*, Behn aligns herself as playwright not with the whore but with a distancing device, a representation. The prostitute Angellica Bianca, wishing to keep up her price and encourage business, hangs out a painted picture of herself which fills its spectators with the appropriate and lucrative desire for the lady herself; since in the end she does not totally possess the man she wants, it appears that this representation may have had more power over men's desire than the corporeal lady can ever achieve. The lady, not the sign, is a whore and she is unsuccessful in her trading, giving more in goods and services than she receives. When a man is taken for a woman presumed to be a whore, the exchange is often associated with his impotence, as it seems to be in *Love Letters between a Nobleman and his Sister* (Part I), when, after his sexual failure, the disguised hero Philander meets the lady's father, who assumes he is a sexually available woman.

Behn's presentation of self in playful whoring mode is confined largely to the prologues and epilogues often delivered by actresses. But these do not represent the whole story of her self-construction and there is considerable evidence that, if she sometimes delivered herself as writing whore, she also desired to create herself as professional economic woman, dealing in her language not her body. Her desire seems paradoxically enhanced by her slightings of women in her prose works which, with her deprecatory remarks about herself as female author, suggest doubts about any general assumptions concerning women, and serve to draw attention to Behn's art as that of a *woman* writer writing worthy of purchase.

The apparently serious assessments of art and theatre occur most obviously when Behn addresses not an audience but a readership without mediation of the actress's sexualized and whorish body. In the prefaces to the printed works which often came out some months after the performance of the play and, forming a kind of commentary and criticism, could take into account this performance, a very different tone appears from that in the prologues and epilogues. In these prefaces there is no need to invoke the convention of female playwright as whore and inevitably there is less contribution from the actress. In the absence of an actual audience, a different sort of rapport with the reader or consumer can be established. One kind of meta-artistic expression for women seems, then, to need the absence of the female body as well as the absence of the spectator, with the result that the voice of the woman writer may be associated with another less femininely sexualized part and be heard without titillation.

In the prefaces the tone is not that of the playful whore or lover, whether performer or simply stimulator, but of the professional writer and literary producer. In daring opposition to the hyperbole concerning art and the artist employed by most of her famous male contemporaries, Behn claims that she was 'forced to write for Bread and not ashamed to own it', that she was a professional not an amateur.[20] What she wrote for this 'Bread' was ephemeral drama. This was a necessary choice of genre mainly because women were excluded from classical education and the code of Latin which kept them from knowledge of the past. So they were condemned to the single 'Fulsom Gingle' of the time. Happily this 'Gingle' was the stuff of theatrical comedy, and comedy, she claimed in her pamphlet to the reader of *The Dutch Lover* (1673), was her particular sign. Comic plays were never the 'grand affair of human life', she wrote: unlike the classical dramatists such as Ben Jonson with whom she was often coupled and compared, she did not think the theatre was intended to improve an audience but simply to divert it with 'the picture of ridiculous mankind'. Deflatingly she gave her opinion that composition was, after all, not 'such a sturdy task'.

In the preface to *The Luckey Chance* (1687) she made further specific comment on one component of that drama which was not the 'grand affair of human life': bawdry. She declared that, like any successful trader, she had studied the market and chosen to deal in wares she had learnt were popular. Here, quite inappropriately in Behn's view, the issue of gender cropped up again, although she insisted she was speaking not as a whore or even primarily as a woman but as a professional economic entrepreneur.

Woman spectators were not necessarily opposed to the display of the female body on the stage: often in tragedy or pathetic plays which included representations of women as constructions of superior virtue – plays thought to be encouraged by female audiences – there was considerable exploitation of bodily parts, especially in scenes of female physical humiliation. But women spectators were assumed to oppose self-conscious bawdry and it was this, rather than pathetic representation, whether chaste or lewd, that many of Behn's plays exploited. There is much modern discussion of the components of the Restoration audience and much argument about the effect of the growing number of woman, if indeed there was such growth. But many contemporary playwrights, including Behn, certainly thought that women constituted a faction, and she was irritated by their apparent expression of dislike for the comic exploitation of the sexualized female body. She found this dislike hypocritical and in retaliation she asserted her right not to be bawdy as a woman, but to employ bawdry as a playwright.

She needed, she affirmed, to be as commercial as possible and to use the current coin whatever it might be. So in the preface to *The Luckey Chance* she expressed the problem of being a 'woman writer' but with no sense that she should have a special gendered voice – rather that her sex seemed to prevent her from marketing freely what men had shown could be successfully sold. The bawdry existed in plays precisely because the audience wanted it, but condemnable bawdry appeared to exist because an issue was being made of gender; consequently the problem lay in the interplay of feminine name and prejudiced audience: 'such Masculine Strokes in me, must not be allowed'. Behn did not present herself as a bawdy writer because of bawdry's inherent and naughty relationship with her sex, but she was nonetheless criticized because of her sex:

> had the plays I have writ come forth under any Mans name, and never
> known to be mine; I appeal to all unbyast Judges of Sense, if they had
> not said that Person had made as many good Comedies, as any one

Man that has writ in our Age; but a Devil on't the Woman damns the
Poet.[21]

Behn's defences of herself as female writer of ungendered bawdry
probably did have some impact; in *The Play-House. A Satyr* Gould is
especially incensed with the defence of Lady Galliard, 'the lewd
Widow' of *The City-Heiress*, who after her seduction acquaints the
'Audience with her flimsy case' (Act IV, scenes 1 and 2). The analogy
of 'the lewd *Widow*', Lady Galliard, and *'chast Sappho'* suggests that
this may also be read as criticism of Behn. Gould diffuses the power
of Lady Galliard's reasoned sexual defence (and Aphra Behn's literary
one) by sexual accusations and innuendo, insisting in contradiction
of his own anxiety that the woman is both lewd and encroaching and
has confused 'luscious Bawdry' with '*Wit*'.

Beyond the presentation of self as commercial operator it is clear
that Behn shared some of the artistic aspirations of her male contemporaries worried about the falling status of art in an age of propa-
ganda. Despite her denigration of comic plays and her deflating of
the pretentions of privileged art, she wished for another self-presentation than that of trader: that of serious artist. She desired a lasting
fame, distinguishable from sexual or feminine fame or infamy and
'bread' alone: a literary approbation for her writing as a poet.

To acquire this other kind of fame she would need to unsettle the
process in which she elsewhere involved herself – the engendering
of art as feminine wiles. She would have to separate authorial sex
and art, as she had tried to separate authorial sex and bawdry. To do
this she would need to take on the authority of 'masculine' art. With
this aim Behn would inevitably approach the stance of the cross-
dresser, another image, like that of whore, that could impinge on the
image of the female playwright, one which could be used by her but
which could also overwhelm her. Here then it is necessary to consider
the powerful image of theatrical cross-dressing in the Restoration.

As female representation in the Restoration theatre necessarily
changed in interpretation with the arrival of actual woman, so cross-
dressing changed from a homosexual titillation or a useful device to
allow the boy actor to take off the constricting female dress. In the
circumstances one might expect it to decline. But in fact, as a female
mode of a woman-in-breeches rather than a boy-in-a-dress, it
remained highly popular, occurring in almost a quarter of all plays
produced between 1660 and 1700.[22] Its value was an obvious one, to
display the female leg, a leg which was otherwise swathed at least in
public in elaborate petticoats. It also made exceptionally erotic the

revelation when the lady was unbreeched, or when she suddenly bared her breast in confirmation of her sex.

If Restoration cross-dressing undoubtedly fed the pornographical and erotic fantasies of the audience it also acquired considerable socio-sexual meaning, since dress denoted role as well as sex and directed not only the body but the mind. But it seems that on the whole during this period the transvestism of a woman in man's garb lost some of its political power. This sort of cross-dressing had been much condemned before the Civil Wars by both puritan and royalist, in theatre and in life, since it tended to symbolize and encourage a world without proper hierarchy and order, the 'world upside down'. Political stability required hierarchy and especially differentiation of the sexes. In the Restoration, however, so sexualized was the image of the cross-dressing actress that cross-dressing itself was easily taken into cultural currency and shorn of some of its political significance. The defence which rendered it politically unthreatening was, as might be expected, a crude reference to male sexual power. In a prologue to *Secret Love*, for example, Dryden wrote that women who passed as men could fight, swagger and swear, supplying all theatrical needs, but were unable to perform the final offstage act. The male part of copulation became the only signified, of which all other acts, theatrical and otherwise, became pallid signs.

The pretty woman in breeches was a boy not a man, so the cross-dressers of most Restoration plays usually avoided the tinge of the threatening Amazon. These cross-dressing women were most frequently spirited girls coming to London or some other metropolis to find romance. They assumed breeches, went masked and behaved madly while keeping their physical honour intact, and they differed markedly from the prostituted and naughty women with whom they often struggled for the chosen man. The passionately lewd older women remained in female dress and lacked the power of disguise, of wit and of control eminently displayed by the pert young cross-dressing and boyish girls who had the intellect to plot and win. Such young things knew their age and were in charge of it within strict boundaries, as Wycherley's young heroine says to her 'reverent aunt' in *The Gentleman Dancing Master* (1672): 'Tis a pleasant-well-bred-complacent-free-frolick-good-natur'd-pretty Age; and if you do not like it, leave it to us that do.' In this world female cross-dressing becomes part of the 'free-frolick'. The playwright, the manipulator of the show, was not, then, analogous to the cross-dresser, whose cross-dressing almost always pointed to the ultimate dress of the feminine body. Perhaps she might be seen as an under-dresser.

Yet despite the potential avoidance of the theatrical images of the whore-actress and the cross-dresser by the female playwright, gender continued to press on her image primarily through the presentation of the artist's creativity as 'masculine'. This presentation was not, however, as excluding as it later appeared to become. Partially because of the extraordinary biological notions of the sexes in the seventeenth century, which represented the female as lesser but the same in kind as the male, with an inverted sexuality, the mirror of the male's, in certain exceptional circumstances there could be a changing of sex, not simply a cross-dressing.[23] So where in the eighteenth century the pen was accepted as gendered and the woman was instructed to write only out of her femininity, it was possible for a woman in the previous period to write out of a 'masculine' part to which she had claim, despite its sexual overtones.[24] So there is neither penis envy nor monstrosity, cross-dressing nor bawdry, when a woman poet desires the fruits of masculine wit for her 'Masculine Part'.

The epilogue to Behn's play *Sir Patient Fancy* asks, as many women would ask during the next century:

> What has poor woman done that she must be,
> Debarred from sense and sacred poetry?
> Why in this age has Heaven allowed you more,
> And women less of wit than heretofore?[25]

Although she did trivialize her art and insist that she was a woman 'forced to write for Bread', she clearly did long for a reputation beyond the moment of commerce and the feminine fame of sexuality. In her later years she expressed a wish to write plays that would last beyond the theatrical performance and have merit away from the body of the actress, dressed, undressed or cross-dressed.

Her clearest statement of this is the famous one in her preface to *The Luckey Chance*. Here she asserted serious masculine art, along with her claim to it, dramatizing herself as both victim and hero:

> All I ask, is the Priviledge for my Masculine Part the poet in me . . . to tread in those successful Paths my Predecessors have so long thriv'd in. . . . If I must not, because of my Sex, have this Freedom, but that you will usurp all to your selves, I lay down my Quill, and you shall hear no more of me. . . . I am not content to write for a Third day only. I value Fame as much as if I had been born a *Hero*; and if you rob me of that, I can retire from the ungrateful world, and scorn its fickle Favours.[26]

Literary fame is here given to the hero, leaving sexual fame and infamy to the actress. Behn wants what the actress cannot have and if she, the playwright, cannot have it, she will – with more melodrama than modesty – pull out of the sexual and theatrical economy altogether.

At the end of her struggling artistic life, Aphra Behn was in a way offered an entry into heroic male art beyond the whore's pleasing of men and the trader's successful bargain, a chance to image herself as an 'ungendered', that is 'masculine', artist. She seems to have been invited by Dr Gilbert Burnet, on his own or another's authority, to write a poem of welcome to the new ruler William III. Burnet was a firm supporter not only of William but also of the new Whig order coming into being after the deposition or abdication of Behn's beloved James II, and he must have invited Behn – whom he appears personally to have despised as 'abominably vile' – because of her known skill at panegyric and public poetry (displayed most significantly in her odes on Charles II's death and James II's coronation). Her reply to this curious invitation was the last poem published in her lifetime.

Despite her repeated insistence on her role as 'masculine' poet, her *Pindaric Poem to the Reverend Doctor Burnet* immediately sexualizes the offer and reinscribes the female artist as whore-provider. But it does so only to deconstruct and unsettle images of both female whore and male artist.

Behn begins by creating the poet as feminine body and employing the images so often used derogatively for female writing and feminine wit. The poet accepts that the fame she has yearned for and the money she desperately needs from writing will now be the reward of her successful seduction by male art and artist. The poem becomes a subtle and ambiguous discussion of this would-be seduction and its implications, of the artist as whore and of the objectification of the female artist. It goes beyond her other statements in suggesting the subversive notion not only of the artist as whore but of the possible whorishness of art.

In the *Pindaric*, the female writer of a lifetime's achievement in drama, prose and poetry becomes not the famous artist but the sexualized actress and female writer facing the timeless male author. To him alone, she now admits, fame necessarily belongs because he alone controls history. Burnet's masculine writing, so politically immoral from the standpoint of her own expressed royalist and Tory politics, becomes 'immortal wit' within its own political world, the world of power and history. What his 'wondrous pen' composes is 'perfect and sublime' art, equivalent to the divine work itself in its transcendental quality. Despite the public poetic achievements that have presumbably led to Burnet's invitation, the female poet's own writing is presented as inhabiting a far lower plain than the male's, avoiding the heroics of history and politics and encompassing only the ordinary and the amorous.

The drama of the *Pindaric* is superficially an enacting of female stupidity – the woman artist like Lady Lambert in *The Roundheads* is presented as taking false for true and failing to understand the ultimate male sexual-political power. She has been offered poetic glory imaged as seduction by masculine art; acceptance will allow her to flourish in the present and keep her name alive in the future.

The display of 'masculine' wit – not sexless now but quite specifi-cally connected with men – almost seduces the female pen into thinking it can write in the same mode, penetrated as it is by the masculine pen's 'fine ideas' rather than the constructions of its own 'Masculine Part': 'since by an authority divine,/ She is allowed a more exalted thought'. The female poet knows that the seduction promises desired fame and poetic 'eternity' through masculine praise and mimicry of the masculine, and she accepts that, without this male mediation in composition and reception, she and her works must remain earthbound, unheroic, inglorious and insignificant. In short she acknowledges now that masculine evaluation through masculine authority gives worldly estimate:

> Scarce anything but you and Heaven
>   Such grateful bounties can dispense
> As that eternity of life can give;
> So famed by you my verse eternally shall live.

The sycophancy clothes what seems the female poet's timely admir-ation, as well as her ultimate comprehension of what it takes to please.

Yet there is obviously another message at odds with the sycophan-tic and self-deprecating stance, which makes the buildup of the poetic and political power of Burnet semi-ironic – the female poet's refusal is not only the result of failure but also an act of understated deflating bravery. She refuses the lucrative and honouring invitation on behalf of her 'stubborn Muse' who clings to a kind of loyalty known to be useless. The fair prosperous wind can make those who sail with it thrive, while those whose sails it does not reach will have neither fame nor prosperity, neither money nor acknowledged artis-tic achievement. The excluded female poet is reduced to the body of the woman, more pathetic forsaken lady than seducing whore, though the layers of ironic sycophancy unsettle all identifications. What remains a basic truth, however, is that she will receive no rewards in cash, fame or pleasure.

Behn ends with a wry paean to the masculine art of Burnet whose pen can flourish and effect change, even as it sloughs off the now old-fashioned heroics of the male and female poet. While needing none of the supplicating contingent role of the whore himself, Burnet's art, it is implied, has become both pimp and whore. At the same time the female poet's gesture of humility aligns her with the classical male poets: both Horace and Ovid, whose verse Behn had rendered into English during her long poetic life, invoke this trope of modesty and self-denigration.

With the end of the Restoration – and the political and literary debasement ratified by the accession of William III in Behn's Tory political view – masculine art became far from heroic. Instead it appeared simply shoddy and powerful, covering stratagems of deception and disloyalty. Fame now fell not to the best and wittiest but to the temporizing and duplicitous. 'Masculine' art as much as trivial 'feminine' commodity became simply the 'Fulsom Gingle' of the time.

So the female poet refused what she had once so desired, seeing it as a last attempt at seduction of a tired woman. She considered the cost of compliance too high: 'loyalty commands with pious force,/ That stops me in the thriving course.' The last stanza of the *Pindaric* makes the point with clarity:

> Tho' I the wondrous change deplore,
> That makes me useless and forlorn,
> Yet I the great design adore,
> Though ruined in the universal turn.
> Nor can my indigence and lost repose,
> Those meagre Furies that surround me close,
> Convert my sense and reason . . .[27]

Yet, with sad realism, she does not put *female* heroics in the place of men's: just before or after this poem, she signed her name to her usual sort of royal commendation, *A Congratulatory Poem to Her Sacred Majesty Queen Mary, Upon Her Arrival in England*, to welcome, albeit with declared reluctance, the entry of the usurping daughter into England. She did not, however, manage such a poem to the real power on the throne, William III.

Behn died about the time of the publication of her *Pindaric to Doctor Burnet*, between the landing and coronation of Mary II and William III at which Burnet, soon to be Bishop Burnet, officiated. It seems possible that, before she died, she herself wrote the couplet carved on her tombstone:

> Here lies proof that wit can never be
> Defence enough against mortality.

Notes

1 Katherine Philips was often called 'the Matchless Orinda' and contrasted with Behn in public reputation. The description of Behn occurs in commendatory poems published in her *Poems upon Several Occasions* (London, 1684).

2 *The Prologues and Epilogues of John Dryden: A critical edition*, ed. William Bradford Gardner (New York: Columbia University Press, 1951), pp. 29–30.

3 *The Diary of Samuel Pepys*, ed. Robert Latham and William Matthews (London: Bell and Hyman, 1976), IX, p. 260.

4 'From worthy Mrs Behn the Poetess, to the famous Virgin Actress', in *Letters from the Dead to the Living*. Interestingly, though the sexual availability of the actress was an endless source of satire and mockery in pamphlets and broadsides, actors who were also sexual objects to the audience and often kept by wealthy ladies were less so.

5 Jeremy Collier, *A Short View of the Immorality and Prophaneness of the English Stage* (London, 1699), p. 13. Not only did the playwright have to struggle with the actress, there was also the theatrical appearance of certain notorious ladies in the audience. Pepys in his *Diary* more fully describes the dress and flamboyance of the King's mistresses, such as Lady Castlemaine in her box, than of any actress on the stage. Little dramas were enacted offstage, as when Lady Castlemaine wished to scotch rumours of her declining hold on the King by ostentatiously whispering to him across others and finally moving to sit next to him, or when the estranged Duke and Duchess of York put on a public show of affection. The audience judged offstage acting as it would the onstage sort: Lady Castlemaine was scrutinized for evidence of dismay at the arrival of a queen for Charles as an actress would be scrutinized for her art.

6 At the same time, however, women's arrival allowed the theatre to become a forum for female articulation once denied women.

7 See the 'Preface' to *The Luckey Chance* (1687) and Wycherley's 'Letter to Mother Bennett'.

8 *The Play-House. A Satyr, Poems* (London, 1689), p. 163.

9 *The Play-House. A Satyr*, p. 165.

10 *The Play-House. A Satyr*, pp. 181–4.

11 *The Roundheads*, Act I, sc. 2, *The Works of Aphra Behn*, ed. Montague Summers (1915; New York: Phaeton, 1967), vol. I.

12 *A Comparison Between the Two Stages* (1702; Princeton: Princeton University Press, 1942), p. 17.

13 'The Female Laureat', *Poems* (London, 1709), II, p. 16.

14 'The Description of a Poetess', BL (Harl) 6913. In *The Mental World of Stuart Women* (Brighton: Harvester, 1987), p. 214, Sara Heller Mendelson identified this poem as Gould's.

15 *A Journal from Parnassus*, ed. Hugh MacDonald (c.1688; London: 'A Letter from Artemiza in the Towne to Chloe in the Countrey', *The Poems of John Wilmot, Earl of Rochester*, ed. Keith Walker (Oxford: Basil Blackwell, 1984), p. 83.

16 *Oroonoko, the Rover and Other works*, ed. Janet Todd (Harmondsworth: Penguin, 1992), p. 330.

17 William Wycherley, *Miscellany Poems* (1704); repr. in *The Complete Works of William Wycherley* (London, 1924), pp. 155–6.

18 Catherine Gallagher, 'Who was that masked woman? The prostitute and the playwright in the comedies of Aphra Behn', *Last Laughs: perspectives on women and comedy*, ed. Regina Barreca (New York: Gordon Breach, 1988), pp. 23–42.

19 Other writers of the time do not exploit the whore-poetess connection, e.g., Katherine Philips. Gallagher quotes Lady Carey in support of her thesis, but she was writing in 1613 and much had changed since the reign of James I.

20 'To the Reader', *The Dutch Lover*, *The Works of Aphra Behn*, I, p. 223.

21 *The Luckey Chance*, *Works*, III, p. 186.

22 See J. H. Wilson, *All the King's Ladies* (Chicago, 1958), p. 75.

23 See Regnier de Graaf, *A New Treatise Concerning the Generative Organs of Women* (1672). Stephen Greenblatt has investigated this construction in *Shakespearean Negotiations* (Oxford: Clarendon Press, 1988). See also Thomas Laqueur, 'Orgasm, generation and the politics of representing biology', *Representations*, Spring 1986.

24 In so far as gender always implied hierarchy, the claim by a woman for involvement with the 'masculine' implied a claim to the highest and most intellectual; at the same time contemporary critics used gender to support distinctions of which hierarchy was only one element. So Dryden saw music as feminine because of its involvement with the 'feminine' imagination and with sweetness, but poetry as masculine because it encouraged virtue and appealed to the intellect.

25 *Oroonoko, The Rover . . .*, p. 329.

26 *The Luckey Chance*, *Works*, III, p. 187.

27 *Oroonoko, The Rover . . .*, pp. 347–50.

2 Spectacular deaths: history and story in Aphra Behn's *Love Letters, Oroonoko* and *The Widow Ranter*

I

Aphra Behn largely avoided theatrical tragedy; consequently she rarely depicted heroic death. Her one tragedy, *Abdelazer*, which, if her poem to the tragedian Sir Francis Fane can be taken autobiographically, she felt 'cold' and 'feeble', has a remarkably villainous pair at its centre; both die in discourses that trivialize their dying, the woman talking of lust, the man of cruelty.[1]

But, outside the tragic theatre, Behn frequently and lengthily represented death. In both theatrical tragi-comedy and in her prose works she could mitigate the simplicity of tragedy, tempering rather than destroying the heroism of a violent conclusion. The represented death might, for example, be noble and honourable, yet at the same time involve grotesque mutilation or absurd blunder. The tempering or mitigating is most obvious when Behn's narrative approaches historical narrative, when artistic representation interacts with related historical event. On these occasions it seems that life insists on clouding the generic clarity of tragedy.

This destabilizing of representation is a mark of Behn's treatment of many subjects, life, sex and death – the drunk cavalier, impotence in passion, or the physical stench of the metaphysically pure corpse – but it may well be the conjunction of grotesque and tragic in the seen, heard historical moment that, in these particular cases, inspires the fictive treatment.

Interestingly, though, such representations are also marked by the reverse conscious influence: the life as represented, pretending to or actually copying historical event, is a life made to imitate art. Against the multiplicities of experience the dying man tries to approximate his death to the satisfying simplicity of tragedy (the masculine possessive pronoun is intentional: women die violently in Behn's work but men are the usual centres of fatal political theatre). The effort, which necessitates some literary self-consciousness, does not diminish the heroism of the death, but it adds a tinge of the absurd.

Towards the end of her life, in the 1680s, Behn created several heroic and oddly anachronistic figures, who form a commentary on the politics of the period. The 1640s and 1650s pressed heavily on the 1680s, and there was constant expectation of a repetition of the royal tragedy of 1649. In this context her stories of humbled princes achieve a kind of typological power.

Two of her heroes, Oroonoko of the short story and Bacon of *The Widow Ranter or Bacon in Virginia*, are set in the New World context which she probably experienced as a young woman in the early 1660s. A third, perhaps in part the inspiration for the other creations, was James Scott, Duke of Monmouth, 'Cesario' of the closing pages of her long three-part 'novel', *Love Letters between a Nobleman and his Sister*, set in a European context. All three are gentlemanly, idealistic and romantic men, quite distinct from the witty, sexy, opportunistic and roving cavaliers of her earlier works, such as Wilmore of *The Rover* or Loveless of *The Roundheads*, both plays set before 1660 when the glitter of restoration could be imagined for the future. The later heroes exist in a decadent world after disillusionment and are distanced by the narrator or by other characters who inhabit a cynical society and wryly contemplate the heroes' heroic simplicity. The spectators marvel at an admirably naïve inability to separate words and meaning, for example, and to desire sex and money above romantic love, or food and drink over death. Each hero is theatrical in the sense that some part of his actions is inspired by gestures described in literature; he acts and speaks more suitably for the stage than for the political event in which he is involved.[2]

Love Letters, *Oroonoko* and *The Widow Ranter* each have a substantial amount of historical parallels. They fictionalize history, as do Behn's earlier works, but they add the new theme of interacting history and formal fiction. At the centre of these artistic constructions, the 'historical' hero consciously presents and projects himself. The relationship between fiction and fact, fiction and faction, fact and faction, literary faction and political faction comes to the fore, then, not only in Behn's choice of subjects from life, but also in her simultaneous definition of them in political and dramatic terms. The heroes create themselves, but they need the models from the past and the audience from the present.

The climax of the self-consciously shaped life is a violent and, to a greater or lesser extent, voluntary death, an artificial process outside natural decaying and ending. The experienced event is almost pure theatre for the inexperienced watcher and is intended as theatre by the voluntary agent/victim. The three heroes all have a death that is brought about before nature could intervene, through suicide or through acts that the politically astute would expect to lead to death; all of them wish to kill themselves and become direct agents of their own deaths. In the case of Cesario and Oroonoko there are parallels between their self-dramatizing and their achieved death; Bacon, Behn's last hero, is also allowed the kind of ending his self-presentation demands, even though this appears to contradict historical record. It is the record that appears a source of the grotesque element in the fictional deaths.

II

Voluntary death or suicide was of immense interest in the seventeenth century. In clearly Christian works, suicide was often expressed as temptation, as in the famous lines of Despair in Spenser's *Faerie Queene*, 'death after life does greatly please', or in Eve's plea in the face of divine punishment:

> Why stand we longer shivering under fears
> That show no end but death, and have the power,
> Of many ways to die the shortest choosing,
> Destruction with destruction to destroy?[3]

Undoubtedly Behn knew Shakespeare's Hamlet and Cleopatra – 'is it sin/ To rush into the secret house of death?' – but she probably acquired the fascination with voluntary death as exaltation of free action more from classical literature than from the native tradition.[4] Under this influence Montaigne, for example, considered that humanity had the self-consciousness to understand itself and its predicament and therefore to consider the arguments for suicide as an appropriate and sometimes honourable course.

What the classical writers provided Restoration authors haunted by death was freedom to doubt the afterlife: if a sense of afterlife were destroyed, there seemed no reason to prohibit the taking or risking of one's own life. Some writers went further than this, exalting suicide as free action. Montaigne himself was much influenced by Lucretius, the Latin poet who had conflated the philosophies of Epicurus and Empedocles and the theory of atoms from

Democritus and was extremely influential in seventeenth-century 'libertine' circles. Lucretius declared firmly that human beings were material entities and that there was nothing after death: 'Dead, we become the lumber of the world. . . . Impartial death confounds body and soul', as Dryden's translation expressed it; happiness should be gained on earth. Lucretius' aim was to counter fears of the afterlife and the actions of the gods by insisting that everything consisted of moving atoms, including human beings, and that the world was controlled by mechanical and rational laws. The soul was therefore as mortal as the body. Consequently in Book III of *De rerum natura* there was emphasis on the absoluteness of death and the absurdity of the 'base craving for mere life'. Suicide became a rational choice when the gratification of ceasing pain or fulfilling honour demanded it. The Christian containment of Lucretius was best revealed in Jerome, who claimed that the philosopher was poisoned by a love-potion, wrote his great poem in lucid intervals during the resulting insanity, and finally committed suicide. So his doctrines were reduced to autobiography and distemper.

Lucretius seems to have been of special interest to mid-seventeenth-century women writers such as Margaret Cavendish, Duchess of Newcastle, and Aphra Behn, both of whom were fascinated with the theory of atoms and the notion that everything mental and physical was formed by their moving and combining in space. In the late 1680s Behn translated Fontenelle's *The History of Oracles* and *A Discovery of New Worlds* from French to English. In the first she largely confounded the dupings of pagan and Christian priests to make a point similar to Lucretius concerning the constructed and superstitious fear of the gods and retribution; in the second she supported the Copernican theory and clearly separated religion from science. This science had little in common with a growing technology in the service of commerce, but more resembled the rationalist and imaginative speculations of the Duchess and of Lucretius himself.

In 1682 Behn must have read Lucretius in the new translation by the young scholar Thomas Creech, for she published a commendatory poem in the second edition: *T. Lucretius Caro . . . De Natura Rerum* (Oxford, 1683). She reprinted the poem in her own volume of collected verse, *Poems upon Several Occasions*, in 1684, but in a substantially different version which may well have represented her original intention. This view is supported by a letter to her publisher Tonson which includes a sentence that might apply to her attitude to changes probably made by Creech before the first printing of the poem: 'As for Creech, I would not have you afflict him with a thing can not now be help'd, so never let him know my resentment.'[5] The version in *Poems upon Several Occasions*, 'To Mr Creech (under the Name of Daphnis) on his Excellent Translation of Lucretius', is more pagan than the one published with the translation, more rational than pious and emotional, mocking 'poor Feeble Faith's dull Oracles' which would be the subject of her later translation. In her poem Behn sexualizes reason into a Lucretian life force that gives freedom over life and death: 'Reason over all unfetter'd Plays,/ Wanton and undisturb'd as Summers Breeze.'[6]

That Creech may indeed have tampered with her poem to render it more Christian and innocuous is supported by the existence of a defensive dedication to the second edition of his translation where he worried about the 'venomed Pill' of this classical philosophy and tried to separate himself from the material he was translating. (For the devotees of Lucretius it was unfortunate that Creech, supposedly suffering from melancholy love, would in 1701 go on to kill himself, thus laying himself open to the charge of being the latest victim of the poisonous pagan.)

Throughout the rest of her poetry, Behn frequently referred to Lucretius with admiration. In 'The Golden Age', taken mainly from Tasso, she makes a Lucretian sense of non-retributive death part of the calm philosophy of the 'golden' state, giving eternity to the moment and imagining each 'Swain . . . Lord o'er his own will alone'. Her concluding line, 'a sleep brings an Eternal Night', echoes the famous non-Christian one from Catullus' poem to Lesbia, 'Nox est perpetua una dormienda'.

While there seems admiration in Behn for the fearless death implied by Lucretius, she also acknowledged weakness and disease and their undermining of the heroic will. In her last works she combined weakness with willed greatness in her masculine heroes, who are contemplated by a female author already contemplating her own unwilled death by disease. In 'On the Death of E[dmund] Waller' she wrote:

> I, who by Toils of Sickness, am become
> Almost as near as thou art to a Tomb?
> While every soft, and tender Strain
> Is ruffl'd, and ill-natur'd grown with Pain.

III

One of Behn's most abiding political obsessions was with James Scott, Duke of Monmouth, Charles II's first and favourite illegitimate son. In the troubled 1680s, Monmouth became a central figure in the plots of those who wished to avoid a succession of the Catholic James. Most dangerous of these was the Rye House Plot of 1683, an alleged conspiracy to assassinate both Charles and James on their way from Newmarket, in which Forde Lord Grey (fictionalized as Philander, the anti-hero of Behn's *Love Letters between a Nobleman and his Sister*) was implicated.

In 1685 on the death of his father, urged on by Grey and his mistress Henrietta Wentworth, Monmouth re-entered England from Holland at the head of a rebellion. The attack proved mismanaged and was unsuccessful. The most famous survivor of the bloody and extensive reprisals was Lord Grey. Monmouth was executed on 15 July 1685.

Like Dryden and other loyal supporters of James, Behn had long been intrigued by Monmouth both as a handsome, skittish cavalier and as the dark shadow of legitimate Stuart power. Both poets had the difficulty of condemning him as an undutiful son while wishing to praise Charles II as a fond father. Behn manages to bring Monmouth's image into poems that appear initially quite impervious to any political message, as well as turning ballads and songs into warnings and allegories. 'Silvio's Complaint: A SONG, to a Fine Scotch Tune' and 'SONG. To a New Scotch Tune' use 'Scotch' tunes and dialect to clarify the poetry's allusion to Monmouth, surnamed Scott and the victor of Scottish campaigns; both are included in *Poems on Several Occasions* (1684), although one at least appeared in a broadside version in 1681. The varied refrain of 'Silvio's Complaint' reads on one occasion: "Twere better I's was nere Born,/ Ere wisht to be a King'. On the last it is most prescient: 'My Fame Renown, and all dye,/ For wishing to be a King'.

By 1682 Monmouth was cropping up everywhere in Behn's work. In that year she wrote prologues and epilogues for *Like Father, like Son*, the title of which was probably based on a notorious Whig ballad accused of inciting regicide, and for *Romulus*, the performance of which directly implicated her in state politics. The main problem occurred in the Epilogue, which included the uncompromising lines:

> . . . of all Treasons, mine was most accurst;
> Rebelling 'gainst a KING and FATHER first.
> A sin, which Heav'n nor Man can e're forgive . . .

The True Protestant Mercury for 12–16 August 1682 records the result:

Thursday last being Acted a Play called The *Tragedy* of *Romulus* at the Dukes Theature and the *Epilogue* spoken by the Lady *Slingsbey* and written by Mrs *Behn* which reflected on the D. of *Monmouth* the Lord *Chamberlain* has ordered them both in custody to answer that affront for the same.

It is not known what action if any was taken, but it is unlikely to have been serious since the Epilogue with the offending lines was not withdrawn from circulation.

Along with the Rye House Plot, Monmouth makes many appearances in Behn's rhyming version of *Aesop's Fables* published in 1687. Now defeated and executed, the young hero enters her verses mainly as a warning against insubordination and mistaken aspiration: Fable XXIV, for example, advises, 'To false ambition if thy thoughts are bent,/ Reflect on a late pittyed president [precedent]'. In Fable XII she changes the lines of her source, Thomas Philipott, from 'oft those ills that wee for others spread,/ Upon ourselves by equall fate are shed' – to 'The young usurper, who design'd t'invade,/ An others right, himself the victim made'. A similar topically political message is yielded by Fable LXXX: 'So fancy'd Crownes led the young warriour on,/ Till loosing all he found himselfe undone', and by Fable LI, which alludes directly to Monmouth's invasion from the West: 'Of Specious overtures lett all be ware,/ 'Twas fair pretences rais'd the western warr'. That she entirely supported James's policy of executing Monmouth is clarified in the moral of Fable L: 'Mercy extended to ungratefull men/ Does but impower em to rebell agen'. In Fable XCIV she indicates that, even had he won and kept his head, Monmouth would have had a poor life on the throne: 'He who by th'Rables power a Crowne does weare/ May be a King, but is a Slave to feare'.[7] In this Behn reveals one of the sources of her implacable opposition to Monmouth's politics, his appeal to the mobile, the rabble, the '*wanton Beast*', as she variously describes the common people. The unstable mass, too crude and uneducated to manage liberty, would destroy any prince weak enough to offer it unaccustomed freedoms: so in Fable XCVIII: 'Ungratfull People thus on Princes fall,/ And given some liberties rebell for all'.

Behn is unremittingly negative about Monmouth in her poetry where she sees him as a political threat and a popular leader. She is equally negative in the first two parts of *Love Letters*, in which Monmouth is merely a shadowy presence, fictionalized as Cesario, lover of the anti-hero's wife and foolish pretender to a throne, whose presumption has led to the undermining of authority and the multiplication of revolts in family and nation. In the third volume of 1687, however, Cesario becomes more central, and her attitude somewhat changes as the doomed prince experiences capture, imprisonment and execution.

Not that she wavers in her political view, which conforms to her expression in the poems that Monmouth's execution is, in terms of statecraft, appropriate for a ruler who is praised in the *Pindaric Poem on the Happy Coronation* for his ability to tame the unruly horse of the people. But, in the final pages, where she enters Cesario–Monmouth's story as responder and spectator of his mortal spectacle, she allows him to gain theatrical authority by in part moving into theatrical tragedy and fiction and out of politics. This happens through a close adherence to reported history. Cesario–Monmouth now becomes interesting as a slightly absurd, tragic man, who, like any Restoration stage hero, refuses the dull conventionality of repentance and contrition and declares his love on the scaffold. Through the dramatic heroism of his death, he can be emptied of one sort of political significance, while making a more subtle and ambivalent political point.

Pamphlets of the time reveal how Monmouth rendered himself a theatrical agent before Behn fictionalized him and they capture the absorption of the dying man in his romantic love. The absorption of obsession gives him an appearance of heroism which his political conduct could not deliver. In *Love Letters*, romantic love, as opposed to sexual infatuation and amorous manipulation, is the site of a doomed authenticity, almost a ludicrous but also wonderful sincerity. It relies on projection that exists within the imaginative realm, making the projector absurd, heroic and unworldly. There is no political or personal future for such love, and in the novel Octavio, to whom the narrator gives her slightly patronizing admiration, foreshadows Monmouth; he ends in a monastery, as removed from political power as the dead Duke.

The national fascination with Monmouth in 1685 is displayed in a variety of genres besides Behn's novel. One example is 'The late rebellions of Monmouth & Argyle, lively represented in a pack of cards. . . . Sept 1685'. Later in 1690 came the play *The Banish'd Duke: or, the Tragedy of Infortunatus*, which made of Monmouth a duped heroic figure dying less romantically than piously. Claiming to be closer to historical event are the pamphlets reproducing Monmouth's written words, purporting to present his speech and delivering eyewitness accounts of actions and gestures, such as *An Account Of what Passed at the Execution of the Late Duke of Monmouth, On* Wednesday *the 15th of* July, *1685, on* Tower-Hill. *Together With a Paper Signed by Himself that Morning in the* Tower, *in the Presence of the Lords Bishop of* Ely, *and* Bath *and* Wells, *Dr.* Tennison, *and Dr.* Hooper. *And Also The Copy of His Letter to His* Majesty *after he was taken, Dated at* Ringwood *in* Hantshire, *the 8th. of* July.

The letter to James quoted in full in the pamphlet is naive and infelicitous in the extreme; it addresses the King who has just defeated him thus: 'Your Majesty may think, it is the Misfortune I now lie under, makes me make this Application to You'. He had no intention of fighting against his uncle, Monmouth claims, but he had unfortunately met with 'some Horrid People' who had persuaded him it was 'a Shame, and a Sin before *God*, not to do it'. Now he has learnt 'an Abhorrence for those, that put me upon it; and for the Action it self'. The childish quality of the letter can be gauged by the ending:

> I can say no more to Your Majesty now, being this *Letter* must be seen by those that keep me. Therefore, *Sir*, I shall make an end, in begging of Your Majesty to believe so well of me, That I would rather die a Thousand Deaths, than excuse any thing I have done, if I did not really think my self the most in the Wrong. . . .

(Similar ingenuousness is revealed in the letter to James's wife, Mary of Modena, whom he thinks 'may have some compassion for me': 'I would not desire your Majesty to doe it, if I sweare not from the bottom of my hart convinced how I have bine disceaved in to it, and how angry God Almighty is with me for it . . .'.[8]) The letters to James and Mary correspond to Behn's description of Cesario's writing 'several the most submissive letters in the world' trying to 'mitigate his treason, with the poorest arguments imaginable'; as if

> his good sense had declined with his fortune, his style was altered, and debased to that of a common man, or rather a schoolboy, filled with tautologies and stuff of no coherence; in which he neither shewed the majesty of a prince, nor sense of a gentleman; as I could make appear by exposing those copies, which I leave to history.[9]

History in its direct copy is not, then, exposed in Behn's fiction, although she uses the literary debasement of Cesario to help towards the defanging of Monmouth's political threat. Her failure to quote from the copies or rewrite them in the text allows Cesario–Monmouth to diminish as political agent while remaining potentially heroic. For, on the scaffold, Cesario plays a part as much in theatrical drama as in history.

Already in the pamphlet Monmouth has become a professional actor. His fantasies reach beyond the scaffold and its political decorum, making his context heroic romance not politics. He refuses to die as a political failure, denying the discourse of the exemplary rebel or the contrite sinner. Instead he insists on entering the imaginative sphere of romance, referring beyond the scaffold and its specific occasion and gesturing outwards at timeless theatre. In the novel *Love Letters*, too, he refuses to cooperate in the official political pageant by apologizing for rebellion, but insists on the tragic-heroic one of romance. It is this inwardness deriving from romantic obsession, both in historical record and in fictional reconstruction, that sets Cesario–Monmouth apart from other convicts.

Like Oroonoko and Bacon in Behn's accounts, the historical Monmouth of the pamphlet is far more concerned with his earthly relationships than with any divine future. All he will state is his role in the romantic melodrama of adultery: that 'I have had a Scandal raised upon me about a Woman, a Lady of Vertue and Honour . . . I have committed no Sin with her; and that which hath passed betwixt Us, was very Honest and Innocent in the Sight of God.' As with religion, so with politics, he simply refuses the demands of his captors. Though he wrote repentance when there was a chance of life, now facing death he will not conventionally recommend his wife and children to the King who is killing him and he approaches the political finale with a taciturnity that is both heroic and childish: '*I have said, I will make no Speeches; I will make no Speeches; I come to dye.*' The myth that sustains Monmouth in the historical pamphlet and in the fiction is the simple one of romance: as Behn put it, 'he spoke, he thought, he dreamed of nothing but *Hermione* . . . even on the scaffold', the moment when the condemned was expected to commit the soul to God, profess religion and bless the King and royal order. The narrator, who had earlier in the novel so attacked the ageing Hermione (based on the historical Lady Henrietta Wentworth) 'being turned of thirty', leaves Cesario free with his romantic image at this crucial moment.

The insistence on the personal, which Behn saw as both admirable and absurd, is particularly revealed in the incident of the tooth-pick case. Just before his death and during his official silence, Monmouth of the pamphlet called his servant and gave him 'something like a Tooth pick-Case, *Here* (said he) *give this to the Person, to whom you are to deliver the other things.*' In this context the item becomes a love token or magic sign with a private significance, out of reach of the scaffold and its political meaning.

Behn follows history closely: in *Love Letters* Cesario gives to his servant 'the enchanted tooth-pick-case . . . and commanded him to bear it from him to *Hermione'*. The significance is here anticipated since the superstitious Hermione had sought to fix Cesario in his love for her through magic; consequently Fergusano (based on Monmouth's follower Robert Ferguson), here said to be a magician as well as a priest, acquired a love philtre which she gave to Monmouth so cunningly that he 'vowed it should be the last thing he would part with in the world'.[10] Novel action is tied together by tokens that move in and out of history. In the fiction Hermione and Cesario almost exchanged gender, he being effeminized by love according to a follower and she being rendered 'manly'. So 'effeminate' had he become that the narrator could only provide wishes for actions or heroize him by fantasizing a classical death: Cesario wanted to fall on his sword and 'like *Brutus'* finish 'a life he could no longer sustain with glory', but he was stopped by love, 'the coward of the mind'. Later she wrote, 'he should have died like a *Roman*, and have scorned to have added to the triumph of the enemy. But love had unmanned his great soul . . .'.[11] By returning the tooth-pick case with its romantic significance, Cesario regains something of his manliness and can die in masculine posture, while still retaining the aura of romance.

In the pamphlet Monmouth felt the axe, fearing that its bluntness betokened the gruesome fate of his predecessor in opposition, Lord Russell, who 'he said had been struck three or four times'. In the event this mutilating was his own fate for, in Bishop Burnet's words: the executioner 'gave him two or three strokes without being able to finish the matter, and then flung the ax out of his hand. But the sheriff forced him to take it up: and at three or four more strokes he severed his head from his body.'[12] Behn chooses not to echo this lengthy violence – although it may have influenced her depiction of Tarquin's execution in *The Fair Jilt* – so as to keep the emphasis on heroic romance.

On the scaffold of *Love Letters*, Cesario, now politically defused, provokes sympathy and pity, not fear and involvement. As with the earlier entry of Octavio into the monastery, the book becomes the account of a public event that distances the character into spectacle and brings into the foreground the attitude or response of the spectator and narrator. It is because there is no difference between the spectacle and the reality, the scaffold and the theatre on this

occasion, that Cesario is both magnificent and unthreatening. Imagi-
natively the spectacle is more significant than the reality because it is
fed by the needs and desires of the spectators. Immediately following
his execution Cesario becomes an icon of unnecessary death satisfy-
ingly stage-managed: 'so that it became a proverb, "If I have an
enemy, I wish he may live like – , and die like Cesario".'

Securely controlled then, the epistolary failure in sense and elegance revealed in his letters to the King and Queen forgotten, Cesario
resumes his 'wonted grace' – : 'at least . . . all that beheld him
imagined so', the narrator wrote of what she had just described from
historical reality. The fact that her presentation has been influenced
by the accounts of the actual death is suggested by the earlier
prescient description through Philander of Cesario's expected end.
This occurred at the conclusion of Part I of *Love Letters*, which was
published in 1684, a year *before* Monmouth's rebellious attempt:

> I would not have him die poorly after all his mighty hopes, nor be
> conducted to a scaffold with shouts of joy, by that uncertain beast the
> rabble, who used to stop his chariot-wheels with fickle adorations
> whenever he looked abroad.[13]

In this anticipation, either Cesario fails to rise to the occasion or the
people upstage him with their volatility. In the depicted ending of
Part III, however, Monmouth, translated into Cesario, becomes the
first of Behn's line of noble and simple or foolish heroes, part of
whose significance is captured in their treatment of the scaffold, the
stake or the battlefield as their own theatrical stage, with themselves
as the most appreciative spectators.

IV

The possibility of historical theatre, of political play-acting, is even
greater in the colonies than in Restoration England or Huguenot
France (where *Love Letters* is purportedly set). Though a more
straightforwardly heroic figure throughout his story than Cesario,
Oroonoko, called Caesar by the colonists, the princely black hero of
Behn's most famous short story, is nonetheless also expanded by
theatrical rhetoric and inflated by Roman precedent. He lives by a
code that is more classical than African or Christian, the virile code
of theatrical masculinity. At the same time this code is also a
simulacrum of the decadent sophisticated English notion of the

primitive code of truth and transparency, a code that is somehow natural rather than acquired, displayed by Swiftian horses or Behn's Indians who cannot lie. None of these can act in a stage way, being too naive to know there is any choice of posture. Oroonoko's death is, then, both an affirmation and a denial of personal theatricality.

There is no clear source for Oroonoko's story of rebellion and violent death, although its context and supporting characters seem based on Behn's own probable stay in Surinam in the early 1660s when William Byam, who becomes the perfidious villain of the short tale, was the deputy governor in charge of the colony. There is, however, an interesting decription of a suicide following an enthusiasm for Roman literature in a curious letter by Byam, entitled *An Exact Relation of The Most Execrable Attempts of John Allin, Committed on the Person of His Excellency Francis Lord Willoughby of Parham, Captain General of the Continent of Guiana, and of all the Caribby-Islands, and our Lord Proprietor*, published in London in 1665. If Behn was indeed in Surinam in late 1663 and early 1664, as seems probable, then some of the events recounted in Byam's letter must have occurred during her stay there and been the talk of the colony.[14] Something of the combination of bluster, blasphemy, heroism, romance, physical violence and absurdity described in Byam's letter may well have informed Behn's depiction of her tragi-comic hero when, in the tragi-comic last days of the reign of James II (another Caesar), she looked back for inspiration to her colonial past.

Various contemporary documents reveal the roughness and insubordination of the Surinam colonists. One example is *A Letter Sent from Syrranam, to His Excellency, the Lord Willoughby of Parham, General of the Western Islands, and of the Continent of Guianah, &c. Then residing at the Barbados. . . .* by Henry Adis. This letter was dated 10 December 1663 and printed in London in 1664, together with a reply from the governor of the colonies, Lord Willoughby, dated Barbados, 23 January of the following year. In contrast to Behn's account in *Oroonoko*, it gives much praise of Byam, 'that worthy person, whom your Lordship hath lately honoured with the Title and Power of your Lieutenant General of this Continent of Guianah' (the title claimed by the narrator of *Oroonoko* for her father and by 'One of the Fair Sex' for the father of Aphra Behn; if true, the title might have gone to Byam after the death of this elusive man). Despite the good principles and government of Byam, Adis speaks of the settlers who, 'by their debauched Atheistical Actions, evidence themselves more brutish by far, than the very Heathens themselves, to the shame and stink of Christianity . . .' and he is shocked by the 'rude rabble', their oaths and 'lascivious Abominations'. Since the principled defiance of the laws and religion which the heroically inspired Allin shows in the Byam letter was obviously unusual (as opposed to the usual drunkenness and rowdiness), it may be Allin that Adis has in mind in his complaint of atheism.

According to Byam's pamphlet, Allin, who had 'good natural parts', displayed exemplary industry when he first came to the colony, but he was also villainously addicted to swearing, cursing and drunkenness. The unusual ingredient of this fairly common mixture was blasphemy. When the accusation including the wicked words was recited in the court, the building's foundations cracked as 'a dreadful signal of Divine displeasure' according to the superstitious Byam, who was 'an Auricular witness'. Allin held 'Atheistical' or anti-Christian principles, a stance close to that of Oroonoko, who repeatedly mocked the doctrinal side of Christianity, as well as the disjunction between belief and practice which he observed among his Christian captors.

The blaspheming Allin was unmoved by the signs of omnipotent fury that Byam witnessed and he was described as outrageously entertaining

> his hours of leisure with Romances, and the Lives of some bold *Romans* and daring valiant ones, which bred in him an admiration (which he often uttered in his discourse) how any man, endued with the least reason or courage, would on any account suffer torment or publick ignominious death, when his own hands with a stab or poison could give him ease and remedy.

Once introduced to his work by the narrator, Oroonoko too became a devotee of Plutarch and he likewise despised men who waited to suffer death at another man's hand. It is clear that Byam in the pamphlet found this reading of romances and Roman heroics distasteful; this accords with the disdain revealed by the fictional Byam for the narrator of *Oroonoko* who delivered these tales to her hero. Perhaps too, if Behn and the narrator may here be supposed one, it was in allusion to this fictional inclination that the historical Byam referred to the lady who may have been the young Aphra under the romance name out of D'Urfée, 'Astrea'.[15]

The greatest resemblance of Allin and Oroonoko comes through their romantic and heroic aspirations, which are hopelessly at odds with the unheroic times. As Monmouth thought to be king with a few plotters and followers, so Allin had ridiculously grandiose notions of what a little hard work could bring: through plantation labour he would get many horses, he would then buy a ship and go to kill 'the Great Turk'. Such schemes Byam called 'swelling Vapours'. Oroonoko thought to be the prince of a black rebellion and found himself simply a renegade slave. At the end he thinks to kill half the colony and ends up killing only his wife.

In November 1663, just at the time when Behn supposedly arrived in Surinam, Allin was found exercising his 'sarcastical wit to the prejudice of Capt Parker'. Naturally in this volatile colony such a rencontre ended in a duel. Allin intended killing Parker and then, inspired by his romantic and heroic reading, stabbing himself and running into the flames to avoid 'an ignominious death'. But desire and reality do not concur and Parker was only wounded. Like Monmouth's, Oroonoko's code of honour leads him to heroic, slightly absurd actions, the rhetoric of which is rather more impressive than the reality. For example he steals a tiger cub, with some difficulty kills the mother, and then lays the cub at the narrator's feet. At another time he makes his assault on a tiger into an act out of old romance, expecting on his return 'trophies and garlands' from the ladies; his action becomes indeed famed 'in story' and his deed 'gave Caesar occasion of many fine discourses of accidents in war, and strange escapes'. So distinct does he regard himself that, when he hears of the electric eel numbing people, he 'had a great Curiosity to try whether it would have the same effect on him'. He does so and is struck 'almost dead'. When he recovers it is the mockery of others, the loss of his position within heroic narrative, that worries him. Ironically it is the narrator who is responsible for the reduction to the absurd: 'we had the eel at supper, which was . . . most delicate meat'.[16]

It is in the actual death that the closest connection is made between Allin and Oroonoko. In both, the grotesque detail triumphs over or fuses with the tragic depiction, with the result in *Oroonoko* that the expectation of a conventional tragic denouement is foiled. When Thomas Southerne turned the events of Behn's short story into a formal theatrical tragedy, he substantially rewrote the death and omitted many of the elements of the grotesque.

After being fooled repeatedly by the colonists, who use language as a weapon rather than as truth or the romantic heightening of truth, Oroonoko decides to end the slavery which no amount of heroic narrative can any longer disguise from him; he intends both to kill his beloved Imoinda, whose body will thus remain pure and purely his, and assassinate the deputy governor Byam, who he believes is staying at the same plantation as himself. In his weakened state, graphically described by the narrator, he imagines not only the killing of Imoinda and Byam but 'all those he thought had enraged him, pleasing his great heart with the fancied slaughter he should make over the whole face of the plantation'.[17] He will then commit suicide.

In the event he manages to kill only Imoinda, who achieves the simple heroism of an accepted and willed death, smiling as she is stabbed. In death and life she remains rather strange to the narrator, who calls her leave-taking very beautiful, 'as the relation of it was to me afterwards'. But, interestingly enough, she herself chooses not to retell this tale, although, as with the account of Monmouth, she draws attention to the omitted narrative. What is given instead is the actual physical detail: 'first, cutting her throat, and then severing her, yet smiling, face from that delicate body, pregnant as it was. . . .'[18]

His own proposed suicide is made almost absurd by his impotent ravings after murder and the physical weakness that keeps him by the corpse; in time 'his strength' is 'decayed' and the reality of starving and suffering takes the heroism out of his grasp. His end is in fact brought about by the extraordinarily loathsome 'stink' of the beloved Imoinda, for in the heat the 'delicate body' has begun to decay. The only theatricality brought to bear on this gruesome situation is his enemies' echoing of *Othello* when their noses lead them to the murderer and the corpse: 'Oh monster! that hast murdered thy wife.'

From now onwards both sides seem determined on male heroics, a determination which brings about an escalation in physical gro-tesqueness: first Oroonoko tries to achieve the suicide he could have committed earlier: 'he ripped up his own belly, and took his bowels and pulled them out . . .'.[19] But even these extreme actions fail to result in death. He returns to the house with the narrator, but his earthy smell proves so strong that it drives her out and, during her absence, he is taken, whipped and placed over a fire like cooking meat. While tied to the stake he asks for a tobacco pipe, which he smokes as 'his members' are cut off and thrown into the fire and his ears and nose hacked off with a blunt knife and burnt.

The actions mock his earlier efforts at suicide and simultaneously echo the heroic and competitive self-mutilation of the Indians which, with his Europeanized eyes, the black hero had found bizarre. This mutilation now links Oroonoko with the 'golden-age', exploitable and naïve natives, making him a sacrifice of all three tangled races.

Only when his second arm is severed does the pipe fall from his mouth as the signal of death. His body is then cut into quarters and sent to the chief plantations, one being refused by a good white man who does not want to display the 'frightful spectacle of a mangled king'. The narrator is the only one to write praise of the hero and his heroic death but, after claiming modesty, she hopes that the 'reputation of my pen is considerabe enough to make his glorious name to survive to all ages.'[20]

The account of the end of Allin allows some comparison with these closing pages of *Oroonoko*. Some months after the events of the story are supposed to have taken place, when Behn's alleged kinsman Lord Willoughby, so conspicuously absent in her narrative, finally arrived in Surinam from Barbados, he enquired about the celebrated blasphemy case of Allin. No doubt, as proprietor of the territory, wishing to encourage colonists, he was sensitive to what so many had told him of the 'lewdness of this Country'. An encounter of Allin and Willoughby followed and in January of 1665, a year after Behn's supposed departure from Surinam, Allin foreshadowed the fictional Oroonoko in compassing the life of the ruler of the colony.

In Allin's case Byam, the object of Oroonoko's violent fantasy, is telling the tale of Willoughby's escape. Both governor and deputy governor are wounded at different times by their foes and both Oroonoko and Allin think to bring about their assassinations while their enemies are at Parham House, owned by Willoughby and around which both men were known to walk. To effect his purpose with the governor, Allin dressed in 'one of his Negroes' coats, almost as if he were impersonating his more famous fictional successor. Both men fail to kill their enemies, although Allin does succeed in wounding Willoughby, as Imoinda had wounded Byam. Both men intend to kill themselves, but Oroonoko finds himself too weak and Allin, stabbing himself, fails to make the blow mortal. Both however succeed in making 'a large Orifice' in themselves. Both are heroic in words to compensate for their failure in deeds, Allin heralding Monmouth's words on the scaffold twenty years later, 'I came here to dye, to kill my Lord, and then my self.' His physical and mental strength comes from his lack of Christian belief for, as he wrote in the letter found on him, 'He that slights his own life may command any mans life in the world; and I have too much of a *Roman* in me to possess my own life, when I cannot enjoy it with freedom and honour.' He had, he declared 'as much courage as ever *Caesar* had'.

Both Oroonoko and Allin suffer a time of torment after their self-mutilating but neither repents anything except his failure to kill, and both avoid Christian comfort. Towards the end both ask for a light for their pipes, although Allin does so to try to obtain wherewithal to discharge his pistol. Both in the end die fairly ignominiously, death coming, as it was for Behn, simply through an accumulation of pains, although Allin helps his on with 'Landocum'.

Because he was considered a suicide, Allin's carcase was treated as Oroonoko's: it was

> dragged from the Gaol by the common Hangman, and Negroes, to the Pillory . . . where a Barbicue was erected; his Members cut off, and flung in his face, they and his Bowels burnt under the Barbicue . . . his Head to be cut off, and his Body to be quartered, and when dry-barbicued or dry-roasted, after the *Indian* manner, his Head to be stuck on a pole at *Parham*, and his Quarters to be put up at the most eminent places of the Colony.

Byam's final comment is succinct:

> Thus died this perverse Atheist, unparallel'd in History, whose pride and passion, and overweening judgment of his cursed Tenet, hurried him to this ignominious end, which his folly fansied should never seize him.

So is Behn's: 'Thus died this great man, worthy of a better fate.' Both Behn's narrator and Byam insist it has been their duty to write their narratives; Byam has been careful 'that onely Truth should direct my pen', while Behn's narrator is 'relating the truth'.

V

The only popular British uprising in colonial America took place in Virginia in 1676; its leader was Nathaniel Bacon, who had come as a young man from England in 1674 to set up as a gentleman planter on the James River. Like his neighbours he suffered various Indian raids on his servants and property; soon he concluded that the governor, Sir William Berkeley, was too lenient on the Indians and too unconcerned for the lives and livelihoods of the lesser planters. Consequently he took up arms against the raiders without waiting to be commissioned for such activity. The rebellion that commenced with this act and included the sacking of James Town has been seen variously as a popular protest against the older aristocratic hegemony, which was accused of appeasing Indians and strangling trade in the colonies, and as one episode in the long struggle of puritanism and royalism, democracy and centralism. On a personal level it was a fight between an ageing legitimate governor and a young populist would-be hero, not unlike that between Monmouth and his ageing uncle, James II. The rebellion was fierce but short. Within a few months Bacon died and it fizzled out. Reprisals by the governor foreshadowed the alleged severity of James to the hapless followers of Monmouth.

Probably towards the end of her life, perhaps even in the final year, Behn turned this colonial material into a play which was performed posthumously in 1690, *The Widow Ranter or Bacon in Virginia*, the first play to be set in colonial America. As in her other accounts of heroes, so here Behn seems fascinated by factual elements, the involvement of fiction and fantasy in historical action and the approach to death as romantic or heroic drama. But, in contrast with the Monmouth story, the historically recorded death of Bacon needs modification to fit it for fiction.

As in the case of *Oroonoko*, it is important for Behn's narrative that her hero be acting within a vacuum of authority. In the short story, Byam the villain is given as little legitimating status as possible, while the real governor, Lord Willoughby, is absent throughout the tale; in the Virginia of the play, the governor and the King's deputy, Sir William Berkeley, who in history struggled against Bacon, is also absent, so that the rebel can assume something of royal authority himself. This accords with the historical Bacon who repeatedly made his appeals direct to King Charles.

In the preface to *The Young King* printed in 1679, Behn claimed that she had 'visited many and distant shores' and one of these just might have been Virginian – ships frequently sailed in convoy from Surinam through Virginia and back to Europe. There are periods of her life unaccounted for in the 1670s and 1680s and a suggestion in the 'Memoirs' published after her death that she had worked for the King on occasions other than the few months in Antwerp.[21] But, although few events can be ruled out of Behn's life, there is no strong evidence that she was ever in Virginia, as there is much evidence for Surinam. It is more likely, then, that she gained information from those who were there in the 1670s or shortly after. The names associated with Virginia recur in her life: Arlington, Colepeper, Berkeley and Scot. The most definite reference to her early years is from Thomas Colepeper, who claims her mother as his wet-nurse; Lord Colepeper, a very distant relative, became governor of Virginia and heard the grievances of Bacon's followers. His predecessor Sir

William Berkeley shares the name of the family Behn had so flamboy-antly exposed in *Love Letters*; as his third wife, Berkeley married in the 1670s the widow Frances Colepeper, who helped her husband against the commissioners sent out by the King in 1677 to investigate the rebellion and its aftermath. (The royalism of Berkeley, like that of Byam, would seem to indicate that Behn should be on his side in the affair, but this was not the case although it is possible that the governor was written out of the story to prevent any hostile depiction of him. The King himself is said to have criticized Berkeley, 'That old fool', for hanging 'more men in that naked Country, than he had done for the Murther of his Father'; this sense of Charles's dis-pleasure at his governor perhaps allowed Behn to present a rebel in a more flattering light than would otherwise be appropriate.) Arling-ton, partly responsible for her spying mission in Antwerp, and Scot whom she went to interrogate there, both had (or belonged to families that had) estates in Virginia and the West Indies. From any people connected with these men Behn may have learnt of the Bacon rebellion.

Another possibility is that she gained her colonial background from Surinam and transferred it northwards. Certainly the colonists of Adis's letter, and indeed of *Oroonoko*, might have informed her presentation of the litigious, illborn, convict-filled society of Virginia.

In *The Widow Ranter*, Bacon is presented as a tragic masculine hero sited not in the unreal exoticism of Renaissance Spain or pre-Columbian America, the proper home for the heroic male in early Restoration drama, but instead in the disgruntled 1670s in the mismanaged colony of Virginia. He is thus forced from being a glowingly simple hero destroyed by social forces in the manner of Dryden's early heroes into becoming a commentary on a murkily complex reality that does not so much destroy as sully and diminish him. In this context masculine heroism and its aesthetic come under closer scrutiny than ever before in Behn's works.

The play is a tragi-comedy, a form Behn had not used since her first dramas twenty years before. In the absence of a governor, Bacon is rebelling against the debased but nonetheless legal political author-ity of the vulgar, uneducated Virginians who, he and his followers believe, have failed to defend the people against the Indians. Like the historical Allin and the fictional Oroonoko, he has a strong sense of what he can accomplish: one of his opponents calls him

a man indeed above the common rank, by nature generous; brave, resolved, and daring; who studying the lives of the Romans and great men, that have raised themselves to the most elevated fortunes, fancies it easy for ambitious men to aim at any pitch of glory. I've heard him often say, 'Why cannot I conquer the universe as well as Alexander? or like another Romulus form a new Rome, and make myself adored?'[22]

It is clear that such ambition now belongs in the theatre, since little can be achieved in a world where an admiring man, such as this speaker shows himself to be, will go on to declare himself an enemy of Bacon, simply because of an 'Interest' he has in the new governor.

Bacon, who has a strong sense of the theatrical heroic, loves and is beloved by a tearful Indian queen whose virgin heart he had apparently conquered before she married the young Indian king. Cynical onlookers within the play, young men who know that marriage and love are partly affairs of money and ease, declare that Bacon needed a princess to love to complete his image. In the course of the play Bacon defeats and kills the Indian king; after her husband's death, the queen dons male attire to escape, but she has no heart for cross-dressing and needs no effeminizing of Bacon to fix him to his role, as Hermione had needed to fix Cesario. She is as 'timorous as a dove', she declares, and she admits that 'I have no Amazonian fire about me'. Consequently she simply causes confusion in the battle. In the end she is mistakenly killed by Bacon before he can sully her by any physical love and he thus preserves her feminine body in the purity Imoinda had briefly obtained. He responds to his fatal error and a sense that he is losing the battle against the authorities by imagining a heroic classical suicide for himself – he is well read in the *Lives of the Romans* – accompanied with the correct heroic dying words and followed by an equally heroic funeral: 'make of the trophies of the war a pile, and set it all on fire, that I may leap into consuming flames – while all my tents are burning round about me.'[23]

After much talk that almost falls into a surprising blank verse in this most prosaic of plays, Bacon does kill himself in the mistaken belief that he has lost the battle. He is provoked into it by fear of what one of his followers describes as 'a shameful Death'. Suicide for Bacon becomes 'a noble remedy for all the ills of life' and he is sure that he will thereby secure himself 'from being a public spectacle upon the common theatre of death'. Like Monmouth he is more concerned with earthly reputation than with repentance, but, dying by his own hand rather than by another's, unlike Monmouth he feels able to utter on his own account the proper political words: 'never let ambition – love – or interest make you forget as I have done – your duty – and allegiance.'[24]

But, like the Indian queen, Bacon is seemingly in the wrong play and in the wrong time. He has actually won the battle, as Cleopatra had not when she purposed to die in 'high Roman fashion', and no one is making a spectacle of him except himself. (Happily however his erroneous death can suggest another Latin parallel and one of his followers stoutly declares that he has fallen like Roman Cassius 'by mistake'.) No legal death is ever performed: no one achieves public hanging in the chaotic colony although many are condemned to it. Without Bacon, his former followers compromise, make peace and are pardoned. His heroic futile death and his beloved's ineptly romantic one are juxtaposed with the feasting to celebrate the opportunistic marriage of one of his followers with a wealthy, tabacco-smoking widow of the town.

Characters within the play comment on Bacon's staginess. Even before his classically theatrical death, he insists, despite the inglorious times, on achieving glory by playing chivalrous roles, uncommon outside the theatre: he demands a personal duel with the Indian chief whom others simply dismiss as a 'mad hot-brained youth', to fulfil his 'romantic humour' according to his followers, and he treats those he conquers with elaborate courtesy. The glamorous and glorious conception of personal power Bacon holds resembles that of heroic drama and indeed of the glamorous Stuart kings, Charles and James. Both Bacon and the Stuarts inspire followers with this glamour and amaze others with their anachronism.

Like Oroonoko, thinking to be the prince of a slave uprising, and Cesario, who expected to be king of three kingdoms, Bacon talks of empire while his contemporaries seek simple solvency. He has the consciousness of the mythologized 1640s, when cavaliering was swashbuckling, or of the 1660s, when such myths were fashioned, the early jubilant years of the Restoration with their fantastic hopes of a heroic golden age and incorruptible power.

Behn's character Bacon believes in a kind of transcendental politics, true for all times and places. This political belief is based on heroic myths and is deeply embedded in masculine classical literature which he takes to be true. He also has faith in the integrity of language: the oath and word of honour. In an obsessively plotting age like the 1680s it was no longer clear that there was any real reference for words at all, or that anything out there in any way corresponded with the verbal representation. This worrying disjunction of words and things was the theme of many pamphlets by Behn's political associates such as Roger L'Estrange. Even more strongly than Oroon-oko, Bacon believed that, if addressed to him or by him, the word must still be true like himself. So, when a clearly false letter arrives from the Virginian council, Bacon believes it sincere where his followers observe its falseness. This easy deception makes Bacon absurd in a world where even his staunchest admirers can see that the personal heroism of a 'great soul' is not the answer to duplicitous statecraft. So with death: he trips himself into it with heroic rhetoric.

The historical versions of Bacon occur in several sources. The most accessible to Behn would have been a pamphlet, *Strange News from Virginia; Being a full and true Account of the Life and Death of Nathaniel Bacon Esquire, Who was the only Cause and Original of all the late Troubles in that County. With a full Relation of all the Accidents which have happened in the late War there between the Christians and Indians*, published in 1677. This has Behn's tone only in the beginning: 'There is no Nation this day under the copes of Heaven can so experimentally speak the sad Effects of men of great Parts being reduc't to necessity, as *England*'; Bacon's ambition acted out on the colonial stage is called indulgently 'the general lust of a large Soul'. But there are other tones: 'when men have been once flusht or entred with vice, how hard is it for them to leave it.' In the last two pages, which record the providential death of Bacon, the tone is harsher: he is 'the great Molester of the quiet of that miserable Nation'. His death is down-graded by the rumour that he was a hard drinker and died of 'two much Brandy'; though the author does not believe this slander, it has been repeated. The pamphlet ends more positively with praise of his 'natural parts', learning and sense:

> Wherefore as I am my self a Lover of Ingenuity, though an abhorrer of disturbance or Rebellion, I think fit since Providence was pleased to let him dye a Natural death in his Bed, not to asperse him with saying he kill'd himself with drinking.

The official view which Behn might have read in manuscript if she were still working directly with government intelligence in the 1680s was *A True Narrative of the Late Rebellion in Virginia, by the Royal Commissioners, 1677*. This included *A True Narrative of the Rise, Progresse, and Cessation of the Late Rebellion in Virginia, Most Humbly and Impartially Reported by His Majestyes Commissioners Appointed to Enquire into the Affaires of the Said Colony*. The report arose out of a commission sent to Virginia after news of the rebellion had reached London in September of 1676. The commissioners arrived in the beginning of 1677 and returned in July to make their report to the Privy Council in October. In this they present themselves as transparent observers, allowing the 'most knowing, credible and indifferent Persons in Virginia' to speak through them and basing their narrative on the 'most authentique Papers, Records, Reports . . .'.[25] Like Byam in his letter and Behn in *Oroonoko*, they claim truth: they wrote what they 'thought most consonant to Truth and Reality'. A source of the Indian queen may be found here in the historical Queen of Pamunckey, who feels the dual allegiance to Indians and settlers which is given in romantic terms to the young Indian queen in *The Widow Ranter*. But this woman flees from Bacon and swerves decidedly from the timorous fictional character in playing a subtle diplomatic part, more concerned with supplies and troop movements than with romance.

The commissioners give Bacon the old-world status of an illustrious family, which Behn's character assumes. Like Behn's creation, this one is ambitious, arrogant and imperious, but unlike hers he manages to hide these qualities till he grew 'powerfull and popular'. He is closer to Monmouth than to Behn's Bacon when he is prevailed on to lead the revolt by appeals to the vanity of leadership, when he seduces 'the Vulgar and most ignorant People' to believe in him, and when he uses the appearance of magic to impress the credulous. Like Allin, Oroonoko, Monmouth and Cesario, he has notions quite beyond the times or his capabilities: 'he pretended and bosted what great Service hee would doe for the country in destroying the Comon Enemy, securing their Lives and Estates, Libertyes', called by the commissioners 'such like fair frauds'.[26] He is a fantasist who returns from a campaign 'with a thousand braging lyes to the credulous Silly People of what feats he had perform'd' and he speaks to them after he has caused 'the Drums to Beat and Trumpet to Sound'; in his rousing words the rebels become the true guardians of 'his majestyes country'.[27]

Like the other heroes and their historical equivalents, Bacon is not impressed with Christianity: like Allin he is described as 'of a pestilent and prevalent Logical discourse tending to atheisme . . .'; the germ of the classically suicidal Bacon described by Behn may exist here. His death is physical and ignoble:

> But before he could arrive to the Perfection of his designes (w'ch none but the eye of omniscience could Penetrate) Providence did that which noe other hand durst (or at least did) doe and cut him off.
> Hee lay sick. . . . of the Bloody Flux, and . . . accompanyed with a

> Lousey Disease; so that the swarmes of Verymn that bred in his Body
> he could not destroy but by throwing his shirts into the Fire as often
> as he shifted himself.
> Hee dyed much dissatisfied in minde. . . .[28]

With this death, close to the physical realism of *Oroonoko*, Behn's character in *The Widow Ranter* has nothing to do, unless it be in the 'dissatisfied' mind.

In other official documents there are hints Behn may have taken. For example PRO document C.O. 1/36.77 suggests that when Bacon first defeated the Indians he took the king's daughter as prisoner. The 'Manifesto' quoted here and called a 'Declaration of the People' took a high patrician tone, suitable for Behn's creation, accusing Virginian rulers of having risen from low extraction and of lacking education and honour, of being sponges on the public treasure.[29]

Other accounts to which Behn could not have had access occasionally suggest she knew more than *Strange News* or even the *True Narrative* could give her and, as suggested above, may either have been to Virginia or have spoken with those who had, although none gives much basis for the fantastic 'Roman' suicide she creates. Among the accounts is *The Beginning, Progress, and Conclusion of Bacon's Rebellion, 1675–1676*, written thirty years after the events it chronicles, by 'T. M.' and printed in 1804. 'T. M.' appears to have been Thomas Mathew of Cherry Point in Virginia, the owner of land in an area troubled by the Indians who so affronted Bacon. He held various local offices and was a member of the House of Burgesses in 1676. Apparently trying to dissociate himself from both Bacon and his opponents, he twice refused a lieutenancy from Bacon though he conversed often with him and had considerable sympathy for his cause. Like the commissioners he presents himself as the reverse of the fictionalist, an impartial businessman used to numbers not words, not a dramatist but a follower of 'the Track of barefac'd Truths'. His language is however not without its tropes: he speaks of his desire to return to the 'Sphere of Merchandize' out of 'the dark and Slippery Meanders of Court Embarrassments' and the Bacon that emerges from his account is one of dramatic gestures and postures. When he faces the governor, for example, he is 'Strutting betwixt his Two files of Men'; later he appears walking 'with outragious Postures of his Head, Arms, Body, and Leggs, often tossing his hand from his Sword to his Hat . . .'.[30] This Bacon has a sense of theatre and spectacle, as does the governor, who bares his breast to be shot during the argument. In T. M.'s account Bacon shows himself fascinated with the rhetoric of heroic suicide and slaughter:

> when Mr Bacon followed the Governour and Concill with the forementioned impetuos (like Delirious) Actions whil'st that Party presented their Fusils at the Window full of Faces, He said 'Dam my Bloud, I'le Kill Governr Councill Assembly and all, and then Ile Sheath my Sword in my heart's bloud' . . .[31]

Given the emphasis on bare truth, it is interesting that, as Byam's account is full of omens and prodigies where Behn's fictional tale avoids them, so here the plain recorder starts his account with 'three Prodigies' appearing in Virginia in 1675, where Behn's dramatic hero has no such divine context. The prodigies begin a process of causation which the fictionally inspired Bacon does not need. But T. M.'s and Behn's images come close in the notion of candour: like Oroonoko, Bacon can be deceived and so he becomes the pawn of his friend, who is described as 'subtile', able to discover 'mens Inclinations, and Instill his Nottions'.[32] Bacon is 'of a Disposition too precipitate' to be a manipulator.

But if T. M. remembers a theatrical Bacon close to Behn's, the death again follows the official narrative in being unheroic and unwilled. He falls sick 'of a Flux' after being wet and 'in a While Bacon dyes . . .'; his followers immediately submit to the governor and some are pardoned. Behn's Bacon, like Macbeth in a more heroic play, hopes to avoid becoming a common spectacle; here 'Bacons Body was so made away, as his Bones were never found to be Exposed on a Gibbet as was purpos'd, Stones being laid in his Coffin . . .'. This is the one account of a rebel that closes without a mangled body.

The History of Bacon's and Ingram's Rebellion, lacking beginning and end, was published for the first time in 1814 and was reputedly written by an unknown Virginian resident with first-hand information. His self-presentation is more vernacular and humorous than T. M.'s and his picture of Bacon even more sympathetic, though he accepts the illegality and barbarity of the rebellious enterprise. Instead of being political allegory boosted by prodigies, his narrative becomes personal and exemplary: Bacon is 'an Epittemey' of Fortune's 'fickle humer'. The Bacon of this account is again charismatic, virile, 'Populerly inclin'd' and malleable, and he indulges in 'elated and passionate expressions', like Oroonoko haranguing the fainthearted. Here too Bacon sickens and dies, 'haveing for som time bin besieged by sickness'; inevitably his death is 'by the hand of good providence'. The only useful additions are the declaration that Bacon follows Behn's dying heroes in avoiding 'Religious duty' and the inclusion of a poem by Bacon's servant which, in its counterfactual statements, comes closest in tone to the play's conception. The servant who attended Bacon's corpse to its secret burial praises him in the Roman terms so important to Behn's character: he has conquered like Caesar and acted like Cato.[33]

Holding less to the particulars of history than in *Love Letters*, Behn in this late play manages to create a death that summarizes the others and both celebrates and anatomizes a masculine heroics embodying and flouting authority. It becomes a statement of her ambivalent attitude to the politics of glamour and personal power, seen as both naive and splendid. The depiction of Bacon's death gains some of its absurdity through the usual posturing and self-dramatizing of the protagonist and some from its deviation from history. Where the heroic, romatically inspired death of Cesario is made a little absurd by the token of the tooth-pick case and the fiercely heroic death of Oroonoko by the pipe-smoking and the grotesque physical failure, in *The Widow Ranter* Bacon's heroic death is senseless in the circumstances of the play and absurd in its replacement of physically disgusting disease with clean suicide.

VI

In all these cases of heroic death, it seems that it is the interpenetration of history and story, fiction and faction (in both its senses), that intrigues Behn. The self is taken outside itself through the ideals of love and heroic politics. The self fictionalized in and outside of history, the self that is annihilated in death, is the mobile, shifting self of Lucretian atomism, a momentary voyeur of itself, taking an anticipatory pleasure before death in the contemplating of its assumption in death into heroic art or after death into folk mythology.

In Behn's presentations there seems no concept of a personal or political grand narrative as context, no concept of history as Christian and providential, often a feature of the purportedly historical accounts which parallel her fictions; instead there is a sense of the aesthetics of a willed or anticipated death than cannot be commodified for the actor though it may be so for the spectator. This moment, contextualized more in classical philosophy than Christian religion, gives an artistic if not a political authenticity to the otherwise unstable selves of the protagonists. They achieve their greatness by moving out of history into myth, in the manner of Mircea Eliade's heroes who transport themselves into a mythical epoch for the moment of their 'exemplary gesture'.[34]

The intrusion of the grotesque and absurd from history into the magnificent causes a coexistence of myth and its undercutting. These moments in which history and fiction involve each other, in which history interrupts generically formal art with precise physical and social circumstances or shadows its effort by simple contradiction, insist that reference be made beyond the fiction and that presentation be known as representation. This insistence is aided by the self-consciousness in the protagonists, caused by their reaching out to classical literary images or tokens. The aesthetic moment of organized death is not for them a Burkean aestheticizing of political truth in a fetishized body, but more an anarchic moment, destabilizing political and literary categories.

The represented, planned and orchestrated deaths of great men are both private and public. They refuse to conform to any Renaissance notion of didactic virtue and instead hold to an anachronistic Roman sense of manly honour. At their ends Oroonoko, Bacon and Cesario are buoyed up by a concept of classical masculine behaviour, not by any need, articulated socially by the priests on the scaffold of Monmouth, to be an exemplar of Christian virtue. All three depicted men refuse Christian death and its inevitable contingency and, dreaming of Roman suicide, try to achieve the Lucretian power to act as they will. Refusing like Lucretius to accept the hidden divine power that 'treads human grandeur down', they create a self that they appear to believe for the moment is not manipulated by others, ironically taking a kind of freedom at their supreme moment of impotence.

Beyond the aesthetics of what might be called the heroic grotesque is the spectating life that continues. The spectators live on in the Lucretian flux, exalted as by great art rather than edified by exemplary behaviour; these men and women are written into Behn's accounts as, with their ordinary selves intact, they leave on the next boat, learn new proverbs or make political compromises. There is a gender division too: at the close of the three works *Love Letters*, *Oroonoko* and *The Widow Ranter*, the heroic men are dead and the pragmatic women live to read, write, watch again, and die from the 'Toils of Sickness'.

The public deaths make a political, as well as an aesthetic and individual, point: they interrogate order and a doomed aristocracy.

The three heroes exist in worlds largely without the proper authority which they themselves try to make. The worlds outside England – the Continent inhabited before Cesario's death, the colonies of Oroonoko and Bacon – are simpler than England; there is a sense almost of childish make-believe in them and people can declare themselves of any class and sex. The proper authority will come from outside and is not represented: the governors are awaited in *Oroonoko* and *The Widow Ranter* and the king is absent from most of *Love Letters*. In such circumstances, there can be a fantasy of proper authority and order, never quite to be depicted. Perhaps in this depiction of England through what is not England there is a desire once again to inhabit the promising world of the late Interregnum, of *The Rover* and *The Roundheads*, where political idealism was still possible. The works would then become a kind of rewriting of the Restoration as a perpetual restoration through desire.

In their enterprise of creating an authority outside legalities, the heroes are admirable, but their mistake is a belief in improper *personal* authority: going beyond the heroism of Plutarch's *Lives*, they try to build an edifice of personal power based on the fickle and degenerate people, slaves, peasants or colonial convicts. In this they must fail for, as the Aesop fable warned: 'He who by th'Rables power a Crowne does weare/ May be a King, but is a Slave to feare'.

Perhaps, too, the three great doomed leaders have a more cynical message in themselves for authority; perhaps they speak less of the historical rebels they represent than of the legitimate authorities that destroy them. In many respects Cesario, Oroonoko and Bacon, probably all creations of the later 1680s, although with historical parallels from earlier times, seem an amalgam of the heroic and theatrical Charles I whose great death on the scaffold so dominated Restoration politics, and of his two sons: the cynical, charismatic Charles II and the doomed idealist James II, about to be deserted by most of the followers Behn had resplendently described in her *Coronation Ode*. After all her public support for the Stuarts, are these late works ways of suggesting the anachronistic, 'fictional' nature of what she admires, a more open expression of that political exaspera-tion to be found in her last published poems, the *Pindaric Poem to Dr Burnet* and the *Congratulatory Poem to Queen Mary*? Is the imaginative spectator of public deaths a less disturbing image of the subject-spectator of the death of a dynasty?

Public deaths and suicides from apparent failure affirm the legal order and serve power in all the works; as failed rebels in their texts, all three heroes are destroyed by legally constituted authority. But the death, judicial or personal, is marked less by the re-establishment of order than by a resumption of semi-order. In proportion as their social context is debased, the men become heroic and tragic, so that Oroonoko in a colony governed by evil deputies is the most heroic and Monmouth in a country with standards of literary expression and proper behaviour the least. Bacon, the most politically justified, kills himself and suggests that authority, in almost Hobbesian terms, remains to be obeyed even when corrupt and base. Power needs constant victims and constant spectacles. There is nothing left politically for the decent character to do but to obey the law and contemplate the image of art: as one admirable character in *The Widow Ranter* laments, 'What pity 'tis there should be such false maxims in the world, that noble actions, however great, must be criminal for want of a law to authorise them.'[35]

Norwich 1991

Notes

1 'On the Honourable Sir Francis Fane, on his Play call'd the Sacrifice', Aphra Behn, *Poetry*, ed. Janet Todd (London: Pickering and Chatto, 1992).
2 *The Fair Jilt* with its depiction of the intended execution of Tarquin fits into this scheme but, since the hero escapes death, I have not treated the story here.
3 *Faerie Queene*, Book I, Canto IX, line 40; *Paradise Lost*, X, lines 1003–6.
4 *Antony and Cleopatra*, Act IV, sc. 14, 80–1.
5 Letter to Tonson, *The Gentleman's Magazine*, V, May 1836, p. 481.
6 *Poetry*, p. 26. From her thorough grounding in Lucretius, Behn no doubt derived some of the boldness of her position as a woman declaring on scientific and linguistic matters.
7 *Poetry*, pp. 239, 235, 258, 248, 263.
8 Reproduced in David G. Chandler, *Sedgemoor 1685* (London: Anthony Mott Ltd, 1985).
9 *Love Letters between a Nobleman and his Sister*, ed. Maureen Duffy (London: Virago, 1987), p. 458.
10 *Love Letters*, p. 419.
11 *Love Letters*, pp. 454 and 456.
12 *Bishop Burnet's History of His Own Time* (Oxford: Oxford Univeristy Press, 1833), III, 56.
13 *Love Letters*, p. 112.
14 For the fullest account of Behn's involvement in Surinam, see William J. Cameron's *New Light on Aphra Behn* (Auckland: University of Auckland Press, 1961).

15 See Cameron, *New Light on Aphra Behn*.
16 *Oroonoko, The Rover*, ed. Janet Todd (Harmondsworth: Penguin, 1992), p. 120.
17 *Oroonoko, The Rover*, p. 135.
18 *Oroonoko, The Rover*, p. 135.
19 *Oroonoko, The Rover*, p. 138.
20 *Oroonoko, The Rover*, p. 140–1.
21 'Memoirs of the Life of Mrs Behn. Written by a Gentlewoman of her Acquaintance', *Histories and Novels* (1696).
22 *Oroonoko, The Rover*, p. 256.
23 *Oroonoko, The Rover*, p. 318.
24 *Oroonoko, The Rover*, p. 321.
25 The pamphlet and subsequent ones are reproduced in *Narratives of the Insurrections 1675–1690* ed. Charles McLean Andrews (New York, 1915). The last quotation is from p. 140. See also Wilcomb E. Washburn, *The Governor and the Rebel: a history of Bacon's rebellion in Virginia* (Chapel Hill: University of North Carolina Press, 1957).
26 *Narratives*, p. 111.
27 Despite their claim of authenticity, the commissioners provide speeches for their characters, presumably following the methods most associated with the historiography of Thucydides: 'As for the speeches delivered by the several statesmen before and during the war, it is difficult for me to report the exact substance of what was said, whether I heard the speeches myself or learned of them from others. I have therefore made the speakers express primarily what in my own opinion was called for under the successive circumstances, at the same time keeping as close as possible to the general import of what was actually said' (*Thucydides*, trans. John H. Finley Jr., Ann Arbor: University of Michigan Press, pp. 94–5). Restoration drama based on 'history' seems an extension of this practice.
28 *Narratives*, p. 139.
29 The 'Manifesto' is printed in *The Old Dominion in the Seventeenth Century: a documentary history of Virginia, 1606–1689*, ed. Warren M. Billings (Chapel Hill: University of North Caroline Press, 1975), p. 277.
30 *Narratives*, p. 29.
31 *Narratives*, p. 29.
32 *Narratives*, p. 40.
33 *Narratives*, pp. 52–4 and 74–7. See also *An Account of Our Late Troubles in Virginia written in 1676*, by Mrs An. Cotton of Q. Creeks, published from the manuscript in 1804.
34 Mircea Eliade, *The Myth of the Eternal Return; or, Cosmos and History*, trans. Willard R. Trask (Princeton: Princeton University Press, 1974), p. 35.
35 *Oroonoko, The Rover*, p. 268.

3 *Pamela*: or the bliss of servitude

I

'Why, what is all this, my dear,' says Sir Simon Darnford, 'but that our neighbour has a mind to his mother's waiting-maid!' This is a cynical if not uncommon view of the subject in *Pamela*, expressed at greater length by Henry Fielding. Numerous maids were deflowered by masters in the first half of the eighteenth century, presuming that a girl in the family might as well be in the family way.[1] And yet Sir Simon's remains a simple response to the complex relationship of service, whose codes and assumptions were much debated in literature. Richardson's *Pamela*, along with the tracts of Swift and Defoe, is part of the debate on service and its meaning for both masters and menials.[2] But, while describing his new pious ideology of service, Richardson uncovered a psychology of servitude that wickedly allowed the social terms – maid, master and mistress – to assume for a while their sexual meaning and his readers not only to adjust their social sense but also to indulge their voyeuristic tendencies.

Lady's maids were for the mid-eighteenth century a difficult group of servants to place. This was especially so for the middle class who could not, like their aristocratic sisters, resort to breeding and birth for distinction. Maids were often as educated as their mistresses; they frequently read the same novels and they probably spoke similarly. Above all, lady and servant were similarly dressed, although the latter's finery was usually the mistress's cast-offs. Daniel Defoe for one was appalled at the confusion of rank this habit led to. He tells of arriving at a friend's house and, on being ordered to salute the ladies, did so and found he had 'kiss'd the Chamber-Jade into the bargain, for she was as well dress'd as the best'. 'Things of this Nature', he commented, 'would be easily avoided, if Servant Maids were to wear Liveries', a frequent plea of the time, unheeded until the next century.[3]

Part of the problem with the lady's maid, as with other domestics, came from an unclear concept of service, which made it possible for Defoe both to salute a servant and to recoil from the act. Many eighteenth-century masters held to a notion of the master as a friend in the sense of benefactor – 'for my dear mother's sake, I will be a friend to you', says Mr B. initially in *Pamela* – and the maid as faithful menial serving the family for loyalty rather than pay.[4] With this concept went the master's complete right over his servant's body, so that Mr B.'s toying with his maidservant and even his raping of her would not, as Pamela fondly thinks, have much discomposed his neighbours. Servants and masters were in this view castes apart and the maid's fall was her own affair. On the other side, however, was a newer idea of service as a job done for money; 'to expect attachment from a servant is idle, and betrays an ignorance of the world', wrote the Reverend John Trusler in the 1780s. The new idea of service grew among servants with the great increase in mobility and wages during the period, which meant that a domestic stayed on average as little as three or four years with an employer.[5] According to the view, servants differed from masters in class, considered as a matter of luck in title and fortune, and not in caste, an absolute unchangeable state of worth and breeding.

In *Pamela*, Mr B. with his boasts of mastery aims to take the most distressing elements of both concepts of service, desiring an unques-tioning servant from the old idea but one whom he can cast off at will as in the newer one. His maid, however, counters with a different concept, involving the best from the old and new ideas, loyalty and self-possession, and adding a religious element that dignifies service, yet firmly limits its extent. It is a concept that avoids earthly while insisting on divine equality and that firmly establishes social hierarchy while allowing another hierarchy to enter. Henry Fielding in *Shamela* declared that the instruction of *Pamela* was that a maidservant should neglect her business and ornament herself, so that, if her master were not a fool, she would be debauched by him and, if he were, she would be married.[6] In fact the exemplary servitude of Richardson severs debauchery and marriage completely. *Pamela*'s new idea of service makes wife and maid one and a wedding of master and servant into perfect social sense. It is for this ideal that Mr B. is brought to bed.

The squire proposes an absolute vertical social structure that can allow with impunity the odd horizontal peccadillo. 'He has *power* to oblige', write Pamela's parents, 'and has a kind of *authority* to command, as your master' (p. 13).[7] Mr B. is repetitious about his great state. 'Consider the pride of my condition', he tells his servant, the 'pride of birth and fortune'. And he enjoys expressing his mastery: 'I will not sue meanly, where I can command' (p. 122). Mrs Jewkes, the Lincolnshire housekeeper, is eager to support the social and sexual power she knows, and Pamela seems naive in underestimating it. He is, after all, a justice of the peace and may imprison a person legally; he owns houses that serve as prisons if the law will not oblige and people who may become priests and gaolers. He is indeed 'the mighty rich' and his maid 'the abject poor' (p. 99).

Pamela, however, counters Mr B.'s hierarchical claim by at first emphasizing the social part of it. But, when she asserts the distance of maid and master, she manages at the same time to elevate her own lowliness by spiritualizing it. In the Christian scheme, the last is first, the servant of the Lord above the wordly master, and the poor blessed beyond the rich. Jonas Hanway, a proponent of the religious concept of service, prefaces his tract to domestics. *Virtue in humble Life: containing Reflections on the reciprocal duties of the wealthy and indigent, the master and the servant* (1774), with a picture of Mary humbly bathing Christ's feet. So there is an edge to Pamela's repetition of Mr B.'s wealth and her poverty, his lordliness and her humility, and the reiterated words 'degrade', 'demean' and 'consequence' grow resonant. 'I am of no consequence . . . that such a great gentleman as you, should need to justify yourself about me' (p. 71), she says humbly, and, with variation, 'I am not of consequence enough for my master to concern himself, and be angry about such a creature as me!' (p. 55). Frequently Mr B. is told not to 'degrade' himself by offering 'freedoms to his poor servant' (p. 14).

These quotations point to another technique of the maid. Pamela uses Mr B.'s desired hierarchy to keep him in his place and sever his social and sexual powers. James Frazer in 'Taboo and the Perils of the Soul' describes how primitive people control their king by hedging him round with rules and observances which seem to contribute to his dignity but which in reality hamper his actions: 'Far from adding to his comfort, these observances, by trammelling his every act, annihilate his freedom . . .'.[8] In a similar way, under the pretext of humble service. Pamela forces her master to the correct stance. She can leave him when he wants her to stay, announcing that 'it doesn't become a poor servant to stay in your presence' (p. 15). Later, as he eyes her lecherously, she can beg to withdraw, 'for the sense I have of my unworthiness renders me unfit for such a presence' (p. 38). Indeed, when Mr B. diverges from the proper path of social mastery, she taunts him back. 'Do you know whom you speak to', he barks; to which she pertinently replies: 'Well may I forget that I am your servant when you forget what belongs to a master.' Again she comments, after one of his encroachments, that he has gone too far for a master to a servant; he must be brought to a proper knowledge of the degrading nature of his conduct. Sexual desire improperly equalizes employer and employed, and undermines social power.

When Pamela speaks Mr B.'s own language of mastery and distance, it becomes less humility than pride of servitude: 'You have taught me to forget myself and what belongs to me, and have lessened the distance that fortune has made between us, by demeaning yourself, to be so free to a poor servant' (p. 17), she asserts. This self-respecting lowliness is nicely represented sartorially; when Pamela assumes her ravishing rustic dress, she is more assured than in the rich array of her mistress.

Pamela's pride of servitude allows her to claim lowliness while enjoying high status. In Lincolnshire, where she arrives not as a maid but as the master's desired object, she is immediately addressed as madam, and her statement of humility to the housekeeper – 'I am a servant inferior to you' – is far from humble in the context of her clear power over Mr B. She stresses her own lowly background and yet creates and re-creates it to her own proud taste. Her parents are so poor she must send them money, and, when she grows great, she must tell them how to leave off slavish ways; she is, however, elaborate and public in obedience to them – obedience which they could not command of her – and she insists on the magical formula of proud humility. When Mr B. calls the Andrews 'low and . . . honest', she corrects him; they are 'poor and . . . honest'.

So Pamela beats Mr B. at his own game by accepting his social hierarchy and glorying in her lower rung. She is a humble servant and by refusing any other role she dignifies and valorizes this status. But Pamela also sets up an opposing hierarchy altogether, one which Mr B. must come to accept along with his own. In this one, social rank gives way to individual qualities with which the maidservant is well endowed: beauty, wit, literary accomplishments, gentility and above all virtue. With these it is an easy matter for a servant to become a wife.

Beauty in the lowly lubricates both a rise and a fall. It is this attribute that initially strikes Mr B. and sets the whole plot in motion, but it also renders the girl a general prey of men: 'you are so pretty', says her master, 'that go where you will, you can never be free from the designs of some or other of our sex' (p. 86). Wit and literacy strike next, for it is Pamela's tongue that piques her master's interest and her letters that keep it. She wins all verbal contests with him and he can end them only by appealing to the social hierarchy he dominates. When she catches the classical allusion to Lucretia, which his educational advantage should leave only to him, he is annoyed; yet ultimately he takes her point. By writing, of course, Pamela manages to control the whole drama of mastery, which she alone interprets. Her letters ultimately seduce and capture her social superior, and it is her diary that transforms her from a waiting maid in Bedfordshire to a fair maid in Lincolnshire. For Pamela, the female needle effectively gives way to the pen and the flowered waistcoat which she embellishes as a servant is succeeded by the embellished prose of the lady in distress.[9]

Mr B.'s mother had educated her maid above her station, and in the eighteenth century a female education delivered gentility. Certainly Pamela is remarkably genteel and, like any well-born lady, she is scrupulous, sentimental, and whimsical. She gains immediate respect from the lesser servants, who see her as a breed apart from themselves. To the irredeemably servile Nan it is entirely believable that Mrs Pamela, the country maid, should not know than a sunflower has no smell. Pamela has, too, the lady's powerful weakness, the happy knack of fainting; and in numerous instances she both preserves her innocence – since Mr B. is no necrophiliac – and asserts her feminine gentility in òne swoon.

But, above all, Pamela triumphs through virtue, that spiritual socio-sexual something which no marriageable lady should be without. It is a wonderful magical possession on which, as Pamela says, depends her 'everlasting happiness in this world and the next'. Initially Mr B. sees it as yet another trick of the 'artful young baggage', but in time he too understands it as the jewel above his own earthly jewels, a quality by which the servant can claim equality with the born lady – in this case the astounded Lady Davers. Most usefully for the servant, the concept of virtue gives a new and powerful master in God and so allows her proudly to nullify the whole social hierarchy on which Mr B. sets such store; in death 'all the riches and pomps of the world will be worse than the vilest rags than can be worn by beggars', she declares ringingly. 'My *soul* is of equal importance with the soul of a *princess*; though my quality is inferior to that of the meanest slave' (p. 164). There is pride in both halves of this claim.

If Pamela has been educated above her state, Mr B. has been brought up below the needs of his. The young master must marry and yet his atrocious education makes it impossible for him to tolerate a social equal or superior. As a child and young man, he was raised in privilege, indulged by his nurses, parents, and masters; any girl of like quality to himself must be similarly treated. A marriage of such spoilt children would naturally be disastrous: 'two people thus educated, thus trained up in a course of unnatural ingratitude, and who have been headstrong torments to every one who has had a share in their education, as well as to those to whom they owe their being, are brought together', describes Mr B. accurately. 'The gentleman has never been controlled: the lady has never been contradicted' (p. 471). Pamela is as aware of this sorry state as Mr B., for she exclaims against 'the lordliness of a high condition . . . what a fine time a person of an equal condition would have of it, if she were ever to marry such a one!' (p. 253).

The answer to this class problem seems not reformation within the class but, as in Jane Austen's *Mansfield Park*, for the master to descend a rung or two to find virtue in the distressed lower orders and so reinvigorate his own class with a virtue unattainable soley within it. The poor must lend virtue to the rich if the line is to continue worthily. In *Mansfield Park*, no woman from the spoilt gentry seems worthy of a gentleman's house, and the family of Mansfield Park must continue with the aid of the virtuous lowly.

Pamela is a proper wife not despite her servanthood but because of it. In Mr B.'s required scheme, a wife is the extension of the maid and Pamela is eager to weld the two roles and keep the lowliness which has after all won her lord. So she continues to call her husband master and she curtsies at her wedding. Indeed her reactions are fitting since, in both hierarchies, his and hers, she is now below the man: Mr B. guards the virtue which she had once used to resist him, for he stands as husband between her and God. 'I should be unworthy, If I could not say, that I can have no will but yours', she sighs and, after some time of marriage, she piously exclaims, 'I will endeavour to conform myself, in all things, to your will' (p. 470). In fact she delights in the totality of her subservience to her lordly husband and stresses again and again that she is entirely the work of his bounty. As a wife, Pamela fervently asserts that her husband will always be her master and that she will think herself more and more his servant. The wife becomes more servile than ever the servant has been. 'How dare you approach me', Mr B. snaps at his new mate, 'without leave, when you see me thus disturbed?' (p. 460), and the once pert Pamela hardly murmurs at the imperious rebuke. So, too, as wife she is prepared to be objectified, to be trotted out for neighbours as the new wonder of the parish where, as a servant, she had rebelled against such degradation. In the novel, then, the servant's pedagogy slides into the wife's handbook, and the maid becomes the mistress by exaggerating servility.

II

But there is more to Pamela than the humble servant, as Mr B.'s sister Lady Davers notes. And, although the exemplary transition of maid to mistress takes place in her humble terms in the social sphere, the sexual one that makes of a maid a kind of mistress is mainly Mr B.'s doing. In this sexual context, submission is not an exemplary virtue, but the mask of a masochistic desire; servitude grows into a sado-masochistic game of mastery and abasement; and the letters which genteely ease Pamela's path into ladyship become the mirror of voyeuristic narcissism for her intended husband.

Sexuality has the effect both of increasing and decreasing Pamela's humility. As sexual object of the mastering role, she can on occasion grow remarkably haughty to others: 'What means the woman', she sneers at Mrs Jewkes, whose superiority she elsewhere asserts. In the early days, when she is merely a serving woman pursued by her master, she is annoyed at Mr B.'s encroachment – 'how came I to be his property?' (p. 129) she demands – and she bridles when she feels at his beck and call. To Lady Davers after marriage she can be quite as uppish as she once was to Mr B., for she has in a way assimilated, before outsiders, Mr B.'s sexual mastery. As Lady Davers wisely if crudely remarks: 'The wench could not talk thus, if she had not been her master's bed-fellow' (p. 406).

As the relations of Pamela and Mr B. grow more sexually charged, Pamela becomes, before Mr B., more involved in his scheme, and her submission to the mastering male increases. This submission is not the humility of a social servant and wife, but, instead, of erotic object and victim. In the sexual scheme, service then moves from the religious concept Pamela sometimes makes of it to enter the sado-masochistic realm in which Freud, Nietzsche and the Marquis de Sade, not Jonas Hanway, can act as guides. For the mastering Mr B., the servant girl is as ideal for a mate as the lowly maid is for the Squire's wife.

Mr B.'s sexual economy is conditioned by his emotional character. This was created in childhood and is both foreshadowed in and moulded by his sister, Lady Davers: 'she'd make nothing of slapping her maids about, and begging their pardons afterwards, if they took it patiently; otherwise she used to say the *creatures* were even with her' (p. 426). This elemental pattern of sadistic activity and humbling is carried into the sibling relationship, although with refinement: 'she always loved to vex and tease me', Mr B. tells Pamela, 'and as I would bear resentment longer than she, she'd be one moment the most provoking creature in the world, and the next would do any thing to be forgiven; and I have made her, when she was the aggressor, follow me all over the house and garden to be upon good terms with me' (p. 436). It is these childhood games of torture and remorse than Mr B. plays as an adult more earnestly with Pamela, fixed as she is through servitude in the humble position. With her cooperation, the sadism becomes more violent and the humbling more delicious. As Freud noted in *Civilisation and its Discontents*, 'the satisfaction of the [sadistic] instinct is accompanied by an extraordinary high degree of narcissistic enjoyment, owing to its presenting the ego with a fulfilment of the latter's old wishes for omnipotence.'[10] Mr B.'s old childhood wishes are certainly discernible in his new adult desires.

The master likes his servant best on her knees in tears, and Pamela frequently obliges him. The description 'I fell down on my knees', usually clutching some part of his lower anatomy, rings through her accounts of her ordeal. The religious emblem of Mary at the feet of Christ, so cherished by Hanway, gives way here to the ravishing figure of Sade's Justine, prostrate before the rampant male. 'The more atrocious the harm he does the weaker, the more voluptuous the thrill he gives himself', teaches Dorval in *Juliette*, 'he revels in the tears that his oppression wrings from the unfortunate . . .'[11]

The more Pamela humbles herself, the more lordly and majestic Mr B. grows. A typical scene finds him spurning her as she cries on the floor. More exquisitely, he demands that she both kneel and beg pardon of her torturer. Seduction, as Pamela notes, becomes a matter of power: Mr B. intends to seduce her because she dreads 'of all things to be seduced'. 'The will to power', writes Nietzsche, 'can manifest itself only against obstacles; it therefore goes in search of what resists it.'[12]

Like the Sadean masters, Mr B. wants mediators, and he frequently demands an audience for his sexual theatre. Indeed, he approaches rape most nearly when other women are present, when, for example, he comes from the closet as Pamela lies in bed with Mrs Jervis or when he plays transvestite to become the sleeping Nan in the women's bedroom.

If Mr B. loves an audience, his desires are even more fulfilled by himself as onlooker, and it is this narcissistic pleasure that the letter-writing Pamela delivers. When Mr B. falls in love largely through her letters, it is the image of himself and Pamela as tyrant and victim that he finds most ravishing. In the brothel at the heart of the novel, the letters function as overhead mirror, where his encroaching wicked-ness and her virtuous resistance are constantly reflected. In letters Mr B. can enjoy his own humbling and re-create again and again the image of his naughty self.

Pamela plays her part of victim so well because she too derives pleasure from the role. Indeed it is Mr B.'s sadism that wins her. The kindly and pious Parson Williams seems in her view a 'poor gentle-man' beside the lordly master, and he has no chance of winning her. Never can she love such a one, she declares, for her heart is quite given to the man who is unrelenting in his persecution, who spurns her as his painted bauble and gewgaw and whose mighty threats of rape prostrate her in a tangle of tears and hair. 'I know not *how* it came', she remarks of her love for her master, 'nor *when* it began; but crept it has, like a thief, upon me; and before I knew what was the mater, it looked like love' (p. 260). But the reader knows exactly how it came, for it is immediately after Mr B.'s cruellest treatment that it arrives. 'A thousand times she had reflected to herself upon the cruelty of this man', comments Sade of his Justine, '. . . the depravity of his tastes, and the moral gulf that separated them; and nothing in the world could extinguish this budding passion.'[13]

At the beginning of her trial, before either Mr B. or Pamela suspected the delicious game they were to enter, the servant had primly announced that '*she* that can bear an insult of that kind [a sexual one], I should think not worthy to be a gentleman's wife; any more than he would be a gentleman that would offer it' (p. 42). But this in the early days, before the lordly gentleman and the delicate lady have been swallowed up in the master and slave. In Sade's *Philosophy in the Boudoir* a character remarks that it is the most delicate and refined person who responds above all, best and immediately, to cruelty. 'With all this ill-usage', says the genteel Pamela wonder-ingly, 'I cannot hate him' (p. 187).

III

The sado-masochistic sexual economy can best be illustrated in a scene from the Lincolnshire ordeal, when the aroused Mr B. arrives at Pamela's prison, intent on her sexual humiliation. The scene is strangely re-enacted with a variation in cast when Lady Davers arrives with a similar but social intent. The related scenes combine the three main characters in the sexual drama and bring together the two types of service. Pamela's social one and Mr B.'s sexual one, each gaining significance and complexity from the other. The first scene is charged with sexuality; the second, taking its elements from the first, is desexualized. With the repetition, the naughty scene can enter the social sphere and serve as public and sentimental entertainment rather than private and sexual excitement.

It was about his supper; for he said, I shall choose a boiled chicken with butter and parsley. – And up he came!

He put on a stern and majestic air; and he can look very majestic when he pleases. Well perverse Pamela, ungrateful runaway, said he, for my first salutation! – You do well, don't you, to give me all this trouble and vexation! I could not speak; but throwing myself on the floor, hid my face, and was ready to die with grief and apprehension. – He said, Well may you hide your face! well may you be ashamed to see me, vile forward one, as you are! – I sobbed and wept, but could not speak. And he let me lie, and went to the door, and called Mrs Jewkes. – There, said he, take up that fallen angel! – Once I thought her as innocent as an angel of light: but I have now no patience with her. The little hypocrite prostrates herself thus, in hopes to move my weakness in her favour, and that I'll raise her from the floor myself. But I shall not touch her: No, said he, cruel gentleman as he was! . . .

I sighed as if my heart would break! – and Mrs Jewkes lifted me up upon my knees; for I trembled so, I could not stand. Come, said she, Mrs Pamela, learn to know your best friend; confess your unworthy behaviour, and beg his honour's forgiveness of all your faults. I was ready to faint: And he said, She is mistress of arts. I'll assure you; and will mimic a fit, ten to one, in a minute.

I was struck to the heart at this; but could not speak presently; only lifted up my eyes to heaven! – And at last made shift to say – God forgive you, sir! – He seemed in a great passion, and walked up and down the room, casting sometimes an eye upon me. . . . And so he went out of the room. . . .

I laid me down on the floor, and had no power to stir, till the clock struck nine: and then the wicked woman came up again. . . .

I got up as well as I could, and trembled all the way down stairs: And she went before me into the parlour. . . .

. . . I call you down to wait on me while I sup, that I may have some talk with you, and throw away as little time as possible upon you.

Sir, said I, you do me honour to wait upon you: – . . . But I was forced to stand behind his chair, that I might hold by it. Fill me, said he, a glass of that Burgundy. I went to do it, but my hand shook so, that I could not hold the plate with the glass in it, and spilt some of the wine. So Mrs Jewkes poured it for me, and I carried it as well as I could; and made a low courtesy. He took it, and said, Stand behind me, out of my sight!

Why, Mrs Jewkes, said he, you tell me she remains very sullen still, and eats nothing. No, said she, not so much as will keep life and soul together. – And is always crying, you say, too? Yes, sir, answered she, I think she is, for one thing or another. Ay, said he, your young wenches will feed upon their tears; and their obstinancy will serve them for meat and drink. I think I never saw her look better though, in my life! . . .

Poor I was forced to hear all this, and be silent; and indeed my heart was too full to speak. . . .

I hope (said Mrs Jewkes), whatever be your honour's intention concerning her, you will not be long about it; for you'll find her as slippery as an eel, I'll assure you.

Sir, said I, and clasped his knees with my arms, not knowing what I did, and falling on my knees. Have mercy on me, and hear me. . . . he said, Don't prate girl! – No, said she, it don't become you, I am sure.

Well, said I, since I must not speak, I will hold my peace; but there is a righteous Judge, who knows the secrets of all hearts; and to him I appeal.

See there! said he; now this meek, good creature is praying for fire from heaven upon us! O she can curse heartily, in the spirit of Christian meekness, I'll assure you! – Come saucy-free, give me another glass of wine.

So I did, as well as I could; but wept so, that he said, I suppose I shall have some of your tears in my wine!

When he had supped, he stood up, and said, O how happy for you it is that you can, at will, thus make your speaking eyes overflow in this manner, without losing any of their brilliancy! You have been told, I suppose, that you are *most* beautiful in your tears! – Did you ever, said he to *her*, (who all this while was standing in one corner of the parlour,) see a more charming creature than this? Is it to be wondered at, that I demean myself thus to take notice of her? – See, said he, and took the glass with one hand, and turned me round with the other, what a shape! what a neck! what a hand! and what a bloom on that lovely face! . . .

I went to the farthest part of the room, and held my face against the wainscot; and in spite of all I could do to refrain crying, sobbed as if my heart would break. . . .

Come hither, hussy! said he: You and I have a dreadful reckoning to make. Why don't you come, when I bid you? – Fie upon it, Mrs

Pamela, said she. What! not stir, when his honour commands you to come to him! – who knows but his goodness will forgive you?

He came to me, (for I had no power to stir,) and put his arms about my neck, and would kiss me. . . .

Yet with all this wretched grimace, he kissed me again, and would have put his hand into my bosom; but I struggled, and said, I would *die* before I would be used thus. – Consider, Pamela, said he, in a threatening tone, consider where you are! and don't play the fool: if you do, a more dreadful fate awaits you than you expect. But take her up stairs, Mrs Jewkes. . . . So I went upstairs. . . . (pp. 191–6)

In *Clarissa* sexuality is delivered to the reader through a mess of nosebleeds and knifings. In the more earthy *Pamela* it comes through food and drink. The dining scene of Mr B. is claustrophobic; there is no let-up in the master, only variation in approach, and no exit for the victim. The episode can be viewed as a kind of drama of cruelty in three acts, with Mr B. and Mrs Jewkes as spectator-participants.

The play begins with the customary tableau of a lovely woman sobbing on the floor before the puissant male who spurns her. The next stage of Pamela's humiliation finds the victim serving the sexual master in parody of the social act of servant and employer. When Mr B. commands her attendance at table to wait on him, she is all meekness and subservience, while so moved by the situation she must clutch a chair for support. All becomes so overcharged with sexuality that the master's desire for a glass of burgundy affects the servant deeply; she can hardly pour it for the shaking of her hand. She delivers the wine as if she were presenting her own virginity, and she seasons it with her humble curtsy. Her attitude inspires the master to new verbal violence, and Pamela as suffering beauty becomes the object of discourse between him and his audience Mrs Jewkes, who makes for her master an affecting portrait of the sobbing girl.

The third act repeats the motifs of the first two. Mrs Jewkes urges Mr B. on to rape by the kind of sexually ambiguous language Pamela had always resented but reproduced. Such speech brings the maid to the floor again, clasping the potent knees of her master, who again spurns her, while he and Mrs Jewkes alternate taunts. The flavour of the mingled insults and caresses is well if unkindly caught by Fielding's *Shamela*: 'Hussy, Gipsie, Hypocrite, Saucebox, Boldface, get out of my sight . . . I was offering to go away, for I was half afraid, when he called me back, and took me round the Neck and kissed me . . .'.[14]

Pamela's crying excites Mr B. mightily. 'Women are really delicious when their tears heighten their charms with all the disorder of grief', remarks Derbac in Sade's *Le Comte Oxtiern*.[15] Pamela's tears are especially potent when they seem to mingle with the wine she had been imperiously forced to serve. It is a heady brew, a kind of emblem of Pamela for Mr B., inebriating and grieving, and the drink becomes an accompaniment to the sexually charged meal. To reverse the image, Pamela herself is like a glass of good wine, for she is turned and contemplated before being sipped; Mr B. gains further mediated pleasure from the reflected image of her beauty in the glass.

Again of course comes the spurning, followed by renewed desire, and it seems that at last acting is over and the real act of rape, so often foreshadowed in all this foreplay, is to follow – at least the exasperated Mrs Jewkes hopes so. Mr B.'s desire and sexual jealousy – he claims to suspect Parson Williams – make him loving and coarse, both delighting in his servant's charms and eager to degrade her into a slut, a hussy, and a tantalizing virgin. But then, suddenly, the master grows tired of the drama he has contrived. No climax is possible for, if it occurred, it would deny any sadistic repetition. Mr B. summarily dismisses his servant like any social master, and Pamela is left to go upstairs alone. It is at the end of this curious episode that the maid first declares her love for her master, and Mr B. begins to move through maintenance to marriage.

The sadistic episode of Pamela and Mr B. at dinner is remade and remodelled in a later one of Pamela and Lady Davers. Through repetition the naughty sexual action in the first episode is desexualized. Standing in for her brother, Lady Davers takes the adult Sadean scene back into childhood and allows a happy social ending, in which all three actors socially not sexually embrace.

Mr B. is out visiting, awaiting the wife he so enjoys displaying to the neighbours. Lady Davers arrives at his house, ignorant of her brother's marriage, but burning to eject his supposed whore. She encounters Pamela, who only half-heartedly asserts her wedded state:

> . . . Prythee, child, walk before me to that glass; survey thyself, and come back to me, that I may see how finely thou can'st act the theatrical part given thee!
> . . . she ate some soup . . . and then, as she was cutting up a fowl, said, If thou *longest*, my little dear, I will help thee to a pinion, or breast, or any thing. But may be, child said he [Lady Davers' nephew], thou likest the rump; shall I bring it thee? . . .

Pamela, said my lady, help me to a glass of wine. . . . I was silent and never stirred.

Dost hear, *chastity*? said she, help me to glass of wine, when I bid thee. – What! not stir? Then I'll come and help *thee* to one. Still I stirred not, and, fanning myself, continued silent. . . .

. . . I moved to the window on the other side of the parlour, looking into the private garden; and her woman said, Mrs Pamela, don't make my lady angry. Stand by her ladyship, as she bids you. Said I, Pray, good now, let it suffice *you* to attend your lady's commands, and don't lay *yours* upon *me*. – Your pardon, sweet Mrs Pamela, said she. Times are much altered with you, I'll assure you! Said I, Her ladyship has a very good plea to be free in the house that she was *born* in; but you may as well confine your freedoms to the house in which you had your *breedings*. . . .

I think myself far from being deluded and undone, and am as innocent and virtuous as ever I was in my life. Thou liest, child, said she.

So your ladyship told me twice before.

She gave me a slap on the hand for this; and I made a low courtesy, and said, I humbly thank your ladyship! . . . Your dear brother, madam, however, won't thank your ladyship for this usage of me, though I do. . . .

Pray your ladyship, said her woman, let the poor girl sit down at the table with Mrs Jewkes and *me*. – Said I, You are very kind, Mrs Worden; but times, as you said, are much altered with me; and I have been of late so much honoured with better company, that I can't stoop to yours. . . .

She [Lady Davers] gave me a slap on the hand, and reached to box my ear . . . she was like a person beside herself.

I offered to go out, and Mrs Jewkes took my hand to lead me out: But her kinsman set his back against the door and put his hand to his sword, and said, I should not go, till his aunt permitted it. He drew it half-way, and I was so terrified, that I cried out, Oh, the sword! the sword! and, not knowing what I did, I ran to my ladyship herself, and clasped my arms about her, forgetting, just then, how much she was my enemy, and said, sinking on my knees. Defend me, good your ladyship! the sword! the sword! – Mrs Jewkes said, Oh! my lady will fall into fits! . . . (pp. 409–19)

The action goes on for several more pages and is terminated by Pamela, who exits by nimbly jumping through the window.

The elements of Lady Daver's scene are those of the earlier one, but, although there are some coarse sexual jokes and much physical violence, the episode is not sexualized. The setting of both scenes is the dinner table, and the action once more the drama of servitude;

the motive is again jealousy, for Lady Davers, married to a weak-spirited husband, has a more than sisterly interest in her virile brother and his bedroom escapades. In both scenes Pamela falls on her knees and clasps her tormentor. In both she is objectified through name-calling – she is insulted as 'slut' – and through being reflected in the mirror at the command of others. In each scene she is ordered to serve wine, although in the later she refuses to do so; in this she is right, for her expressed view of service is that it entails a proper hierarchical relationship but not a use of the lower by the upper orders for their own gratification of power. The refusal underlines Pamela's complicity in the earlier scene where her presence is far from necessary to deliver Mr B.'s dinner.

There are other differences between the two scenes as well, the most obvious being their endings; in the first episode the only escape for Pamela was Mr B.'s boredom or surfeit, while in the second she can jump through the window, so making her own exit. A far more striking difference, however, is the object of humiliation; for, although superficially Pamela is the victim in both scenes, in the second it is actually Lady Davers who is brought down. By refusing to convince her sister-in-law of her marriage, she allows her to enter a scene of aggression and humiliation that parallels her youthful rituals. Ultimately of course the humbling, at different levels, of both women is delivered in Pamela's accounts to Mr B., who, now publicly married, is largely deprived of his sado-masochistic games.

In the first drama, Mr B. was sexually aroused by his servant's humble service; in the second his sister is excited to social wrath by Pamela, who now refuses to wait on the woman where she had been honoured to attend the man. Indeed the wife has taken on some of the master's haughtiness, and Beck, the lady's maid, who does little more than her duty, encounters a very lordly Pamela, who actually taunts her with lowly birth. Like her brother, Lady Davers offers physical violence, but Pamela counters not with subservience but with mock humility. Again like her brother, Lady Davers descends to insults and threats, but before all the terrible tantrums Pamela is merely 'quite frightened'. There is none of the overwhelming physical response of the first drama.

The absence of sexual tension in the scene – on Pamela's side at least (Lady Davers's need to touch the object of her brother's lust is another matter) – is stressed by the sudden entry of male activity, which momentarily stops the social play-acting and reveals its hollowness. The exhibition of the half-sword is an extraordinary act of the hitherto foolish nephew, ordered about by his aunt and mocked by Pamela. Her extreme reaction – even to possible fainting, her usual response at high sexual moments of the novel – connects the scene to the earlier one of aggressive sexuality and reveals the asexual social nature of the rest of the drama. Pamela is here a child at play, running when things turn nasty to her mistress-mother to protect her, and the form she clasps is maternal. In the earlier scene the knee she clutched was mastering and there was a lecher and bawd to exploit her.

Pamela escapes to the waiting Mr B. and his friends, carrying in her head the entertainment which Lady Davers had produced. At first she is coy about presenting it, for Mr B. had told her an exemplary tale of a woman who destroyed sociability by wailing too long about her broken china. But, like the libidinous ladies of Wycherley's *Country Wife*, who beg the hero for more and more of his china, Pamela's audience demands increasing amounts of her story. 'So we talked a full Hour and a half, about my Vartue', says Shamela, and Pamela's audience could not have escaped with less on the subject of her wifely triumph.[16] The episode with Mr B. was re-created in her private journal, meant initially only for her own eyes; here the relating is a public performance.

Pamela enjoys her telling, relishing both her slight and temporary humbling as a knowing servant and Lady Davers's much greater and longer one as an ignorant lady. Although it naughtily echoes the earlier scene of sexuality, the uxorious Mr B. also enjoys the relation. Indeed husband and wife provoke each other into creating the other woman's humiliation: 'Well, but said he, I suppose she hardly asked you to dine with her; for she came before dinner, I presume. . . . No, sir, dine with my *lady*! no, indeed! Why she would make me wait at table upon her, with her woman . . .' (p. 424). When Pamela stops for breath in her narrative, Mr B. urges her forwards: 'Tell me, then, Pamela, said he, did she lift her hand at you? Did she strike you? But I hope not! A little slap of the hand, said I, or so. – Insolent woman. She did not, I hope, offer to strike your face? Why, said I, I was a little saucy once or twice; and she would have given me a cuff on the ear, if her woman and Mrs Jewkes had not interposed' (p. 438). If Mr B. himself seems to flag, Pamela goads him by growing reticent: '[I was] *wenches* and *creatures* out of number, and worse than all that. What? tell me, my dear. Sir, said I, I must not have you angry with Lady Davers.'

Mr B.'s delight in his wife's performance is social. It is shared by his friends, who are sentimentally improved by it. It differs markedly from the way he relished the gaze of his servant, Mrs Jewkes, on

Pamela's humiliation. In the earlier scene, he was frequently in a rage: when he read its account, he was overcome with remorse and love. No such emotions attend his consumption of the later scene, and he cannot even grow angry with his choleric sister. In its telling and retelling, the episode with Lady Davers modifies the one with Mr B. and rids it of both sexuality and servitude. Two women are sparring – ultimately they are equal through gender as the nephew's sword shows and as Pamela herself stresses – and neither actor is really a servant. The new scene can be taken tolerantly; it is after all a rendition of the old drama, suitable not for master and maid, but for married man and exemplary wife.

In the first encounter with Mr B., service is sexualized; with Lady Davers it is desexualized. Pamela largely contrives the scene by her handling of her sister-in-law, whom she provokes to reveal her unattractive side and then delivers to her brother and assembled neighbours. It is as if Pamela needed both to steal the power from the early unwifely and anti-social scene, itself an adult version of the youthful one, and also weaken the sister-in-law who, in a way, has been her rival and predecessor with Mr B.

In the repetition without sexual charge, the scandal of the first scene is reduced, and covert wifehood becomes the message of the action, instead of covert whorishness. With Lady Davers, Pamela shows the limits of service when not sexually inspired, and her respectable and pious view triumphs as she becomes a socially accepted wife, receiving the decent kisses both of the neighbourhood and of the B. siblings. The sexual scheme in which she had fully played her part is vanquished and Mr B. finds he is properly embracing a servant-spouse and not a seducible chamber-jade. Yet Pamela tries to fulfil her husband's narcissistic and voyeuristic desires as far as they are compatible with chaste wifehood, and in her recorded encounter with Lady Davers she gives Mr B. a shadowed version of the elemental scene he enjoyed so much. She has, also, left him her epistolary accounts in which the naughty drama of servitude is lovingly described. These are eagerly perused by his sister, who comments wisely to Pamela: 'I believe, if the truth were known, you loved the wretch. . . .'

New Brunswick, NJ, 1978

Notes

1 See Lawrence Stone, *The Family, Sex and Marriage in England 1500–1800* (London: Weidenfeld and Nicolson, 1977), pp. 642–7.

2 For example, Swift's *Directions to Servants* and *A Dialogue between a Member of Parliament and his Servant* and Defoe's *Every-Body's Business is No-Body's Business* and *The Great Law of Subordination consider'd*.

3 *Every-Body's Business is No-Body's Business, or, Private Abuses, Publick Grievances: Exemplified in the Pride, Insolence, and Exorbitant Wages of our Women-Servants, Footmen, etc.* (London: W. Meadows, 1725), p. 17.

4 See *The Family, Sex and Marriage*, p. 97.

5 For a general view of servants and their status in this period, see J. Jean Hecht's *The Domestic Servant Class in Eighteenth-Century England* (London: Routledge & Kegan Paul, 1956) and Dorothy M. Stuart's *The English Abigail* (London: Macmillan, 1946).

6 Henry Fielding, *An Apology for the Life of Mrs Shamela Andrews* (Berkeley: University of California Press, 1953) p. 16.

7 *Pamela or Virtue Rewarded* (New York: W. W. Norton, 1958). Page numbers in the text refer to this edition.

8 *The Golden Bough*, Part II (London: Macmillan and Co., 1911), pp. 1–8.

9 See John A. Dussinger's 'What Pamela Knew: An Interpretation', *Journal of English and Germanic Philology*, LXIX (July 1970), pp. 377–93, and Margaret Doody's *A Natural Passion: A Study of the Novels of Samuel Richardson* (Oxford: Clarendon Press, 1974) for elaboration of some of these points.

10 *Civilisation and its Discontents, Complete Psychological Works of Sigmund Freud*, trans. James Strachey and Anna Freud (London: Hogarth Press, 1961), XXI, p. 121.

11 *Juliette, Selected Writings of de Sade*, trans. Margaret Crosland (London: Peter Owen, 1964), p. 221.

12 Friedrich Nietzsche, *The Will to Power*, trans. Anthony M. Ludovici (Edinburgh: T. N. Foulis, 1910), II, p. 130.

13 *Justine, Selected Writings of De Sade*, p. 49.

14 *Shamela*, p. 48.

15 *Le Comte Oxtiern, Selected Writings of de Sade*, p. 193.

16 *Shamela*, p. 43.

4 Marketing the self: Mary Carleton, Miss F and Susannah Gunning

'Poor I, have been for many Years a Noun Substantive, obliged to stand alone.' So Laetitia Pilkington sees her unmanned condition in the 1740s, nominal, described and circumscribed. And, yet, her very act of writing and self-creating betrays her knowledge that she is not entirely a poor noun, but also a very active verb, a writing woman who chooses sometimes to trace wittily the features of the learned lady and sometimes, as here, to create with equal wit the image of distressed and undeclinable femininity.[1]

Women have always been able to sell their bodies, and adorn and embellish them to gain a better price. But the literary image of woman was, until the Restoration, largely a male affair. From the 1660s onwards, women entered the literary market in increasing numbers and created images of womanhood to sell either their works or themselves or both. Inevitably, these woman-created images were shadowed by male ones, already inscribed in literature and in the language itself, and the eye that viewed them was often intended to be man's. But, as the novel and its female audience expanded, the appeal was increasingly directed to female readers as well.

Autobiography had a large catchment area in the eighteenth century, taking in the formal account of Gibbon, the spiritual wrestling of Methodists, and the scandalous and gossipy histories of compromised ladies. The novel too spoke to the public's desire for gossip, when it pretended truth to reality and titillated with disguised names. The line between fiction and fact was extremely fine, and fiction shaped autobiography as well as the reverse, but the autobiographer tended more than the novelist to plead plainness and literary naïvety, to allow events to flounder at the end in ambiguity, where the novelist felt constrained to render justice, and to employ beyond the needs of entertainment a rhetoric of explanation and justification.

Autobiography, more or less fictional and more or less entertainment or vindication, became a favoured female form, delivering self-esteem while presenting even the most pitiable weakness. As Patricia Spacks wrote in *Imagining a Self*, 'Autobiographies affirm identity. The autobiographer, attesting his existence by the fact of his writing, lives through his explanations, tacit or explicit, of how he came to be the person he is.'[2] To women they provide for the first time a listening public, denied them in law and government, and a market place in which to sell their mental image. Literature alone could trumpet female wrongs and demand redress through attracting sympathy to a female image or gain vengeance through the very act of publication. Through the vindications of three women, I want to show the growth in the female power of literary self-selling and follow the change in created image, as taste in women veered from wit to sensibility and from ingenuity to ingenuousness. Many sensational and scandalous ladies could illustrate the theme, from Lady Sarah Bunbury, 'the Innocent Adultress', to Mary Tonkin, the professional and disgruntled spy. I have however chosen Mary Carleton, the German princess, from the Restoration period, Miss F of the ruined reputation from the mid-eighteenth century, and Susannah Gunning, of the great Gunning mystery, from the end. The first and last of these grew famous on their scandals and one can test their images against other literary ones; Miss F exists mainly in her prose. Each woman makes not an autobiography in Roy Pascal's sense, 'a search for one's inner standing' and 'a wrestling with truth', but a vindication, a mask, a saleable self that would attract customers and make them act on her behalf.[3] 'I have discovered', wrote James Boswell, summing up an eighteenth-century view of personality, 'that we may be in some degree whatever character we choose.'[4] The vindicating ladies support this discovery, choosing their roles if not their fates. But each created in conformity with the times, and the characters that could be profitably chosen were few.

In 1663 a princess arrived in London, hot from her escape out of Germany. She was fleeing an unwanted marriage into which her relatives were pressing her. Accompanied by a wealth of sparkling jewellery and a bundle of aristocratic letters, she established herself with noisy secrecy at an inn, where she dazzled the innkeeper and tempted him by her unprotected state to consider her a glittering catch for a relative. Speedily she was courted by a yound lord, who arrived to fall in love, dressed resplendently and travelling in a carriage decked with liveried servants. The father was willing, the son eager, the lady decently backward, and the marriage was hastily celebrated. Only then did the bride discover that the groom was no lord but a poor law student, whose family had laid out a large part of their substance on the lordly show.

But worse was to follow: a few weeks after the wedding, a letter arrived from Canterbury declaring the 'German Princess' an 'absolute Cheat' and revealing her humble and criminal past. She was it seems the daughter of a 'jolly Fidler' of Canterbury, befriended by more affluent families who were attracted by her charm and prodigious ability with languages. She learnt to pilfer from these families and soon grew an accomplished thief. She married a shoemaker, tired of him, and in 1658 married a second man. The first husband failed to testify against her and she escaped prosecution for bigamy. The Carletons, doubly incensed by her fraud and their own failed fraud, were not so lenient and this time Mary was arrested for bigamy.

The Carleton case became a sensation and Mary with it. Despite many accusations of duplicity, she stuck to her aristocratic story and was soon visited in prison by a crowd of 'many hundreds', among them the susceptible Samuel Pepys. He was much impressed with her charm, and declared her innocent. When the case came up, Mary Carleton proved the cleverest in a bungling court. The prosecution failed to produce or properly question the most incriminating witnesses and she was consequently freed. She renewed her charms on John Carleton, who wavered; then, bolstered by his angry relatives, he stood firm. She was financially alone, with only her sensational image by which to live. Speedily she capitalized on it by writing in whole or in part two pamphlets in which she tried to impose on the public, as before on her husband, and to gain from them the maintenance lost from the Carletons.

Whatever the literary merits of her pamphlets, they failed to deliver affluence, for Mary Carleton's life is in the mode of the rogue narrative rather than the noble vindication. Soon she was exploiting not the image but its sensational failure and was acting herself on the stage, representing her original presentation in a satire written about her own fraud. After this social tumble, her life is dark for seven years until rudely illuminated in a conviction for theft. Transported to Jamaica, she used her famous charm to prevail on men again and managed to escape. Recaught the following year, she was hanged in 1673.

At each stage of her colourful and created life, Mary Carleton was the subject of journalistic pamphlets, biographical writing and scurrilous or ribald poems, but my concern here is solely with the second of the two works of 1663.[5] This is an adroit and stylistically proficient pamphlet, to some critics suggesting collaboration, as though a convincing female picture must be male-drawn. But Mary Carleton's obvious cleverness and linguistic skills argue her authorship of much if not all of the work.

The Case of Madam Mary Carleton (1663) is self-promotingly dedicated to prince Rupert, suggesting some analogy in rank as German princes and some respectability in the author deemed worthy of royal partronage.[6] For the woman it provides the image of appealing femininity before the puissant male. The lively account that follows is the invitation, mingling wit and pathos, girlish innocence and risqué sophistication. It is a mixture in keeping with other Restoration images created by women with men in mind. It is unlikely to have been seriously presented a century later.

The Case begins by comically describing two German suitors who press the author to marriage, an entertaining prelude to the more serious business of princess-presentation. This begins with an appeal to British patriotism, for her escape, she claims, is to the land of freedom. Virtue in distress should not and will not be left distressed in Britain. Then follows the wonderful episode of the Carleton wooing and duping, tonally various, but on the whole gravely presented. The gravity is in keeping with the dignified pose Mary Carleton generally strikes in *The Case*, of an injured innocent, 'a foreign and desolate woman'. The pose, together with the learning – the Greek, Latin, French, Italian, Spanish and 'Oriental Tongues' she claims – argues nobility in the author, as does the very skill with which she makes the argument. All combine to refute the 'vile and impertinent falsehood, that I am of a most sordid and base extraction' (p. 30).

The image relies a little on distress certainly, but Mary Carleton is not at all the trembling lady of sensibility of a later era, but a strong, serious, maligned woman who reveals her strength by her writing in trouble and in her general outrage at woman's oppressed situation. So she complains at being a *femme couverte*, unable to act legally for herself, and she castigates British law giving the husband power over marital property. The dignity wears a little thin when one remembers that she has three husbands and that there is no marital property in dispute. The same effect occurs when she bewails the lot of noble girls like herself kept passive and sedentary in genteel convents, when she has in fact had the criminal and lower-class freedom of any boy.

The dignity of the Carleton image is further eroded by her need not only to vindicate herself but also naughtily to appeal as a sexual woman of wit. So with *double entendre* she pruriently describes her exposure. She was, she recounts of her arrest, 'divested and stript of all my clothes, and plundered of all my jewels, and my money, my very bodice, and a pair of silk stockings, being also pulled from me' (p. 69). In another description she again sees her predicament in terms of undress before the male eye: 'See the fickleness and vanity of human things, to-day *embellished*, and adorned with all the female Arts of bravery and gallantry . . . now disrobed and disfigured in mishapen Garments, and almost left naked, and haled and pulled by Beadles and such like rude and boisterous fellows, before a Tribunal, like a lewd Criminal' (p. 73). The accounts of her 'undoing' are meant to titillate, hinting at rape; they are sensational and unsentimental. Allied to this slightly risqué appeal and rather at odds with the great delicacy of apprehension she professes is an occasionally coarse humour. Although her name is Maria de Wolway, she announces, the lewd will call her De Vulva.

In *The Case* Mary Carleton presents herself both as a distressed and maligned lady, buffetted by the common herd and worthy of noble support, and as a witty desirable woman begging for a different kind of protection. The image of spiritedness, calculation, and delicacy is complex, and the two functions of vindication and attraction not totally reconcilable. But the Restoration could accept sexual and calculating women and Mary Carleton was perhaps wise to be both appealing and alluring.

By the 1760s female purity was far more in vogue than it was a century before, although a dash of spiritedness could still be invoked. The pamphlet Miss F wrote to vindicate herself is both sincere and duplicitous, judgements inappropriate for Mary Carleton's more flamboyant narrative, which aimed to sell the lady through the reader's collusion in her noble role and through her ambiguous fascination. Because she needs to establish her truth to impose on the public, Miss F, unlike Mary Carleton, risks the charge of deception.

Miss F can afford no prurient interest and she sets up for entire purity. Yet she must incriminate her persecutor and, to describe his naughtiness, show herself indelicately aware of his procedures. So she posits a naive early self and a writer grown sophisticated with misfortune. The dashes for names give authenticity to scandal and yet allow some modesty. Identity is concealed from the unknowing and made provoking for those who might guess the noble cad.

A letter from Miss F addressed to a person of distinction. With a new ballad to an old tune. Sent to the author by an unknown hand describes the loss of the author's reputation through Lord ——. It is published not from resentment, the author claims, but in vindication, 'to remove the prejudices the public . . . have conceived against me' (p. 4).[7] It replaces the 'misrepresentation' of Lord —— with a true presentation; Miss F's public literary image should cast out the private verbal image Lord —— has created. In a more general plea, Miss F hopes to 'undeceive some who detest vice, and a bad heart, in the person of any man'. Yet her telling generates her hostility and she admits to craving vengeance: 'if you have injured me', she writes towards the end of the pamphlet, 'this letter will, I hope, do me some justice' (p. 34).

The events as Miss F relates them begin when she meets the elderly Lord —— at Bath, where he professes friendship. She, all naive girlhood, suspects nothing, on account of his 'age and condition'. Her father, sniffing profit from the attraction, encourages the nobleman, who soon declares 'most passionate and tender love'. In London Miss F's neighbours are dazzled three times a week with 'the parade of a coronet chariot'. Soon Lord —— proposes what one assumes father F wished; he swears 'inviolable love' to Miss F and offers her £800 a year. Still engagingly naïve, Miss F declares her pity for Lord ——, not imagining a married man of his rank, near sixty, could be deceiving, although she admits to being a trifle startled at his stories of previous conquests. On her father the effect of the dishonourable proposal is predictable – he calls his daughter a fool for not accepting the money, since she could take it without necessarily complying with the terms. The disagreement between Mr and Miss F leads in time to a separation.

Over Miss F is the shadow of *Pamela*, although Miss F is not so fortunate in her parent. Like Pamela, she is a naïve young girl pursued by a socially superior man of inadequate morals. Like Pamela too, she rather unaccountably stays when she should go – continuing to receive the nobleman out of compassion since, as she records, he begged her to do so with tears 'trickling down' his 'aged cheeks'. With this aspect of Lord —— Miss F has some trouble; all is perhaps not entirely lost with him and she needs still to flatter – had he been unmarried, she would have preferred him to anyone else, she declares – but she needs also to revenge herself, so she adds spitefully, 'despite his age and person'.

So begins Miss F's fall from reputation. The injustices she claims are personal and professional, although, as she stresses, the two are one for a woman, since Lord ——'s open visits in the noble carriage and her Clarissa-like removal from her father's protection have blighted her marriage chances. Not able to play the market there, she eschews the other female commerce of selling her body for a maintenance and settles on a career in music. Weighing this against the careers of whore and mistress, she admits that singing will bring in only a fraction of what prostitution would have done. By such a comment she proves both her purity and her attractiveness.

The singing career is soured by the iniquitous Lord ——, who would rather have her exhibit her body to him than her voice to the public. He prevents her from meeting a possible patron and 'by misrepresentation and calumny' destroys the modest female mask she needs to create in order to sell her singing. False stories circulate in society and make her unacceptable. When she tries a subscription concert, she applies to Lord ——'s wife, but it is Lord —— who replies, refusing even the £5 she had asked. On the night, he throws a party to lure away her audience. She summarizes her wrongs: 'I have suffered in my purse and reputation'; in her world the two are the same.

Miss F's pamphlet ends with a poem, which under the cover of a more formal genre allows Miss F, the probable author, to simplify and heighten herself and her persecutor through the elemental categories of the ballad. The poem sees an amorous aged earl courting a 'lovely maid'; it concludes smugly: 'Dishonest love can never bear / True virtue's pride and scorn; / Repulsed, its refuge is despair / Or to revenge will turn.'

Miss F is much concerned to vindicate her choice of profession, and she makes some telling points about the selling of self involved in singing and prostitution. 'A young woman may sing in public, or . . . be a public singer, with virtue and innocence', she asserts, 'and be looked upon in as favourable a light, as a surgeon or midwife' (p. 17). Both minister to others and sell their skills not their bodies. Interestingly, she catches that it is female display or independence that shocks, not the profession of singing itself, and that it is public display for her own gain not the private display for one man's gratification that antagonizes. When she sang for a crowd in Lord ——'s house, it was proper; when she pockets the proceeds, it is not. A man can regard with equanimity the selling of his daughter to a man, but find himself dishonoured when she markets herself. Surely, she declares sarcastically, singing 'is almost as reputable, as it is to be, or thought to be, your L—d—p's mistress (p. 27). It is the economic power of woman that subverts the sexual order. Had Miss F asked for Lord ——'s protection, she would she knows have received it; a request for independence is, however, crudely refused.

What Miss F actually does to help and sell herself is to write her pamphlet and many of her arguments for singing apply to this work. In a curious way, writing combines the roles of mistress accepted by Lord —— and of public singer, anathema to him, and it takes on the power of both. Through writing Miss F can create herself as a desirable object, but remain pure while on display. At the same time, writing is public entertainment, like her singing, and it too brings her income. Miss F sells something less than her body as in prostitution, but something more threatening to the man, her skill and the name she takes from a man, so affronting the relatives who share it. Writing then is an economic act for Miss F, delivering prosperity and revenge. 'I shall have the satisfaction', she writes, 'to find that this letter, with all its faults, from the truth it imparts, will make good the deficiency of your L—d—p's subscription' (p. 32). Here, as so often in female vindications, is the assertion of truth, somehow guaranteed by the inadequacy of writing. As the style is denigrated, so the content is magnified. The performance, Miss F argues elsewhere, is not 'worth two-pence', but the matter is worth a great deal more. At least enough to cover the expense of printing and 'put the Five Guineas', refused by Lord ——, 'clear in my pocket'.

Mary Carleton needed to entertain and attract, so she became virtuous and slightly ribald as well. A century later, no ambiguity is allowed except what leaks from the narrative, but some humour can leaven the gravity. A real mistress, Miss F indicates, would have been showered with presents, but the only gift Miss F had of Lord —— was a boar's head, 'rather an odd, first, and only present, from a L—d to his beloved mistress' (p. 14). She would, she avers 'have eat it, had it been eatable'. There is, too, some spirit in Miss F, some threat beyond the economic one. The open end of the 'true' narrative leaves this threat dangling, and the final effect, despite hints of duplicity, pathos and humour, is ominous: 'What crime had I been guilty of . . . to induce you to treat my humble request with such contempt and disregard?'

And so to the Gunninghiad, as Horace Walpole labelled the furor in the family of General Gunning. These singular events provoked a spate of affidavits and true narratives, the most interesting of which are two anonymous pamphlets presumably by men: *A Narrative of the incidents which form the mystery in the family of general Gunning* and a 'Friendly letter to the marquis of Lorn' by 'a Knight of Chivalry', and *A letter from mrs Gunning, addressed to his grace the duke of Argyll*, her brother-in-law, all dated 1791. My concern is with the *Letter* of Susannah Gunning, the general's wife, but the female image she creates can be illuminated by the response in the other two accounts.

The anonymous *Narrative* catches the popular taste in scandals and the rhetoric which justifies it: 'No circumstance', it ringingly announces, 'has occurred in the variegated circle of Fashion, for a long series of years, that has excited public attention, in so high a degree, as the recent dissentions which have prevailed in the family of General Gunning. – To see a young lady, in the bloom of youth and beauty, banished from the house of him whom Nature had designed for her protector – to see the parent become the accuser of his child – the husband, of his wife – was to witness a spectacle of so strange and singular an aspect, as would not fail to work, in either sex, on every passion of the mind. The malignant sneer of Revenge has been excited – the benevolent tear of Pity has been moved – and the rancorous smile has been raised on the distorted features of Envy.'[8] As the *Morning Post* put it more succinctly, the Gunning events were the 'public conversation of the town'.

From the detailed, conflicting accounts, it is impossible to summarize exactly what happened, especially since, as the *Narrative* comments, 'the conduct of all parties concerned is . . . strange indeed'. General Gunning and his wife had an unhappy marriage, which produced one daughter, Elizabeth, a lady of 'substantial excellence' according to the *Narrative*. She was well connected through the remarkably aristocratic marriages achieved by her father's beautiful sisters. Possibly she was courted both by the Marquis of Blandford and by her cousin, the Marquis of Lorn. According to the general's side of things, she was lovesick for the reluctant Lorn (the maiden all for-lorn as a contemporary ballad inevitably put it); to nudge him toward matrimony, Elizabeth is supposed, either with her mother's help or with that of the Bowens, hangers-on of her father, to have forged not only love letters but also notes to and from the Duke of Marlborough, releasing herself from the Marquis of Blandford. This naming of the rival was, in the general's view, to have acted 'as a stimulus' to Lorn's love. In the opposing version, however, the general, caring nothing for his wife and daughter and wishing to spare himself the expense of their maintenance and of the inevitably large dowry, framed Elizabeth with the help of his creatures, the Bowens, so that he could eject both women. Although this explanation seems rather ingenious, the author of the *Narrative* clearly if negatively favours it: the question 'What *interest* can a parent *possibly* have in impeding the felicity of his child?' is answered, 'It is *possible*, that a parent – we must not be understood to allude to any existing or even probable case – whose daughter's attractive charms have procured her the offer of an union with the man of her choice – may, from motives of *avarice*, object to the connection, and, though opulent himself, may seek to impede her felicity that he may not open his purse' (p. 45).

Whatever the case, letters were forged and affixed with seals not usually used by the Duke of Marlborough but obtained from his house, while the name Lorn took on an 'e', which, as Elizabeth pointed out, she was unlikely to have given her cousin. Messengers were bribed by one side or the other and the Bowens implicated by each. They accused Elizabeth, 'this vile daughter of your's', of bribing them to forge letters, so fooling her mother, who in turn accused the Bowens of colluding with the general in his daughter's undoing. To complete the circle, an anonymous letter allied Elizabeth and her father. Certainly the general took a high moral and convenient tone over the affair, and his wife and daughter speedily left his house. (His tone was made discordant by his payment of a large fine shortly after for 'criminal conversation' with his tailor's wife). Elizabeth grew ill and Susannah set about writing her vindication.

Each of the three writers on the Gunning mystery presents a careful self-image. The author of the *Narrative* is impartial and judicious, investigating on behalf of the public and its right to know; the Knight of Chivalry enters as the honest man, a mingling of rough and rude Miller of Dee – 'I want no man's fortune, I court no man's interest' – and the Sternean sentimentalist, the champion of distressed virtue – 'I will be thy friend, dear girl; I will protect thee, said I . . .'[9] The most elaborately embroidered image is however of Susannah Gunning and her 'angel' daughter.

The hyperbolic nature of Susannah Gunning's prose can be gauged from descriptions of Elizabeth. She is, with much italicizing, 'my *innocent*, . . . my glorious child', 'my *proud heart's* darling', the 'beloved object', the '*suffering angel*', 'the innocent darling of my heart', 'my soul's treasure', 'the rich gem', an '*angel* child', 'the *glory* of her family, *beloved* by her friends, *revered* by her acquaintance, *adored* by the children of poverty, and the sweet soother of distress'. She is a 'sweet injured angel', 'my darling, my innocent lamb', and a 'perfect being' of 'immaculate pureness'. Again the Richardsonian image threatens, this time of Clarissa, but Elizabeth has a mother to extol her. 'So *invironed* by malice, yet so free from revenge. – So pursued, *yet* so uncontending. – So persecuted by every *possible* mode of *slander*'.[10]

The superhuman image of Elizabeth grates on the Knight of Chivalry, her supporter, who calls Mrs Gunning a 'foolish mother' and a 'nonsensical woman'. Yet the image is not altogether foisted on the daughter, whose words as quoted in the *Letter* confirm the heroic virtue; her answer to the general's one conciliatory approach has the unwise ring of her mother's hyperbole: 'Turn'd from your doors defenceless, pennyless and robb'd by you of what is and ever will be dearer than my life – my character'; it ends pertinently though not ingratiatingly, 'you call me unfortunate, I am unfortunate; who has made me so?' Like a proper heroine of sensibility, Elizabeth does not scandalously act herself on the stage or take to public singing, but instead falls ill.

Susannah Gunning sometimes sets up as wronged wife, alluding – improperly according to the *Narrative* – to the general's frequent infidelities. Mainly, however, she is a mother, and her work, appealing to the heart of the reader, is replete with sentimental tableaux of sacred motherhood. Since her daughter did not die, as might have been sentimentally expected, Mrs Gunning is forced to imagine the death. She would, she claims, have 'grieved like a *mother*', but pleasurably so, since she would have anticipated a heavenly reunion. To describe herself, she forsakes the italics of her daughter's description for capitals. She is 'A HAPPY MOTHER'. Susceptibiity to these domestic images becomes the test of sensibility in the reader. 'Terrific is the picture I am *forced* to exhibit – it must be a *mere* body indeed who can look upon it *unmoved*' (p. 94).

Mrs Gunning makes the usual vindicator's assertion of truth. Her aim is 'to unfold as much as is in *my* power the wonderful and *monstrous* arts and *deceptions* formed as if by magic, to raise a mist that has enveloped all our senses, and *for a time* obscured the divine face of Truth' (p. 4). She will lead the reader through 'labyrinths of *error*' to 'the unencumbered plains of *certainty*'. To underline further her truth-telling, she, like Miss F, claims to have suppressed '*ten thousand* times *more* than I have expressed'. If she were not reticent, she could fill volumes, each more mysterious than another'. Any warmth in the telling, 'more . . . than propriety in general allows to my sex', proves not insincerity in her but its opposite, since its excuse is motherhood. The motherhood has a licence beyond the lady and all excess merely confirms the image.

As the *Narrative* truly comments, Mrs Gunning's is not 'a simple narrative of plain facts', for she brings to her creation all the arts of fiction. Gothic elements abound: the plot is a 'horrid mystery', the general a gothic villain echoing Manfred in his wicked power and Lovelace in his machinations; dialogue is darkly menacing, '"then," exclaimed he "she will be ruined for ever"' or 'by whom have you been imposed on to believe her guilty? My blood freezes with horror!!!' This last speech ends with Mrs Gunning's favourite emphatic device after italics, three exclamation marks.

The writing is theatrical, with much direct speech. The allegedly hypocritical Mrs Bowen, constructing herself as confidante, wails, 'Oh, my dearest Mrs Gunning! *you* have been – deceived! you are *cheated*! you are abused! . . . your daughter is a wretch!' (p. 49). Susannah in turn takes the theatrical line: 'Bold wicked woman!' she addresses Mrs Bowen, 'how dare you enter my house.' Often the act is made dramatic by a combination of description and interpretation so popular in the epistolary novel. When Mrs Bowen kisses Mrs Gunning's hand, 'I did *not immediately* withdraw it, but felt as if it had been *fastened on* by a *serpent'* (p. 55). Writing itself becomes high drama: 'I even *tremble* with horror when I reflect on the *irresistible* power that *now* bids me retrace them [the events] on paper' (p. 91).

The appearance of fiction is heightened by those realistic elements that gave factuality to fiction in the eighteenth century. The account quotes from memoranda written to the moment and mingles hindsight with partial sight. Minute particulars of the crucial days are given and the pen moves between the characters to give a multiple point of view, each commenting on the account of the other. Letters are quoted to inform, but they also, as in Richardson's novels, act in the plot: correspondence is forged and pens appropriated. Yet Mrs Gunning must avoid letting her narrative acquire the illusionary nature of fiction which often emerges from the multiple clashing accounts, for it prevents an entire surrender to the story. She wants the help of fiction, but she needs to control its effect; she is after all selling not only the work but herself.

So she tries to dissociate her writing from the novel, especially when she is indulging most heavily in its sentimental techniques. By so doing, she emphasizes the truth of her narrative and heightens its appeal. The reader's heart must bleed the more because the truth is presented and because the writer is not a novelist but an actor, or rather sufferer, in the tale (p. 102):

> Heretofore, when *fiction* has guided my pen, my heart has been softened by comparison and my tears have flowed over distresses of my *own* creating; but *Nature* has appointed me to a task which I am totally incapable of performing – as a mother I cannot hold *her* pencil – the *colours* alone *blind* me, to lay them *on* is impossible! *one* expression, though I *die* in the *repetition* of it, shall not be withheld, and *may* it touch with *agonizing repentance* the heart of *him* to *whom* it was addressed – 'O! papa! papa! it is *you* who *falsely* accuse me?' – and to her *own heaven* her eyes were directed, streaming with the bitter tears of anguish.

And so on, for the word 'mother' has opened Mrs Gunning's most flamboyantly baroque vein and the appeal to truth censors any reticence of fiction that might have closed it.

In part she is unsuccessful in her bid to dissociate herself from the novel, for the novelettish side of the *Letter* disgusts at least one reader, the author of the *Narrative*, who complains that Mrs Gunning 'has often disfigured the page of truth by the ebullitions of passion, – ranted where she should have argued – appealed to the feelings instead of the judgement – and disgusted her readers by clogging a narrative of facts, that ought to have been exempt from every species of extraneous embellishment, with indecent invectives, superflouous insinuations, ill-timed raillery, and with fulsome effusions of maternal dotage, which, however excuseable in the nursery, are certainly misplaced in a pamphlet intended for public perusal' (p. 42).

Susannah Gunning was rather sensitive to the charge of fictionalizing suggested by the *Narrative* author and asserted by her opponents. For in her youth, as one of the Miss Minifies, she had indeed penned a series of extremely popular novels, full of villainous men, heroic girls and forged letters, elements uncomfortably close to those of the Gunninghiad, as her enemies were quick to point out. So hyperbolic and sentimental were these productions that the term 'Minific' was created from them. An example of the tone can be taken from *Coombe Wood* (1783), in which girls are angels threatened by the 'dark mist of dishonour' and men display 'avarice, design, and the guilt of murdering virtuous affection'. Some of the fictional speeches could have done duty in life, for Elizabeth might well have said with the heroine: 'I love my cousin . . . I have been taught to consider him as my brother. I admire his fine accomplishments; and I doat on his virtues; but, *marry* him: Lord help me!'[11]

During her marriage Susannah Gunning on the whole refrained from fiction, unless one takes the general's part in the Gunninghiad, but her writing past has two effects on the present. First, it inspires opponents to discredit her through the accusation of fiction. In her *Letter* she is coy about her authorship, as the annoyed Knight of Chivalry notes, and she is able to be so through her opponents' slip in accusing her of writing *Waltham-Abbey*, whose plot is 'made up *they* say of *tricks*, of *stratagems*, and of *forged letters*'. She was not the author, as she enjoys pointing out, but she did write *Barford Abbey* (1768), which is a similar confection. Secondly, her successful novel-writing past fixes her in the sentimental style of the 1760s and 1770s, still much in vogue in 1791, but also being energetically mocked by writers professing reason or common sense. Of this changing taste,

Susannah Gunning knows nothing, and this lack of awareness allows her to disgust some male readers but also to present herself, primarily to women, in the single and simple role of mother, unmarked by any diverting ambiguities or nuances. In the next century, motherhood would clearly triumph over spirited nobility and virtue in distress as woman's most saleable and justificatory image to other women.

Made rudely self-supporting, Mrs Gunning, like Miss F turns to selling her skills on the market, although, unlike her predecessor, she takes no pride in her independence. She makes no mention in her *Letter* of any possible fate other than vindication or death from dishonour. Yet she prudently finished a novel begun years before and in 1793 published a new one entitled *Memoirs of Mary, a novel.* In 1788 Mary Wollstonecraft had put her life into *Mary, a fiction*; Mrs Gunning with similar transparence draws on her experience, for the novel features an old woman dotingly fond of 'her heart's darling', who is innocence itself, yet stigmatized by perfidy.[12] The difference of course is that stylized simple fiction can deliver a happy ending, only allowed to the complex Gunning ladies if their images are accepted and bought.

If Susannah Gunning avoids emphasizing her fictional art, she does follow Mary Carleton and Miss F in pointing to the power writing has given women, to describe and do, not merely exist to be described. Accepting her own skills, she knows her power over her husband and she expresses it in the style so denigrated and yet so potent: 'When to the score of *premeditated* coldhearted *determined* villainy is *added* the vast sums of folly, *beyond* all *calculation*, that have been expended to *support* that *unfathomable* villainy, how will the *perpetrators* of it *shrink into themselves* when they see *not only* their *hearts* but their *heads* laid open to *public* inspection!' (p. 77).

Like Mary Carleton and Miss F, Susannah Gunning is creating her female mask of truth to cover the male-imposed one of fraud. As Miss Minifie's novels powerfully press against Mrs Gunning's life, so the image of her life is pressed into the modes of fiction. Indeed, to appeal to the public, all the writers must construct their masks according to what society applauded. Vindicators cannot be innovators; they must be not original artists but bestsellers.

In the 1660s the eye that looked and the money that bought were male. Mary Carleton knows she must sell herself as heroic female but she can spice her portrait with sexuality. Her scandalous self-display is not allowed to Miss F, who may laugh a little but still remain energetically naïve. Mrs Gunning, knowing her largely female fiction audience, abolishes the risqué woman and capitalizes the mother.

Energy and spiritedness fall before self-pity and passivity. Yet she is as fully aware of actively using female stategies as her predecessors, for she, like them, is going to market in and for herself. If the coin she uses is conventional, it is so because the coin she wants in return is conventional too.

Southampton, 1982

Notes

1 I am indebted to the entry on Laetitia Pilkington by William H. Epstein in *British and American Women Writers 1660–1800*, ed. Janet Todd (Totowa, NJ: Rowman & Allanheld, 1985).

2 Patricia Meyer Spacks, *Imagining a Self: autobiography and novel in eighteenth-century England* (Cambridge, MA: Harvard University Press, 1976), p. 1.

3 Roy Pascal, *Design and Truth in Autobiography* (Cambridge, MA: Harvard University Press, 1960), pp. 182 and 15.

4 James Boswell, *Boswell's London Journal, 1762–1763*, ed. Frederick A. Pottle (New York: McGraw-Hill, 1950), p. 47.

5 For a full description and discussion of the Mary Carleton narratives, see Ernest Bernbaum, *The Mary Carleton Narratives 1663–1763*, (Cambridge, MA: Harvard University Press, 1914).

6 *The Case of Madam Mary Carleton* (1663) expands the earlier account, *An Historical Narrative of the German Princess* (1663). For other versions of the events in 1663, see *The Lawyer's Clarke Trappan'd by the Crafty Whore of Canterbury* and *The Great Tryall and Arraignement of the Late Distressed Lady* . . . Page references to *The Case* are in the text.

7 *A Letter from Miss F Addressed to a Person of Distinction. With a new ballad to an old tune. Sent to the author by an unknown hand* (London, 1761). Page references are in the text.

8 *A Narrative of the Incidents which Form the Mystery in the Family of General Gunning. With biographical sketches; and strictures on the 'Vindication' of Mrs Gunning, comprising copies of all the letters, affidavits, &c. &c. The whole placed in a new point of view* (London, 1791), p. 1.

9 *Friendly Letter to the Marquis of Lorn, on the Subject of Mrs Gunning's Pamphlet, with some explanations of the Gunning mystery never before published. By a Knight of Chivalry* (London, 1791), p. 11.

10 *A Letter from Mrs Gunning, Addressed to His Grace the Duke of Argyll* (London, 1791), p. 146. Page references are in the text.

11 *Coombe Wood* (Dublin, 1783).

12 *Memoirs of Mary, a novel* (Dublin, 1794).

5 'A martyr to her exigencies': Mary Ann Radcliffe

Perhaps no one so well knew the economic limitations of the sentimental ideology of femininity in the late eighteenth century as women who had to provide for themselves and a bevy of children. The plight of such women clearly pushed against the culturally constructed image of the passive and sensitive lady and so was difficult to convey in the literary forms of that culture. The kind of autobiography written by Rousseau in his *Confessions*, which emphasized adolescence and the inner life, even if available to respectable women, would hardly have been a model for the presentation of an existence that was moulded mainly by external factors. The dramatic peak of such a life was not the awakening of sexuality or the experience of social isolation but the foolish marriage and the absconding spouse. The sentimental novel in its mythic or in its solipsistic form could not easily be bent to accommodate the sadly unsentimental dilemma of long years of care, of feckless rather than wicked husbands and of painful childbearing and tedious child-rearing.

Nonetheless, there were women who did try to express something of the social and economic reality. To do so they chose the old form so handily used by women in the past, the memoir as vindication and appeal. Mary Ann Radcliffe in the beginning shared an ideology of femininity and a name and probably a fictional activity with the famous gothic writer Ann Radcliffe, and allowed her publisher to exploit the confusion. But her experience and her response to it distinguish her completely from the retiring, domestic and ladylike Ann. Unlike Mary Carleton or Miss F., who well knew from the outset of their dubious stories the difference between the current mask of woman and the economic and social reality, and equally unlike Mrs Gunning, who resolutely kept the mask in place throughout her rather anachronistic vindication of her conduct, a woman like

Mary Ann Radcliffe learnt about the difference only as she went along. Writing at the same time as Mrs Gunning, she was without well-placed relatives and friends to take her into suitable narratives – or indeed to take her in on a literal level when her various and repeated misfortunes left her homeless.

Mary Ann Radcliffe was typical of unfortunate women in the lower middle class, women who fell below even genteel poverty. Such women were most likely to see the absurdity of a belief in the chivalric, romantic and sentimental picture of women presented by the novels of the day of the sort she herself probably wrote, as well as to understand its stultifying effect on any possible economic effort.

The Memoirs of Mrs Mary Ann Radcliffe (1810) proclaims itself didactic but its initial overwhelming desire, like that of Wollstonecraft's first novel, is for pity. The moral is much repeated: that immense misery can come from '*one* inadvertent step at the beginning of life'. The author is concerned to establish veracity; she is not writing a fiction, she insists, and her story, in the first person, will be 'the plain narrative of an unfortunate individual, whose life of adversity, it is fervently hoped, may prove a useful lesson to the younger part of her readers'. Her style may be described as 'old-fashioned jog-trot': 'full of parentheses, and dashes, to the end'. Such haphazard writing assures authenticity, she proclaims – in true sentimental manner – but it is the authenticity not of inner emotions but of experienced life in society: 'the whole are facts, – real facts! to my sorrow'.[1]

This history is not the sensational Gunninghiad unfolding in high places, but a sorry tale of domestic disappointment. The woman, now over sixty and beyond the reach of sentimental heroinism, looks back on a difficult life, regarding with some amazement and fascination the silly child she once was, a child whose mistaken apprehension of the world has determined her trajectory. The narrative departs both from the flamboyant fraud that could be recounted in the Restoration and from the scandalous divorces of society ladies, writers and actresses; instead it describes the whittling down of spirit through domestic waste and fecklessness.

Radcliffe's elderly Anglican father had married a young Catholic woman, who, as the history unfolds, reveals herself as a simple credulous soul, the 'poor dear woman' of her finally conscious daughter; when the father dies, he leaves his daughter a reasonable property under the management of two guardians. She is piously raised but, at the age of fourteen, like one of Delarivier Manley's ingénues, she meets a fortune-hunter, Mr Radcliffe. The opposition of her sensible guardians is apprehended in fictional terms: it 'all . . .

seemed vastly like a novel'. But the older narrator has learnt a
different mode and she comments as a conduct-book author and
sister of Burney and Austen: 'How cautiously ought parents and
guardians to guard against *first impressions*.' Sentimental romantic
fiction conveys dangerous images to the young girl; love has become
not the overwhelming sexual passion experienced by the early
eighteenth-century innocents of Manley or Eliza Haywood, or the
love of social power of the sophisticates depicted by Aphra Behn, but
simply the romantic enjoyment of unearned attention. The young
Radcliffe elopes and marries out of utter childishness, and the ring
that destroys her life is simply a piece of adornment, 'so mightily
becoming' on her finger. By the age of sixteen she has a daughter;
seven more children follow and she comes to understand that her life
was determined by 'that one forenoon's frolick'.

Her awakening from the fictional romantic and sentimental dream
is expressed in the change in her presentation of Mr Radcliffe. The
wicked fortune-hunter of the early pages becomes, as the story
progresses, simply the good-natured, feckless husband, far more of
a trial to the struggling wife than any outright villain – as many a
Victorian woman writer would discover. It is a realization for which
no reading in fiction or upbringing in piety had prepared her: that
troubles and difficulties are 'attendant upon an improper union even
with *a good man*, and a kind husband'. There is nothing morally
wrong with Mr Radcliffe apart from his manner of getting a wife; he
is simply lazy and inept in business, with a '*penchant* for parting with
money' – her money, of course, since, even with her guardians'
efforts, it was impossible entirely to circumvent those ordinary laws
that transferred all a woman's property to a man on marriage. He
cannot even be blamed, for his 'inactive turn' is, after all,
'*involuntary*'.

Sometimes Mary Ann Radcliffe tries on a sentimental image, like
that of victim. She looks at her 'poor dear helpless children' and
trusts in God for aid. But, as creditors grow pressing, as sharkish
lawyers take what little she has left, and as the kind-hearted Mr
Radcliffe who loves his glass does nothing at all, she steers herself
out of the more traditional role, knowing, however, that she may
well be ridiculed 'for an usurped authority over her husband'.

So at the age of twenty-six, with little property left, without
servants and with numerous children, she accepts the place of
breadwinner for which nothing in literature or education has prepared her. She tries a 'genteel coffee-house' and a boarding estabish-
ment with no great success. At one point she begins a deal over land

with a neighbouring nobleman; as she sets off for this last attempt, she overturns in the mud and has to drag herself 'over the plowed fields, ruminating as I went along on the comforts of matrimony'.[2] Repeatedly her miseries are simply physical, not the sentimental ones of wounded sensitivity and attempted seduction but the common ones of illness and homelessness. Finally she decides to dispose of the husband, who is by now simply another child to care for – fortunately the 'poor dear forgetful' man finds some sort of position in a family – and of the children – the boys are sent to school and the girls to her mother – so that she can go to London to try for work.

There she has no greater success; she aims by turns at being a governess, a milliner and a housekeeper, and she resolutely answers any advertisements she can find in the newspapers. In this sorry state her only comfort seems a sentimental retelling of the past that she has already presented realistically:

> I must now endeavour to fortify my mind against the recital of that ever memorable day when keen adversity forced me from my husband, parents, and chidren! to seek an asylum in a distant part, and save the remnant of my patrimony to clothe, feed, and educate those pledges of our affections, on which I set so high a value, that the most menial occupation I could have submitted to for their sakes.[3]

The falsity of this comforting simplification becomes clear when she returns to Scotland. The older children prove exceptionally demanding. One has 'an hysterick fit' and needs the constant care of her mother; others marry unsatisfactorily, returning to her for help as she struggles on down the hierarchy of trades.

By the end, her story has failed to give any clear moral of prudence or to teach any sentimental emotion, but it has made a political and social point, that 'an unprotected female is the most pitiful object upon earth'. Her own marriage was certainly a mistake but it is society's laws that make it an unmitigated disaster – as underlined when her daughters grow up and inevitably err. Women are excluded from training in trades and yet made the primary carers of children who must always be put before their own interests. The only comfort is the bleak one of the knowledge of typicality – her heart bleeds to see the innumerable requests for work, 'such columns of female wants in the public papers!' No more images or new trajectories are suggested, simply political reform; the government should switch attention from erecting prisons to making 'a suitable provision to support and keep' miserable women off the streets. The sentimental demand for personal pity with which the narrative began has given way to concern for women in general, for the independent and unprepared among her own unfortunate sex.

So the moral of the autobiography becomes another of her works, *The Female Advocate*, first published in 1799 but printed again with the memoirs. This makes precise proposals, like Priscilla Wakefield's, for ejecting men from what should be female trades such as millinery, mantua-making, hairdressing and stay-making, for persuading the government to put money into female training, and for urging wealthy women to refuse service by men and to patronize other women. By the end of the memoirs there is no sentimental atmosphere left; she and the friend to whom she has written her account are just 'two old women', powerless survivors who will nonetheless go on tinkling their ideas like small bells in a parish church.

One such tinkle is this *Female Advocate*, which is subtitled 'An attempt to recover the Rights of Women from Male Usurpation'. Its uncompromising reference to Mary Wollstonecraft's *A Vindication of the Rights of Woman* of 1792 is justified by the statement, reminiscent of Mary Hays's *Appeal to the Men of Great Britain in Behalf of Women* (1798), that the book, although published only in the reactionary year of 1799, was written seven years before, that is at the radical time of Wollstonecraft's work. At the later date Radcliffe must, again like Hays, separate herself from the famous 'Amazonian' feminist by insisting on the personal rather than the political genesis of her proposals: 'All women possess not the Amazonian spirit of a Wollstonecraft; but, indeed, unremitted oppression is sometimes a sufficient apology for their throwing off the gentle garb of a female, and assuming some masculine appearance.' Like Wollstonecraft, she worries her way into seeing the ideology of the passive female as the creation of a particular age and suitable only for a particular class and experience.

Radcliffe is acutely aware that women are excluded from most civic rights and that, although the country has improved economically, women do not share in the improvement: 'What statute is there, which grants that men alone shall live, and women scarcely exist?'[4] She notes that political and private happiness are invariably connected but that the humanitarian temper of the times that has reached slaves and animals has not yet embraced women. She comments unsentimentally on the ferocious lot of prostitutes and those who are prevented by the Vagrants Act even from begging. Yet, although she uses legal and rational political language to make her proposals, she has no rhetoric but the sentimental one with which to generalize specific misery; so she becomes rhapsodic whenever she contemplates the figure who represents her own case, the helpless middle-class woman unprepared and untrained for life.

Perhaps the most moving aspect of the presentation is the embedding of *The Female Advocate* in the memoirs, which continues after the conclusion of the political tract. By now Radcliffe is old, necessarily and invariably opportunistic, ready to judge people only by what they might do for her. Her end is in many ways like the beginning of her married life – except that she now has rheumatism. Her pastry business is no great success, her daughter's school is failing, and all her endeavours seem like Penelope's web, done only to be undone. Her final activity is writing for money. Subscriptions to her work straggle in and the work itself peters out as her life darkens towards its end; her only remaining comfort is a friend recommending '*a second glass* of her very best currant wine'.[5]

New Brunswick, NJ, 1979

Notes

1 *The Memoirs of Mrs Mary Ann Radcliffe: familiar letters to her female friend* (Edinburgh: for the Author, 1810), p. 171.
2 *The Memoirs*, p. 67.
3 *The Memoirs*, p. 108.
4 *The Memoirs*, p. 434.
5 *The Memoirs*, p. 543.

6 Mary Wollstonecraft and the rights of death

I

The French Revolution was a political upheaval in which it seemed possible to 'reconstitute human nature by giving it a new stamp', in the words of the Abbé Grégoire in 1794. Old customs and laws were declared abolished, and morality, religion and habit were agitated. I want to look at one area of change, the attitude to suicide, a topic of interest throughout the eighteenth century. In the rational, heroic spirit of the early Revolution, the act was decriminalized, purged at an instant of guilt, the taint of religious sin and the imputation of civic crime, to become for a time part of the political repertoire – though, curiously, penalties were briefly reimposed in the mid 1790s. So, if suicide were committed rationally and with classical panache, following Socrates and Cato, it might at this time be a valorous and noble deed, as it was deemed in the Martyrs of Prairial, who, one after the other, stabbed themselves with Roman posturing on the steps of the Convention.[1] Since there was no longer any need of religious guilt and, for some time, no sense of an external authority, is it possible to speak of a right of rational death to accompany the many rights of life? If there were such a right, classbound though it must undoubtedly be in its classical expression, would some women have this right?

Revolutionary living was not much open to women, as was noted by Olympe de Gouges, whose eagerness for the revolutionary rights of woman in life brought her to a speedy and involuntary death by the Revolution's instrument, the guillotine. What of *dying* in rational revolutionary manner? Was that available to women? In England the main proponent of extending the enlightened rights of men to women was Mary Wollstonecraft, author of the revolutionary *Vindication of the Rights of Woman*, published in 1792; just three years later she rowed down the Thames to Putney Bridge to where she expected fewer people and deeper water, drenched her skirts and jumped into the river. What was her attitude to suicide, and did the Revolution change it? Since reason was associated with men and feeling with women, when a woman killed herself, did it have to be in emotional not rational style? Since suicide may be seen not only as heroic act but also as the antithesis of struggle and action, is it in fact peculiarly suited to combine with the feminine codes of stasis?

I want to argue that Mary Wollstonecraft was profoundly affected by the French Revolution (or, rather, that nexus of ideas which acted in those events) and that, although her suicide attempts are usually regarded as a feminine emotional backsliding from the more masculine rational stance of *The Rights of Woman*, they may *also* be seen as both rational and revolutionary.[2] Yet everything that Wollstonecraft wrote is marked by her struggle with deeply ingrained notions of irrational, emotional femininity as women's especial trait and burden; so her attitude to suicide cannot entirely escape her conditioning, and the divided but heroically struggling message of her published work is, I believe, caught in the seemingly private writing of her suicide note.

The suicide note is an odd document, almost tactless to investigate. The suicidal person, so disgusted with life that death is preferable, still feels compelled not to quit it without this final dramatizing of the self, a last appeal or justification to a despised world. While death itself is certainly personal and hidden, the articulation of it in language and the *manner* of death are just as certainly public and conventional. They may then be specific to the sexes, time and place, and follow fashion, example or literary pattern; in other words a person may quite well be alienated from a more idiosyncratic trajectory and propelled by fictions or persuasive 'facts'. 'Suicide is very contagious', wrote the suicidologist Émile Durkheim. In 1772, fifteen patients hanged themselves 'from the same hook in a dark passage of the hospital. Once the hook was removed there was an end of the epidemic.'[3] The suicide note is the most personal, intimate, spontaneous and, one would think, least fictional of documents, and yet it turns out to be as constrained by genre, gender and precedent as any novel or romance. What then was the fashion of suicide in 1795 when Mary Wollstonecraft took her intentionally fatal plunge, and what sort of language would be expected from her in the suicide note she left behind?

Before she went to France Wollstonecraft accepted that death on purpose was morally wrong. In early letters written out of deep self-pity in her dependence as a governess, she frequently longed for 'eternal rest' and desired 'to go to sleep – with my [dead] friend in the house appointed for all living'.[4] Yet she never thought to anticipate this rest. Later in London, now an independent author, she grew passionately fond of the married painter Henry Fuseli. When in 1792 she was refused entrance to his household to act as spiritual wife to his legal wife's fleshly one, she did not turn to suicide as answer to her seemingly platonic longings. In life, so in literature. In her early book for children, *Original Stories*, an infantile man kills himself in passion. His daughter finds him dying: 'Horror seized her; another pistol lay charged on the table; she caught it up, but religion held her hand.'[5] In *Thoughts on the Education of Daughters* she sternly disapproved the camp theatricality of death on stage: 'The hour of death is not the time for the display of passions . . .', she remarked. 'The worst species of immorality is inculcated and life (which is to determine the fate of eternity) thrown away when a kingdom or mistress is lost.'[6] In her first novel, *Mary, A Fiction*, she drove her sensitive, miserable heroine, named for herself, to an emotional impasse, finding sexual love in or out of marriage disgusting and waiting for an involuntary death to make it impossible. Suicide was still no option.

But the real-life Mary was more resourceful than the fictional and, if she did not consider self-slaughter, she did cut through her anguish over Fuseli's rejection by setting off to revolutionary France. Under the political onslaught over the years she modified her notions of suicide. By the time she returned to England early in 1795, as unsure of morality as of immortality, she had been devastated by another love, now clearly sexual, for the American Gilbert Imlay. In the summer and autumn she tried to kill herself, with no recorded thought of a Christian afterlife or of the state's disapproval, first probably with laudanum, and second with a leap into the Thames. It would seem to many conservatives when they heard the story that radical notions and the Revolution had liberated her for sex and its corollary, sordid suicide, and that the rights of women she advocated included a shocking 'chaos of errour and of crime', in the words of the anti-revolutionary novelist, Fanny Burney.

Yet a look at her writings up to this point suggests a rather different, more complicated message than a mere confusion of sex, sin and suicide: her point appears to be that irrational supine death, suffered or imposed on by others, may be associated with sexual obsessiveness and femininity and is indeed error and imprisonment for women; rational voluntary death, however, is quite divorced from sexuality and feminine emotionalism, and might not be error and crime at all but a very real optional route and liberty. The progress of the Revolution as understood by English radicals could well illustrate the point. For the Revolution was not, as the hostile reactionary insisted, a single event, but at least a double one, consisting, first, of respect for rational upright virtues, which might well be exemplified in rational suicide, and, second, of a ghastly reassertion, notably in the mid- and later 1790s, of everything that had been clearly and lamentably marked in the French character in the old regime – namely effeminacy, camp theatricality, diseased licentiousness and supine death saturated with sexuality. With some intricate reasoning, this nexus of ideas was symbolized by that embodiment of the national death-wish, the guillotine with its impotent victims – cruelty and effeminacy could, it seems, be as firmly linked by rational radicals as by conservatives and reactionaries. To investigate Woll-stonecraft's attitude, complicated because it crossed so many categories – psychological, political and literary – I want to look at the divided effect of *A Vindication of the Rights of Woman*, seemingly her greatest rational work, addressed directly to the Revolution in which it hoped to intervene with its proposals on education, and written just before she left for France. I want not so much to tease out its covert inclinations and declare them its real doctrine, as to note its ringing surface message in defiance of these inclinations. To consider Wollstonecraft, her suicide attempt and her note, I must also look into general eighteenth-century attitudes to suicide, which caused great argument and debate. Taking Foucault's point that discourse on a subject suggests not popularity but a problem, the debate indicates much anxiety in the 1790s in particular. Her reviewing for the *Analytical Review* shows that Wollstonecraft was well versed in this debate and must have felt the anxiety. So that her act and the writing of it cannot escape the contemporary intellectual context.

II

To the poet Percy Bysshe Shelley, life was a dome of many-coloured glass that could be shattered to reveal Romantic eternity. But for women the circle of confined life was less attractively escapable, its shattering less possible partly because it already included a kind of death. Wollstonecraft's friend Mary Hays, suffering her own version of the common female trap, made her heroine in *Memoirs of Emma Courtney* ask, 'Why do we suffer ourselves to be confined within a magic circle . . .?' Later in the book, feeling hemmed in on all sides by society and her own prejudices, she wrote 'I perceive, indignantly perceive, the magic circle, without knowing how to dissolve the powerful spell.'[7] The circle, which women themselves accepted, was suffocating; it muddled living and dying, preventing understanding in life and confusing the hope of eternity in death.

Wollstonecraft did not consider suicide in *The Rights of Woman* because she believed she had made reason the antidote to the spell of femininity. Reason was the exit from the 'magic circle' of constraint within which the feminine woman felt obliged to rest. It is common to see her as mistaken in this and to note her progress from error to understanding of her own femininity and impotent reason through her experience in revolutionary France and subsequent suicide attempt. In France she watched the Revolution progress from rational hope to a new language of irrational violence; her most personal encounter with it was a glimpse of the guillotine above a pavement wet with blood. Undoubtedly she learnt a good deal about personal relationships: in Paris she fell passionately in love with Imlay and watched, seemingly helpless, as her pen wrote desires that would make a devotee of *The Rights of Woman* blush for their author. She wanted, for example, her 'tendrils to cling to the elm by which I wish to be supported'; perhaps she embarrassed even herself: 'This is talking a new language for me!'[8] Undoubtedly, too, her role of guide and assertrix of cold reason and the rights of woman soured under the affliction of abandonment, and she even at times pleaded for a renewed fantastic femininity, for 'Phantoms of bliss' to enclose her again in 'the magic circle' – she uses here the same words as Mary Hays – of feminine obsession and insentience. But it does not seem necessary to include her rational suicide in this intermittent retreat, for her act differed markedly from the deathly longing of emotional femininity of the sort Hays described and the young Wollstonecraft lugubriously imagined in her first novel, *Mary, A Fiction*, the sort that remains insistent even in *The Rights of Woman*.

Wollstonecraft was much aware of the complicated intertwining of culture and the mind, of metaphor and material or, as she expressed it, of the human propensity to put 'a jargon of words in the room of things'. Yet she lets words squirm through the vigorous vital message of male oppression in *The Rights of Woman* and enervate her challenge. Consequently, though there is much anger, there is no closing of argument in the book, no positive firm ground to stand on. As it preaches vigour, effort and life, insistently the opposition masses: sexual passivity, aristocracy, effortless cruel power over others, and indolent femininity. Rigorously demanding sense, uprightness, activity, health, rationality and struggle for everyone, Wollstonecraft's rhetoric finds appalling, disgusting and, at the same time, fascinating a kind of infantile powerfulness of indolence, an inactivity, a femininity with its stays unfastened lying before corrupt and powerful masculinity, the victim swooning before the guillotine. Over and over again feeling is luxurious, prone, relaxed and scandalously voluptuous in front of rigid morality. The sensuous abstractions she uses to make her points, signifying far beyond any concrete noun, sometimes almost obliterate the stern political abstractions she advocates: reason, liberty, and equality. The revolution in female manners she yearns for, which should be allied to the real transformation across the Channel in the early rational Revolution, is often vitiated by fantastic repetition, a circling, a revolving indeed, but back and down.[9]

And death mingles with all that is most sternly disapproved: imaginative pleasure is sexual, like a feast; feasts bring disease and death in their cups and dainties. The body of the woman in lust is a feast, the dish for every male glutton to eat of. Passion is sickly, gross and voluptuous; it inflames, exhausts, drives mad and relaxes to insentience. Lust is the desperate effort of lascivious weakness flying towards death.[10] In fearful images, hell becomes the spirit continually hovering with abortive eagerness round the defiled dead body, desiring but unable to enjoy without the organ of sense. Against such slippery horror, willed, rational, active suicide would seem a noble act rather than an abject surrender, paradoxically close to the life of improvement, effort and reality which is the overt message of *The Rights of Woman*. For, after all, the book states that it aims to co-opt the rights of men for women and allow them liberation. It is a book which on its intentional surface is a handbook in the avoidance of imprisoning, deathly, sexual obsession, both passion and the defining of the self through sexuality. This obsession has been enjoined on women, and has become both the disease of femininity and the 'magic circle', fascinatingly feared, but not quite seemless, or Wollstonecraft would not have written her didactic book.

Again in the history of the early French Revolution, which she composed in the mid-1790s in France, there is a similar concatenation of words and ideas: woman, supineness, luxury, indulgence, power, bloatedness, consumption, enervation, sloth, lasciviousness, licentiousness, effeminacy and sexuality. There is, however, less disjunction between surface message and inclination here, more political harnessing of the power of deathly sensual image, and in the end less obsession. The old French regime is not only politically incorrect but voluptuous and luxurious in its culture. Its power exists on the prone defiled body of the fantastically powerless people, and both head inevitably towards the involuntary cruel death of the Revolution. Louis XIV is theatrical and indulged, Louis XV indolent and licentious. The ambiguous queen Marie Antoinette, with her strange ruinous predilection for handsome women, blights the court, which in turn is a harlot sapping the nation's masculinity and making it effeminate; royal government is effeminacy dying of intemperance. The French court is resurrected in the failed revolutionaries, those men who have betrayed the rational liberty of the virtuous revolution; both courtiers and revolutionaries belong to a nation of women, fickle, theatrical, debauched and infantile.[11] The guillotine, involuntary death not suicide, becomes their appropriate symbol and finale. As Wollstonecraft implies many times, the French Revolution would have been more successful if it had not been French.

Had she lived on, she would probably not have cared for twentieth-century male psychoanalysts (believing, for example, the Oedipus myth a silly tale with no proper significance, but her words almost demand their intervention. In *Beyond the Pleasure Principle*, Freud writes of the strong human instinct to return to the inanimate state, the pre-oedipal away from fathers. 'Seen in this light, the theoretical importance of the instincts of self-preservation, self-assertion and of mastery greatly diminishes.' He makes the image of the baby, deliciously passive and helplessly erotic, sinking back satiated from the mother's breast and falling asleep with flushed cheeks, the infantile and foetal desire at the core of adult being, the desire to go backwards to insentience.[12] The suicidal poet Anne Sexton calls this deathly sexy longing the almost unnameable lust; Wollstonecraft recognizes this lust but refuses to appease it.

Despite her initial disapproval of suicide, as early as January 1790 she had made a distinction between sorts of willed deaths which supports the overt messages of both *The Rights of Woman* and *The French Revolution*. In a review of a poem called 'Suicide' by Mary Dawes Blackett she addressed the problem of suicide directly and went against the message of the poem, which accepted the 'resignation of a love-sick woman, who patiently waited for her dismission, after every joy was fled', not far from the infantile acceptance of the irrational woman in *The Rights of Woman*. Instead she made it clear that she admired the suicide who 'rushed on death, and daringly broke loose from life', the person who grasped fate with a bold hand.

III

Wollstonecraft's complex attitude is embedded in the debates of the time. In the eighteenth century, England was widely regarded as the special home of suicide, the pious blaming this association on religious infidelity, the impious on social malaise, melancholy, unbalanced humours, and a climate of fog and rain. Suicide was physicalized into part of the English malady and autumn became its season – though there was scant evidence for either claim.[13] It was a disease 'from acrimony of the blood producing false images', according to William Rowley in 1788, and should be treated with tonics, bleeding and rest in bed.[14]

Whatever the personal treatment, the prevailing state attitude was Christian, and Christianity made the act sin, not sickness, by calling it self-slaughter or -murder, an impulse from the devil. The corpse was therefore dishonoured in vampiric ways, burial with a stake on the public highway. In addition, the state criminalized suicide and diverted the property of perpetrators to itself. In England the act remained sin and crime throughout the eighteenth century (staking and burying on the highway was officially stopped in 1823 and forfeiture in 1870) but the attitudes were modified and, by the latter half, penalties were almost invariably avoided, even in the clearest of cases. Verdicts of unsound mind grew commonplace.[15] Although suicide still provoked horror and demanded burial in unconsecrated ground, a secular attitude prevailed in many spheres – along the Thames and by the Serpentine humanitarian groups sensibly set up suicide stations to resuscitate the living, if possible, and, if not, identify the dead.

But two new attitudes were available for the literate classes, which I will call the rational or sensible and the romantic or sentimental. The enlightened stoical attitude, the rational, from which the French revolutionaries took their argument and practice, is expressed by David Hume and William Godwin, the romantic by Goethe's *Sorrows of Young Werther* and by certain remarks and texts of the younger Romantic poets.

In opposition to common opinion, the law of the land and orthodox Christanity, Hume regarded suicide as both a noble Roman habit and a native liberty. Why do we think that a 'man who tired of life, and hunted by pain and misery, bravely overcomes all the natural terrors of death . . . has incurred the indignation of his Creator?' When pain and sickness, shame and poverty in any combination are overwhelming, when a person has weighed up the benefits of the future against the misery of the present, then he has the right to proceed to end his being and not consider either God or society, since he is not obliged to do a small good to others at the expence of a great harm to himself.[16]

William Godwin, for a few months before her death the husband of Mary Wollstonecraft, sought to refine Hume. In the first version of *Political Justice* he saw suicide as neither criminal nor sinful. But he distrusted the Humean motives for escape from life, pain and shame, for pain, he wrote, was momentary and disgrace imaginary. In a later edition, he grew utilitarian and familial, insisting that the would-be suicide consider the net pain caused to the self and the misery to remaining relatives.[17]

If Durkheim's fifteen hanged themselves from a single hook, something is working with despair. In the literate classes no longer impressed by the devil, fiction and fashion were blamed. Indeed even Hume's essay had legendary effects – a friend was said to have gratefully returned it to the author, then shot himself. Earlier in the century, Addison, criticized for sympathetically portraying the noble Roman suicide Cato, was blamed when years later his relative, a literary hack in financial distress, filled his pockets with stones and jumped into the Thames, leaving behind him one last limp verse: 'What Cato did and Addison approved/ Cannot be wrong'.[18] To which Charles Wicksted Ethelston replied in 1803, 'Shall we err because Cato err'd?'

Ethelston's rejoinder occurred in 'The Suicide: Occasioned by Reading "The Sorrows of Werter"'. Here he refers to the greatest of the sentimental or romantic suicides. In Goethe's tale, Werther, narcissistic, passionate and hypochondriacal, makes suicide the act of a great soul who believes in the present and will not wait for tomorrow, who dies for love and an indescribable 'inner raging'. He has no Humean justification of poverty or shame, nor does he stop to consider his Godwinian relatives, being 'lost in the bliss of flinging my torments and my suffering' down the abyss, feeling the almost unnameable lust. Unlike both Hume and Godwin he manages to invest his act with religious, irrational anxiety – the Hamletian fear of the 'undiscovered country' – and he luxuriates by imagining and visualizing his dead body: 'when you read this . . . the cool grave will already cover the stiff remains of the restless, unhappy man'.[19] He dies, he declares, absolutely for his beloved Lotte, sparing her no pain, and gaining exquisite comfort from her projected tears and trembling after he is gone. Before he leaves he indulges in one last

ecstatic literary session, reading the melancholy pages of the sentimental Ossian to his beloved. Suicide has implicated literature and
demanded the critic more than the doctor, lawyer or priest.

The young would-be satirical poet Chatterton killed himself rationally for money it seems, but his act was appropriated for romance,
and Sir Herbert Croft, in *Love and Madness*, began the legend in 1780.
The English translator of Werther linked the two young men,
declaring that Werther's 'feelings, like those of our Chatterton, were
too fine to support the load of accumulated distress'.[20]

English versions of Werther, mindful of the national malady,
prefaced the work with cautions against readers following the hero.
The young Shelley saw himself in the mould, worrying like Werther
at having too much capacity to feel, too avid a desire for disintegra-
tion: 'How much rather would I expire in the struggle! Yes, that
were a relief! Is suicide wrong? I slept with a loaded pistol and
some poison last night, but did not die.'[21] At the height of the fracas
when he announced he intended to abandon his pregnant teenage
wife and take instead the sixteen-year-old Mary Wollstonecraft
Godwin, Wollstonecraft's second daughter, he followed her mother
by catching up a bottle of laudanum, crying, 'I never part from
this.'

Are the rational and romantic modes open to women? The pro-
nouns and rhetoric have been resolutely male but, since the
romantic or sentimental is so frequently associated with the feminine, this kind of suicide, if not the rational, should at least be an
option.

Socio-historical studies usually consider gender, and their empirical findings make even romantic suicide uncommon for women.
Richard Cobb in his study of Parisian suicide in the Revolution,
mainly of the lower orders, noted that women killed themselves far
less frequently than men and that their suicides did not respond to
national events, shortages and wars. They drowned rather than
shot or stabbed themselves, fearing, Cobb speculates, mutilation of
their bodies, expecting these to be displayed in death as in life.[22]
Durkheim's huge misogynist study of suicide in 1911 bore him out.
While men hanged themselves for choice, women overwhelmingly
chose drowning first, then came poison; self-indulgently they
avoided 'methods entailing effusion of blood and disfigurement of
the person'. But again he noted their smaller numbers, which
indicated for him the rudimentary sensibility of the female. For social
collective life involved man where woman merely watched: he was
the product of society, she of nature. 'With a few devotional practices

and some animals to care for, the old unmarried woman's life is full.'[23]

The eighteenth century itself had noticed different and gendered deaths, female drowning and poison, male pistols and ropes. A satirical writer, James Tilson, inspired by England's suicidal fame, advertised in *The World* in 1756 that he had erected a 'Receptacle for Suicides', in which was 'a commodious bath for disappointed ladies, paved with marble and fed by the clearest springs, where the patient may drown with the utmost privacy and elegance' – again the seeming emphasis on sentimental aesthetics and the displayed female corpse; a pistol loaded with dice was provided for gamesters, a sword for officers and, for the lower orders, halters and nooses. Actors of ambiguous gender were supplied with poison.[24]

Literary men did not concur with empirical sociology and its inferior numbers of women – though they did agree with the diagnosis of narcissism – and the romantic female suicide, from Dido to Anna Karenina and Madame Bovary, has been the stuff of myth and fiction; a cat or two to care for could not have helped. In English heroic drama and she-tragedies, suicide and its verbal prelude expiated and completed the sexual act in which the women have indulged, as with the once impudent whore Calista of Nicholas Rowe's *The Fair Penitent*. She kills herself, having appealed to her would-be lover:

> Then when you see me meagre, wan and chang'd,
> Stretched at my Length, and dying in my Cave,
> On that cold earth I mean shall be my Grave,
> Perhaps you may relent, and sighing say,
> At length her Tears have wash'd her stains away.

Mary Wollstonecraft, who knew this speech well, did not approve it, no doubt seeing Calista as one of those women quite openly operating within the magic circle in life and death. Its rhetoric is the common deathly one of forsaken or excluded women, licensed to speak passionately only in this extremity, all luxuriating in the idea of the man's gaze upon their dying or dead selves.[26] Such women demand an absent lover to come and watch; he must be made to face the woman as corpse or semi-corpse, and match her sorrow or repentance with his own. As with Werther, language is magnificent and theatrical, obscuring the feminine choice that is implied: suicide of the woman, not murder of the man. The same magnificence of language is allowed to the death-yearning Clarissa of Samuel Richardson's novel, more seductive to reading women than Calista, alone and starving, entering into her divine father's house through her coffin. Providence is on her side, preventing sinful suicide but giving easeful, involuntary death.

But all of these are women created by men. Their attitudes, influential though they were on actual women, were projections of men. In addition, their deaths act through men: Brutus avenges the suicide Lucretia and brings about a Roman revolution; Morden avenges Clarissa and helps, according to some critics, the revolution of the rising bourgeoisie.[27] What of women writers?

In the mid-seventeeth century, Margaret Cavendish, Duchess of Newcastle, created a She Anchoret to give her own views on religion and government to an eagerly waiting world. The Anchoret is irresistible to a neighbouring king but as a celibate she refuses his hand. He threatens war and, to avoid national conflagration, the philosophical lady decides rationally to poison herself. She succeeds of course and is accorded an immense state funeral, in time becoming the eighth wonder of the world.[28] This is suicide both rational and fantastic, needing no man for posthumous champion or male necro-philiac gaze for validation. By the eighteenth century suicide was more humdrum. Delarivier Manley knew that manipulating clever-ness in a fallen world was what women needed, and the good and silly were left to commit romantic or emotional suicide as their unmoved seducers urbanely re-entered the salon.[29] In the sentimen-tal later century, fictional suicide became less common for women by women, too energetic an act for their much proclaimed femininity, and Clarissa's ambiguous enervated death became more the mode. Even the romantic suicide of Werther usually seemed to be closed to them, although there were of course exceptions, actual women suicides in England and on the Continent dying with Werther beneath their pillow.

Mary Wollstonecraft would not have approved of this posturing. She would not have wished guilt and outside authority removed from the act for such effete theatrically to take their place. Rational suicide should not be such a staging of the self; unless politically necessary, it should involve as little self-display as possible. Ironically such an act was most clearly imaged for women by Edmund Burke, whose political views Wollstonecraft had so loudly condemned in both her *Vindication of the Rights of Men* and *A Vindication of the Rights of Woman*. He envisaged the fallen Marie Antoinette, 'with the dignity of a Roman matron', saving herself from the last disgrace with the 'sharp antidote' hidden in her bosom.

IV

So to return to the drenched skirts, the vigorous rowing and the plunge at dusk. Nothing could be further from sexy, dreamy, self-regarding death, that travesty of the noble revolutionary suicide, that expression of impotent irrational narcissistic femininity which, in *The Rights of Woman*, knowing its attraction, Wollstonecraft thought woman's chiefest wrong. In such context, might not a right be active death, a grasping of fate with a bold hand, a rational suicide connected to a rational portrayal of the self? Although the Revolution had in the end failed to inspire proper principles in the citizens of France, who seemed largely to have given up their struggle for reason, universal free-will and equality, so reinstating power and powerlessness under the authority of the guillotine, yet it might be possible individually to take a rational stand and so become worthy of the original rational principles of the Revolution. If so, how could the act express itself in language? If for death the same hook is irresistible, no doubt the same goes for words. So if *The Rights of Woman* could not avoid revealing as well as attacking feminine wrongs, might it not be impossible to kill oneself, even rationally, without cliché, without a touch of Calista and Werther?

This is the letter Wollstonecraft wrote to Imlay before she set off for the Thames in, as it happens, a rainy autumn:

> I shall make no comments on your conduct or any appeal to the world. Let my wrongs sleep with me! Soon, very soon, I shall be at peace. When you receive this, my burning head will be cold.
>
> I would encounter a thousand deaths, rather than a night like the last. Your treatment has thrown my mind into a state of chaos; yet I am serene. I go to find comfort, and my only fear is that my body will be insulted by an endeavour to recall my hated existence. But I shall plunge into the Thames where there is the least chance of my being snatched from the death I seek.
>
> God bless you! May you never know by experience what you have made me endure. Should your sensibility ever awake, remorse will find its way to your heart; and, in the midst of business and sensual pleasure, I shall appear before you, the victim of your deviation from rectitude.[30]

In its intention to intervene in life, this writing is sincere and rational. If it fails to please at all, its faults – insensitive though it seems to note them – are not those of excessive emotion, but of cliché and literariness. As a suicide note sent and delivered, it must be agent and action; yet, like *The Rights of Woman*, it jostles metaphor and material, fictionalizing on the very verge of secret fact.

But in the end it resists many of the obvious literary urges. There from the despised theatrical Calista is the dream of posthumous power through language and projection. Yet it is much changed. For where the fictional character imagines the man utterly repentant over her prostrate corpse, Wollstonecraft visualizes herself appearing and, surely upright, to the recumbent man amidst his sensual pleasure, awakening not imposing sorrow. The body, so much the concern and appeal in romantic suicide, is of importance here only in the rational need for disposal and concealment: it should fall into the deepest, most inaccessible water and should not be dredged up to be gazed upon by men. The romantic verbal extremes – chaos and serenity, burning and cold, peace and remorse – are there certainly, but she wishes them overcome by assertions of calmness and rationality. Religious fear, so clear in her early works, has quite departed and, although forsaken, she does not assume much of the language of romantic forsaken women bound in their 'magic circle' of obsessive love and longing. Instead, the letter's contrasts are familiar from *The Rights of Woman*: she, the suicide, is stern, moral, rational; he, the living, sensual and effeminate, threatened with ghosts.

I am not intending to make Wollstonecraft's suicide attempt a literary and heroic revolutionary event – that would indeed be a 'jargon of words' substituted for the room of things. But I am suggesting, on the one hand, that, as the fictional Werther dies in the midst of Ossian, so the real woman, intending to die, cannot avoid the expected language of women, however expressive of their wrongs, and, on the other, that the rights of woman might, for a disappointed Wollstonecraft in 1795, include the revolutionary right of rational death.

V

But she does not die. She bubbles up to the surface – as so many women do, the female failure rate being much larger than the male – and goes on living. She does not, however, repudiate her intended death. In her first letter after her unwanted rescue, she wrote: 'I have only to lament, that, when the bitterness of death was past, I was inhumanly brought back to life and misery. But a fixed determination is not to be baffled by disappointment; nor will I allow that to be a frantic attempt, which was one of the calmest acts of reason. In this respect I am only accountable to myself.'[31] No external authority is allowed, from religion, the state, or individual men. Much later, relating the event to William Godwin, she declared she would not try drowning again because of the pain, but she never implied that she would avoid all other methods.

Yet, in George Eliot's patronizing words Wollstonecraft did live on to experience 'some real joys' before 'death came in time to hinder the joys from being spoiled'.[32] Inevitably there is a change in attitude for, however initially desired, the French Revolution had brought no millennium, and in her final book, *Maria, or The Wrongs of Woman*, it dwindles into 'French principles', synonym of bourgeois adultery for English conservatives. In addition, drowning had brought no comfort. From Imlay's reaction to her intended death, it was clear that he would rarely have been haunted with his 'deviation from rectitude'. She had tried out this rational right of suicide and found it still rational, then, but not as powerful as she had imagined. What was there to do?

She could take Durkheim's advice, get a pet and join ordinary women too limited to consider dying before their time. Or she could re-examine death with renewed rationality and investigate how much her search for it, rational though it might have been in appearance, had been fuelled by her irrational fascination for what she most condemned. In *Maria, or The Wrongs of Woman*, death, both rational and sensual, does in fact grow dismal: 'Death I had hailed as my only chance of deliverance', writes the miserably married heroine with many of her creator's traits, 'but . . . I shrunk from the icy arms of an unknown tyrant', though still more inviting than the unwanted husband's.[33] Yet, with divine irony, the book that, despite this oblique refusal of drowning, would nonetheless have as its ultimate or penultimate episode a suicide remains unfinished, for sex brought involuntary, feminine death to the author in childbirth.

After the event, her husband William Godwin, wrote her life with reverential and tactless frankness, thereby achieving two things: he fixed the horrifying connection of suicide and female rights in the reactionary English mind, and he gave his wife's story the sentimental and romantic cast she had spent most of her intellectual life combatting. She became in his words 'a female Werter'.[34] It was incongruous that Godwin, who was one of the advocates of rational suicide and an apparent admirer of his wife in vindicating mode, should have made an event she described as entirely rational into a sentimental surrender. In his depiction her suicide attempt edged closer to Werther's than to that of the revolutionary martyrs or to the rational act described by Hume and Godwin himself, while her letters to Imlay, which Godwin printed in his edition of her *Posthumous Works*, including the suicide letter quoted above, were prefaced by his compliment that they were superior to the fictional Werther's great epistles. Both Wollstonecraft and her act were pushed back into a romantic or sentimental frame: her melancholy letters became the display 'calculated to make a man in love with its author', and her suicide attempts became part of her feminization from the 'harshness' and 'ruggedness' of *The Rights of Woman* to a gentleness of spirit and 'a softness almost more than human'.[35]

But the public did not agree with this softening of Wollstonecraftian suicide, and it was widely accepted in the late 1790s that, if men were driven to self-destruction by Tom Paine, women were propelled by the Mary Wollstonecraft writ large in parodies of Godwin. The *Anti-Jacobin* made her name synonymous with suicide although it vacillated in its review of her life between disapproving her act and blaming her for failing at it. But the disapproving Fanny Burney was clear and consistent. She aimed directly at diffusing the rational and suicidal legacy of Wollstonecraft, filtered through Godwin, by mocking the conjunction of fiction and fact, suicide and system; so she ridiculed both the French Revolution and the revolution in female life and death it had inspired. Parodically following Godwin, Burney muddled Wollstonecraft's rational suicide with the romantic sort, and conflated her involuntary death with involuntary sexual obsession, when in her last novel *The Wanderer*, set in the Revolution, she made her feminist character Elinor repeatedly fail at suicide. Driven wild by sexual longing, rejection, foolish French systems and *The Rights of Woman*, Elinor tries three theatrical times to commit what she terms her 'sublime act of voluntary self-extinction', angry like her original at those who would save her.[36]

On the third failed occasion, progressing in eccentricity, she procures a coffin-shaped tablet in a church as her suicide letter. But by now a grotesque humour is entering the picture, as she cries, 'I am food, for fools, – when I meant to be food only for worms!' Her life is turning from tragedy to farce under the repetition and her creator's insistence. At the end she is co-opted into orthodoxy and her mounting rhetoric leads to religion, not revolution. She learns that she 'has strayed from the beaten road, only to discover that all others are pathless'. She will no longer be a female revolutionary and seek death as a noble moment of free-will, but instead she will call for a man to guide her on her way through the remainder of a life she must lead. The revolution, French and feminist, is well and truly over. In France Napoleon, lacking prescience of his own suicidal needs – he would try to kill himself with poison when events turned sour – rolled the revolution back for others towards reactionary England and suicide was recriminalized. Guilt and authority fell into place again and obedient women died when they ought.

Cambridge, 1989

Notes

1 See John McManners, *Death and the Enlightenment* (Oxford: Oxford University Press, 1985), p. 418, and Dorinda Outram, *The Body and the French Revolution: sex, class and political culture* (New Haven: Yale University Press, 1989).
2 For the former view, see Claire Tomalin, *The Life and Death of Mary Wollstonecraft* (London: Weidenfeld & Nicolson, 1974).
3 Emile Durkheim, *Suicide: A Study in Sociology*, trans. John A. Spaulding and George Simpson (London: Routledge & Kegan Paul, 1968, p. 97.
4 *Collected Letters of Mary Wollstonecraft*, ed. Ralph M. Wardle (Ithaca: Cornell University Press, 1979), p. 134.
5 *Original Stories, The Works of Mary Wollstonecraft*, ed. Janet Todd and Marilyn Butler (London: Pickering & Chatto, 1989), vol. IV, p. 427.
6 *Thoughts on the Educaton of Daughters, The Works of Mary Wollstonecraft*, vol. IV, p. 46.
7 Mary Hays, *The Memoirs of Emma Courtney* (New York: Garland, 1974), vol. I, pp. 168–9.
8 *Collected Letters*, p. 248.
9 See Mary Poovey, *The Proper Lady and the Woman Writer* (Chicago: University of Chicago Press, 1984), pp. 48–81.
10 *A Vindication of the Rights of Woman, The Works of Mary Wollstonecraft*, vol. V, especially Chapters 2 and 3.
11 *A Historical and Moral View of the French Revolution, The works of Mary Wollstonecraft*, vol. VI, pp. 25–9 and 72–4.
12 Freud, *Beyond the Pleasure Principle*, trans. James Strachey (New York: W. W. Norton, 1975), p. 311.
13 See Roland Bartel, 'Suicide in eighteenth-century England: the myth of a reputation', *Huntingdon Library Quarterly*, 23, 1960, p. 145; Charles Moore, *A Full Enquiry into the Subject of Suicide* (London, 1790).
14 William Rowley, *A Treatise on Female, Nervous, Hysterical, Hypochondriacal, Bilious, Convulsive Disease: Apoplexy and Palsy: with thougths on Madness, Suicide &c* (London, 1788), p. 343.

15 See Michael MacDonald, 'The secularization of suicide in England 1660–1800', *Past & Present*, 111, May 1986, pp. 50–100; Donna T. Andrew, 'Debate: the secularization of suicide', *Past and Present*, 119, May 1988, pp. 158–65.
16 *Essays on Suicide and the Immortality of the Soul ascribed to the late David Hume Esq.* (London, 1783), p. 9.
17 Compare the first edition of *Political Justice*, Bk II, ch. 2, appendix 2, with second and third editions; see also his views in the letter on suicide in the Abinger Mss, C527, Bodleian Library, Oxford, where he again reiterates the right of suicide but insists that suicide is regrettable when a person kills himself 'for a temporary suffering'.
18 See the entry on Addison in the *Dictionary of National Biography*.
19 *The Sorrows of Werter: a German story*, trans. attrib. David Malthus (3rd edn, London, 1782), II, pp. 104–5.
20 'The Secularization of Suicide', p. 83.
21 Edward Dowden, *The Life of Percy Bysshe Shelley* (London, 1866), Appendix A, II, p. 544.
22 Richard Cobb, *Death in Paris, 1795–1801* (Oxford: Oxford University Press, 1978).
23 *Suicide*, p. 385.
24 *The World*, 6 September, 1756.
25 Nicholas Rowe, *The Fair Penitent* (London: Edward Arnold, 1969), p. 53.
26 See Peggy Kamuf, *Fictions of Feminine Desire* (Lincoln: University of Nebraska Press, 1982).
27 See Ian Donaldson, *The Rapes of Lucretia: a myth and its transformations* (Oxford: Clarendon Press, 1982).
28 Margaret Cavendish, Duchess of Newcastle, 'The She Anchoret', *Natures Pictures Drawn by Fancies Pencil to the Life* (London, 1656).
29 See the story of Charlot in *The New Atalantis, The Novels of Mary Delarivière Manley*, ed. P. Köster (Gainesville: Scholars' Facsimiles & Reprints, 1971), vol. I.
30 *Collected Letters*, pp. 316–17.
31 *Collected Letters*, p. 317.
32 'Margaret Fuller and Mary Wollstonecraft', *Essays of George Eliot*, ed. Thomas Penney (New York: Columbia University Press, 1963), pp. 199–200.
33 *The Wrongs of Woman: or, Maria, The Works of Mary Wollstonecraft*, vol. I, p. 154.
34 William Godwin, *Memoirs of The Author of 'The Rights of Woman'*, ed. Richard Holmes (Harmondsworth: Penguin, 1987), p. 242.
35 *Memoirs*, p. 249.
36 Fanny Burney, *The Wanderer Or, Female Difficulties* (London: Pandora Press, 1988), pp. 340 and 760.

7   Thoughts on the death of Fanny
Wollstonecraft

In October 1816, at the age of twenty-two, Fanny Wollstonecraft (her correct name though she was better known as Fanny Imlay or Godwin) travelled to Swansea to kill herself. In October 1795, her mother Mary Wollstonecraft had tried for the second time to commit suicide by jumping off Putney Bridge into the Thames.

Fanny was named after her mother's best friend, Fanny Blood, whom, from the age of sixteen, she loved 'better than all the world beside'.[1] Their meeting illustrates the literariness in which Wollstonecraft and her daughter both lived; in his *Memoirs* of his wife Mary Wollstonecraft, William Godwin saw it as an encounter of two fictional characters, the romantic Werther and the domestic Charlotte from Goethe's sentimental novel, *Young Werther*.

Like the girl named after her, Fanny Blood had a short life, much of it dominated by her friend. After Wollstonecraft had rescued her sister Eliza, who seems to have had a postpartum depression, from both matrimony and motherhood (the abandoned child, Mary, died shortly after), together with Fanny, Eliza and the younger sister Everina, she began a school in Newington Green. It was interrupted by the sickly Fanny's voyage to Portugal to marry, followed ten months later by Mary Wollstonecraft's journey to help her ailing friend through childbirth. After Fanny's death, Wollstonecraft returned to England to find her school in ruins, Eliza and Everina perhaps learning the first lesson about the dangers in reliance on their sister.

Wollstonecraft then became a governess on Lord and Lady Kingsborough's estate in Ireland, where in depression she took comfort in the writing of a novel entitled *Mary, A Fiction*, which rather cruelly anatomized the friendship with Fanny. In the book the friend, who dies unmarried, is found emotionally and intellectually wanting by the sensitive but strong-minded heroine.

Fanny Blood comes again to the fore in the troubled relationship with an American merchant, Gilbert Imlay, that followed Wollstonecraft's literary success with *A Vindication of the Rights of Woman* and her lonely trip to revolutionary France. The result of the relationship was a daughter, conceived when Imlay was in Paris and she in enforced exile as an Englishwoman in a village outside the barrier of the city; the couple playfully referred to the baby as the 'barrier girl' and named her Fanny after Fanny Blood. She was a child of the Revolution, of free unmarried parents, and was fittingly registered not in May 1794, but in Floréal.

Over the next months in Le Havre and Paris, during Imlay's ever more frequent absences, Wollstonecraft wrote describing the little girl, imagining the cosy domestic scenarios from which she had rescued Eliza, and recording Imlay's only endearing joke, that such a strongly sucking baby would grow to finish off her mother's work and write a second *Rights of Woman*. In Wollstonecraft's letters, at seven months Fanny is seen cutting a tooth, trying to stand up, and wanting to be bounced; she was 'ready to fly away with spirits' and appeared '*wonderfully* intelligent'.[2] Only intermittently – when nurses were incompetent – did the mother think herself a 'slave to the child', a pardonable exaggeration in a lonely and especially cold first winter in Paris. When a competent nurse, Marguerite, was found, the child became less burdensome, and most of the time the mother was gleeful over the baby's 'life and spirits'.[3]

When she finally returned to London in the spring of 1795, Wollstonecraft learnt conclusively that Imlay was unfaithful and she responded by probably taking an overdose of laudanum. Her sisters, whose lives she had been aiding and ordering, almost certainly knew nothing of the attempt; they therefore responded with wounded self-esteem and bitterness when she wrote to tell them that their dream of a future life together should be abandoned since her 'domestic happiness' might be interrupted by it. The sisters exclaimed correctly, 'Mary cannot be *married*!!'[4]

Imlay's unusual response to the appeal of the suicide attempt was to send Wollstonecraft as his wife and agent on a business trip to find a cargo of French silver – an illegal one during war between England and France – lost in a stolen ship in Scandinavia. In the summer of 1795 she therefore set off with Fanny and Marguerite for Sweden.

On the journey to the boat the baby was in lively form, disturbing her mother throughout and imitating a mail-horn. As she travelled through Scandinavia, Wollstonecraft dramatized and pitied herself; she claimed she felt anew the presence of long-dead Fanny Blood, hearing her voice 'warbling' on the moors before her. The living Fanny was for a while left with the maid in Tonsburg, since the roads were bad and the child's teething painful. Perhaps Wollstonecraft found her a burden again, but, once separated, she thought sentimentally of the child and her miserable feminine predicament in a masculine world where feminine sentiment would lead only to sorrow.[5]

On her return to England she rediscovered Imlay's infidelity and, with more purpose than the previous time, she left instructions for Marguerite to inherit her clothes and to take Fanny back to France, expecting no financial support from the father. She then threw herself from a London bridge, warning in her suicide note to Imlay, 'Should your sensibility ever awake, remorse will find its way to your heart; and, in the midst of business and sensual pleasure, I shall appear before you . . .'.[6] After her rescue she declared that nothing would again induce her to take the suicidal route of drowning.

In time she made of her business trip a romantic volume of travels, which attracted the critic of sentiment William Godwin, who had been repulsed by the aggressive *Rights of Woman* and by what he took to be its garrulous, assertive author. When in April 1796 Wollstonecraft called on Godwin uninvited and alone, he was ready to receive her with friendship. The pair became lovers and Wollstonecraft tried to foster feeling between the bachelor, who had largely eliminated children from his social utopian vision, and the three-year-old 'Fannikin'. When she became pregnant again, they married, to the amusement of the conservative.

Meanwhile Wollstonecraft successfully nursed Fanny through chickenpox and made little books of lessons for her, avoiding the Christian religion with which most small children of the time were indoctrinated. In her mother's letters, Fanny appears playing with her toy rake in the fields near their home in the suburban development of the Polygon in London, hearing from Godwin staying with the china Wedgewoods that he was in 'the land of mugs'.[7] From time to time Wollstonecraft fantasized abandonment, but by this stage her suicidal fantasies included the child; both would be at the bottom of the ocean together.

Wollstonecraft was by now working on her final novel, *Maria or The Wrongs of Woman*, in which the autobiographical heroine writes her life to give her absent baby some notion of herself should she die before they can be reunited. At the end, abandoned like her creator, Maria attempts suicide with laudanum, to be saved, in only one of several ending fragments, by an appeal to live for her rediscovered child. It seems likely that Fanny would in time have read this novel, in which the account meant for the baby actually goes to the deserting man and in which the mother, in most endings, deserts her child through suicide, despite having listened to a disastrous life-history of a mistreated girl left without a mother.

In August 1797 Wollstonecraft began labour with the baby that would become Mary Wollstonecraft Godwin Shelley. But the birth went wrong and as the days passed Fanny was sent to stay with a friend. So she missed the moment on 10th September when her mother died a death 'that strongly marked the distinction of the sexes, by pointing out the destiny of women, and the diseases to which they were peculiarly liable'. Wollstonecraft was buried where she had been married five months before. Fanny, hitherto called Imlay to disguise her mother's status, was adopted by Godwin and relabelled 'Fanny Godwin'.

And now, according to Coleridge, 'cadaverous Silence' fell on Godwin's house as he scratched a living with his pen, having two babies to feed. 'When Fanny interrupts my reading with a request to hold her on my knee and tell her a fanciful tale, I confess I must curb my temper', he admitted.[8] But he was not careless of them and he was concerned to give attention to both. He seems to have retained Marguerite for a while and hired a housekeeper, who adored Mary though not Fanny. In time he taught the children lessons from their mother's books, taking on masters to teach them languages. And he allowed them a period in his study after the silent morning.

His first literary effort after his bereavement was his *Memoirs* of Wollstonecraft, a labour of considerable love but the frankness of which brought down much mockery on his head; inevitably it proclaimed Fanny a bastard. Despite viewing marriage as 'property – and the worst of properties', Godwin felt the need of a wife in his domestic predicament, and he tried several ladies before being discovered himself by Mary Jane Claremont, a 'widow' with green spectacles and a past as unconventional as Wollstonecraft's, but more discreetly hidden. Fanny was just seven when Mrs Claremont moved in with a son and a daughter, Clara Mary Jane, called Jane at first, then Claire. There were four children from four different fathers to support. Soon a son, William, was born to the couple. Despite endless financial worries, Godwin seems to have been moderately happy with his new wife, though she was never favoured by his daughter, who later called her 'odious' and 'filthy', or by many of his friends, one of whom termed her 'that damn'd infernal bitch'. Marguerite had disappeared.

When Fanny was thirteen, Mary ten, the Godwins moved from the semi-rural Polygon to unfashionable Skinner Street, where there was a smell of fish, fur and oil as well as of material from milliners. Godwin and his wife had started a publishing venture and needed the extra room for books. It was a doomed financial venture that, without any particular mismanagement, swallowed up all the money available despite much hard work.[9] The younger girls, Mary and Jane, almost the same age, went alternately to school, but Fanny, the eldest, remained at home. She seems to have been the most useful domestically. Mary complained that Jane was favoured by her mother and never asked to work, and she was chided by Fanny for her moods. But lack of formal schooling was no great impediment to education, and much could be gleaned from lectures and theatres, to which Godwin sometimes took the children, as well as from the occasional tea with famous writers. There was, too, some connection with her mother's past. Her publisher, Joseph Johnson, before he died, directed a bond of £200 for Fanny's use, though there is no evidence she ever received it.

When she was about eleven, according to Godwin's diary, he appears to have had a serious talk with Fanny, probably the moment when he informed her of what she may already have known, that she was not his child. Perhaps this led to an increase in the diffidence and pliancy that people noticed in her by now, the earlier spirits seemingly dormant or quashed. Mrs Godwin complained that she sacrificed her nerves to her adopted children and no doubt took her feelings out on the least defended of the girls. Godwin, however, appreciated Fanny's good nature and eagerness to please, and he praised her domestic help; on one occasion he wanted her to stay behind with him as a kind of housekeeper when the rest of the family went away. He made a distinction, however, between his natural and adopted daughters: 'My own daughter is considerably superior in capacity to the one her mother had before. . . . My own daughter is, I believe, very pretty.' He noted Fanny's 'faculty of memory'.[10]

When in 1812 the young Percy Bysshe Shelley encountered Godwin, the older philosopher was fifty-six. Shelley admired Godwin's past struggles and radical domestic and political ideas, while Godwin, no doubt appreciating the youthful eagerness of his new disciple, also valued his potential wealth and status as the heir of a baronet. Shelley had been just nineteen when he had rescued the pretty and seemingly malleable sixteen-year-old Harriet from boarding school by marrying her. A child was born not long afterwards. He had been reluctant to marry, but Harriet had allegedly threatened suicide if unrescued and unmarried. Still Shelley aimed at more communal living than marriage suggested, of the sort that seemed adumbrated in the writings of Wollstonecraft and Godwin. Consequently he had when first married encouraged a twenty-nine-year-old teacher to join him and Harriet as another 'sister of my soul', but he soon found her ugly and demanding; later he wrote to Godwin to invite Fanny to visit, but Godwin refused the invitation.

Harriet saw Fanny at Skinner Street as a sensible, plain girl, while Fanny in Harriet saw 'a fine lady' dressed in silk. Fanny was the first of the Godwin girls to encounter Shelley, since Godwin had responded to the feud between his wife and daughter by sending Mary for an extended stay in Scotland. Fanny soon became on familiar terms with Shelley and, when on one occasion he left the Godwins abruptly, she scolded him gently. In turn he wrote to her playfully, admitting, for example, his lack of conventional humour: his intended laughs became sardonic grins, disgraceful to a Cheshire cat. He noted her timidity and countered her initial fear of writing to him by the reassurance that, despite being 'one of those formidable and longclawed animals called a *Man*', he was inoffensive and lived on vegetables.[11]

Soon he had met the other girls, all to be equally infatuated by his glamour, noted Mrs Godwin. In the summer of 1814 while Fanny was away in Wales, probably with the Wollstonecraft aunts Eliza and Everina, and Harriet in Bath with her baby, an intimacy grew between Shelley and sixteen-year-old Mary. Soon he regarded her as the person nearest to his soul, another Mary Wollstonecraft whom he admired, a living illustration from her parents' books. With some candour he announced that he saw her as a dream of *himself* – when he spoke of her he felt, he said, like an egoist expatiating upon his own perfections.

True to his communal and libertarian principles, he accepted his new romantic feelings and seems to have believed that all of them could settle down together. Separation when love was dead was not immoral and constancy was no virtue, according to the notes to the poem *Queen Mab*, dedicated to Harriet; one should not, he argued, spend the loveliest season of one's life in unproductive efforts at loving one no longer loved. When Harriet came back to Skinner Street and proved unequal to her new role as friend to the lovers, she found herself sinking in her husband's estimation from soul-mate through 'noble animal' to loathesome beast.

Hating secrecy, Shelley quickly told his mentor of his joy and discovered the father rather than the philosopher. Although Shelley pointed out that he had followed Godwin's words on marriage in *Political Justice*, Godwin countered by declaring he had read the wrong text, the first instead of the second edition, which changed some aspects of the philosophy to suit the changed, more conservative times. Free love should exist only in a perfect society, and the present was imperfect. Godwin, however, remained true to his belief that wealth should go where it was most needed and that Shelley should consequently continue helping the financially faltering but deserving Godwin household with advances of money. After some hysterical behaviour, Shelley offering death pacts with laudanum but trying nothing, he and Mary, together with Jane, left the house for the Continent. Godwin was outraged and the public, which he now feared, was gleeful; a rumour spread that the old radical had sold his daughters to the baronet's heir, Mary for £100 more than Jane. Undoubtedly the Miss Wollstonecrafts in Ireland heard of the scandal, seemingly a repetition of their sister's scandals which had blighted their earlier lives and, they claimed, made them dread the discovery of their name.

Fanny returned to find only the pregnant Harriet left. But, loyal to her sisters, she made no known approach. Meanwhile Shelley still dreamt of group existence and he invited Harriet to join himself and the two girls, but it seems that no invitation went to Fanny, although Percy and Mary were at the time reading her mother's *Mary*, with its anatomy of her namesake. Soon the trio returned, their money gone, and Shelley was at the door dunning Harriet for money to support his entourage. Mary was pregnant was well as Harriet, and he had to keep both women as well as Jane, who, Mary later said, 'poisoned' her life when young. So entangled was he with bailiffs and creditors that he and Mary had to part for much of the time, meeting only in secret. Yet they managed to dine out and to read Wollstonecraft's love letters to Imlay. He also found time to think of rescuing other girls. Fanny became useful as a go-between, trying hard to please both households, helping, soothing and running errands.[12]

Godwin was angry with Fanny for her loyalty to Mary, threatening silence if she visited her, yet making her demand money of Shelley. Mrs Godwin, finding that she still had contact with the delinquents, refused to let her down for dinner if she continued seeing them, although by now she was a girl of twenty, while Mary scorned what she took to be Fanny's poor spirit. A few incidents suggest the painfulness of the time for Fanny: one cold October evening, for example, torn by her loyalties, she waited outside the rooms of Mary, Percy and Jane while they dined inside, then sent up a nervous message about approaching creditors. Shelley and Jane ran down and caught Fanny so tightly she screamed out. On another occasion Percy and Mary visited Skinner Street knowing that an early morning call would raise only Fanny, whose position seemed a cross between a servant's and a child's.

When Mary's baby was born, Mrs Godwin dispatched Fanny with baby linen, but the baby soon died. Harriet's baby was born and lived. By now Jane seemed troublesome to both households and so Shelley sent her off for a stay in Lynmouth, where he had earlier been with Harriet. Trying to gain some respectability, Godwin claimed that she was staying with friends of her family. In pretentious, comically self-deluding letters, Jane wrote to the melancholy Fanny left in Skinner Street, informing her about the beauties of nature and about her own joy in solitude and quietness; she advised cheeriness. By now Harriet was sounding like Mary Wollstonecraft in depressive, self-dramatizing mood. She desired, she wrote, a quiet grave, and she lamented her blasted mind: 'Is it wrong, do you think, to put an end to one's sorrows?'[13] But again it seems that the two lonely women failed to meet.

1816 is frequently seen as the *annus mirabilis* of English Romanticism, origin of *Frankenstein*, *Childe Harold*, and the 'Hymn to Intellectual Beauty', written or begun during the summer of Byron and Shelley, Mary and Jane in Switzerland. Fanny hinted that she might like to come to visit but no one appears to have taken the hint. Mary sent her a portrait of Byron and, when she returned, brought her back a gold Swiss watch.

In Skinner Street Fanny, now over twenty-one, was blamed by Mrs Godwin not only for being a drag on the household, but also for being the only uncorrupted girl, so preventing her compromised daughter, Jane, from returning home. There were few options for a person whom the public saw as the sister of two whores and who had no expectation of a dowry for marriage. So she had to rely on blood relations, her aunts Eliza and Everina. They had expected to take Fanny in to teach with them in Dublin and it appears that she was eager to go. But they had already told Godwin that they had travelled to Ireland to escape the notoriety of their sister, and, following the scandal of the Shelley-and-Mary elopement, Everina, the harshest of the sisters, visited Godwin and seems to have withdrawn the invitation to Fanny. Mrs Godwin told Fanny that Shelley had Mary found her ridiculous and laughed at her.

All these blows must have hit Fanny forcefully and she complained of her 'dreadful state of mind'.[14] She seems to have been sentimental and sensitive and much concerned with the feelings and opinions of others. Constantly she thought of Mary and Jane, warning Mary not to trust servants and worrying even at the end of September about obtaining a pianoforte for Jane. She also worried generally over the poor and starving, without having any of her mother's early belief in philanthropy and her later qualified faith in social change. Fanny thought that England needed not little philanthropies, but a revolution in the whole system, and she saw no hope in politics.

Meanwhile the Godwin finances were as dire as ever and made more precarious by the elopement which Godwin might have expected to end his call on Shelley's generosity. In fact Shelley remained true to Godwinian principles of money and owned his obligations to support his mentor. Consequently in early Autumn he sent a large cheque, though for less than Godwin had asked. But it was tactlessly addressed to Godwin himself in a public way that the recipient deplored. Desperate to keep some reputation as a shocked father, Godwin sent it back, demanding discretion and a new addressee. Shelley duly complied, but before the second cheque arrived Fanny had gone.

Perhaps she pretended that the Miss Wollstonecrafts in Dublin did in fact want their niece to come to them, although the money she had left in her pocket a few days later, only 3s 6d, would argue that she had no intention or possibility of travelling to Ireland through Wales. She dressed herself in her mother's stays and took with her the gold watch Mary had brought her from Switzerland, a red pocket handkerchief, a brown berry necklace and a small leather purse. Possibly she also carried some laudanum or used some of her initial money to pay for it later. At Bristol on 8th October she wrote letters to both Shelley and Godwin households declaring that she was going where she would no longer be a burden to any: 'I depart immediately to the spot from which I hope never to remove.' She then travelled on to Swansea, where she checked into an upper room at the Mackworth Arms. It was 9 October 1816. In a way she followed the Godwin of *Political Justice* on suicide, remembered her relatives, and weighed pain against pleasure when she took an overdose of laudanum and successfully ended her short life.

The Cambrian of Swansea, which on 12th October reported the 'melancholy discovery' at the Mackworth Arms of the 'most respectable looking female' who wanted no help from the chambermaid, also printed her note, which it claimed had the name torn off:

> I have long determined that the best thing I could do was to put an end to the existence of a being whose birth was unfortunate, and whose life has only been a series of pain to those persons who have hurt their health in endeavouring to promote her welfare. Perhaps to hear of my death will give you pain, but you will soon have the blessing of forgetting that such a creature ever existed as

Unlike her mother, Fanny probably quoted life rather than literature in this note, and she avoided Wollstonecraft's threatening posture: 'in the midst of business and sensual pleasure, I shall appear before you.' Unlike her mother, she succeeded at suicide.

II

On receiving Fanny's letter from Bristol, Shelley dashed there from Bath twice. It is just conceivable that he went to Swansea and saw the dead body. If so, perhaps he is implicated in the final anonymity. Certainly it remains unclear who tore or would want to tear the name from the note. Possibly the inn servants to avoid the taint of suicide, but there seems no obvious point to this since the note itself indicates suicide, although as was usual in these days the coroner entered the words 'Found dead', so that the body could be buried as a pauper's not a suicide's. Possibly Fanny herself tore it off, feeling her own lack of legitimate identity or wishing in the end to spare the Godwins further scandal. But it is just as possible that Shelley himself did see the body and the incriminating name and, fearing the effect on them all, did what surely Godwin would have wanted. There was time for him to visit Swansea after the suicide was known and he seems to have been uncharacteristically obedient to his future father-in-law during these days and careful to follow family policy.

Godwin's desire in the matter is clear. Having received his suicidal letter from Fanny he set out on 10th October for Bristol, but was interrupted by the *Cambrian* report of the discovery of a body with a Swiss gold watch and stays initialled MW. Consequently he returned to London on the 12th. By then both Shelley and Mary in Bath had heard the news and Godwin, frantic from scandal, begged Shelley to stop any pursuit, not to claim the body or to expose them to publicity. On the 13th he wrote to Shelley:

I did indeed expect it.

. . . My advice and earnest prayer is that you would avoid anything that leads to publicity. Go not to Swansea; disturb not the silent dead; do nothing to destroy the obscurity she so much desired that now rests upon the event. It was, as I said, her last wish; it was the motive that led her from London to Bristol and from Bristol to Swansea.

. . . Think what is the situation of my wife and myself, now deprived of all our children but the youngest [their son William]; so do not expose us to those idle questions, which to the mind in anguish is one of the severest of all trials. We are at this moment in doubt whether, during the first shock, we shall not say she is gone to Ireland to her aunt, a thing that had been in contemplation. Do not take from us the power to exercise our own discretion. You shall hear again to-morrow.

What I have most of all in horror is the public papers . . .

We have so conducted ourselves that not one person in our home has the smallest apprehension of the truth. Our feelings are less tumultuous than deep. God only know what they may become.

It is a remarkable closing of ranks over the dead woman's body.

III

No doubt there were many reasons why Fanny killed herself. Critics have speculated that she had learnt all of a sudden that she was illegitimate. But this seems unlikely in a house of inveterate readers, where presumably Godwin's *Memoirs* of Wollstonecraft and the letters to Imlay were both available. And it seems a somewhat Victorian notion that anyone would find the discovery of illegitimacy a reason for suicide. There is, too, the evidence in Godwin's diary of serious conversation with the child Fanny which suggests an early revelation of her status.

Another possibility was the one promoted by Mrs Godwin: that Fanny was in love with Shelley. Certainly she had been the first to know him and she might have taken his bantering for special attention; she had, in addition, been a great reader of romances. But her devotion to Shelley, Mary and Jane through the two summers since the elopement argues against a single attachment. It is true that she reverenced Shelley's poetic art but in a rather impersonal way, seeing poetry as a benefaction of the human race: 'It is impossible to tell the good that POETS do their fellow-creatures, at least those that can feel', she wrote a few months before her suicide. 'Whilst I read I am a poet. I am inspired with good feelings – feelings that create perhaps a more permanent good in me than all the every-day preachments in the world.' But her enthusiasm made her feel less rather than more worthy of particular affection or attention: 'Laugh at me, but do not be angry with me for taking up your time with my nonsense.'

Her self-esteem was not aided by this diffidence about what she herself wrote and it was perhaps not an easy household in which to think well of oneself artistically or intellectually: as Jane later remarked, 'In our family, if you cannot write an epic poem or novel, that by its originality knocks all other novels on the head, you are a despicable creature, not worth acknowledging.' In addition, while her devotion to her mother was well attested, Wollstonecraft's legacy cannot have been an easy one, as the more assertive Mary also found. In May of her final year Fanny had met Fanny Blood's brother and heard of his continuing admiration of Wollstonecraft: 'I have determined never to live to be a disgrace to such a Mother', she wrote. In a way she succeeded in the one thing her mother failed at and by a method Wollstonecraft had not rejected.

Fanny's depression seems most likely to have come from a sense of being unwanted in all quarters, from her lack of claims on the impecunious household, from the true or invented mockery of Shelley and Mary relayed by Mrs Godwin, and especially from the withdrawal of the invitation from her aunts following the Shelley scandal. To these factors can be added the genetic inheritance of Wollstonecraft melancholy, which had revealed itself in Eliza's post-partum breakdown and in the frequent and suicidal depressions of both Marys.

And there is, too, the contagion of suicide. Fanny knew her mother to have attempted it twice and she must have known of Shelley's frequent threats. In various editions of *Political Justice* Godwin sup-ported a right to rational suicide, once the interest of relatives who would be disgraced had been consulted, and when pain had been proved irremediable. In a long undated letter to an editor, presum-ably meant for publication, Godwin reiterated his point: 'Soberly and impartially speaking, the power over my life with which nature has endowed me, is a talent committed to my discretion . . . the being that made us has with equal clearness, endowed us with the empire over our own life or death.'[15] He did however stress that one should first examine oneself to see if it is possible to triumph over sufferings.

The letter may have responded to public suicides but, before Fanny or Harriet, he (and probably Fanny) had had more personal experi-ence of suicide. Between 1810 and 1814 Godwin had helped sponsor the Cambridge education of a young man called Patrickson, a sort of predecessor in disciplehood to Shelley. Letters in the Bodleian Library show the growth of the young man's depression in the alien world of Cambridge, and his final letter describes his long struggle with low spirits and loneliness before he shot himself at about the time of the Shelley and Mary elopement. As with Fanny later, the Godwinian influence left him with no 'hope of future happiness', and his position in life with no 'respectable settlement' made present happiness impossible.[16]

IV

Fanny's death made hardly a ripple and there has been no equivalent of the defence mounted for Harriet by writers from Mark Twain (*In Defence of Harriet Shelley*) to Louise Schutz Boas (*Harriet Shelley: Five Long Years*). Jane wrote to Byron, about to be the father of her child, that she was not much moved by news of Fanny's death: 'I passed the first fourteen years of my life with her, and though I cannot say I had so great an affection for her as might be expected, yet she is the first person of my acquaintance who has died and her death so horrible too . . .'[17] As his letter indicated, Godwin invented lies to cover up the death. He put it about that Fanny had died of a cold in Wales. Mrs Godwin, more privately, regarded her as another victim of Shelley's escapades. By now contemplating suicide herself, Harriet probably never knew the truth, so that the incident had no bearing on her own journey a few weeks later to the Serpentine. For his part Shelley made Fanny into a poem entitled 'On F. G.', accepting that Fanny died of love for him (and, incidentally, suggesting that he had seen the grave):

> Her voice did quiver as we parted,
> Yet knew I not that heart was broken
> From which it came, and I departed
> Heeding not the words then spoken.
>   Misery – O Misery
> This world is all too wide to thee.
>   . . .
> They sit – the dead return not – Misery
> Sits near an open grave and calls them over
> A Youth with hoary hair and haggard eye –
> They are the names of kindred, friend and lover,
> Which he so feebly calls – they all are gone –

Fond wretch, all dead! those vacant names alone,
This most familiar scene, my pain –
These tombs – alone remain.[18]

The most extensive though oblique response came from Fanny's half-sister Mary, who, with the new Godwinian care for appearances, hardly mentions the death in her journal or letters (and indeed she hardly mentioned Fanny in later years in any of her surviving papers). She had, she wrote, a 'miserable day' when she must have learned the news in Bath, but she continued writing *Frankenstein*. Interestingly she was finishing chapter 4 at the time; in chapter 5 is the story of Justine, which might have some bearing on her attitude to her dead half-sister.

Justine is a girl taken into the muddled Frankenstein house of orphans as part daughter, part servant because her unloving mother hated her. A kind, frank-hearted, grateful little girl, especially liked by Frankenstein – but not of course thought of as a wife – she loves the little William and adores the new mother whom she most resembles, though she is not quite as beautiful. Yet when this mother dies, attended in her illness by the kind Justine, the more privileged children are too much occupied to notice the poor girl and her grief.

In due course she is blamed first for her siblings' death by her own mother, who went on hating her, and then for the monster's murder of the child William because she had about her the adored adopted mother's portrait, once William's. Justine is tried for the imagined deed and the more accepted daughter, Elizabeth, is upset but fails to act, and she feels a momentary guilt when Justine is condemned to death: 'I wish that I were to die with you.' But in the end Mary Shelley makes Justine first admit to guilt, even though innocent, letting her feel like Fanny that her birth was 'unfortunate', and then to echo Mary Wollstonecraft's final words and the final words of her mother, Fanny's grandmother: 'Learn from me, dear lady, to submit in patience to the will of Heaven!' This seems comforting to the Frankenstein household as Justine is judicially murdered, but is far from the spirit of Fanny's suicide note.[19]

In *Frankenstein* Justine is put to death by the law. In the next novel, the depressive *Matilda* written following the death of her children, Mary Shelley wrote of a woman driven to isolation and suicidal longings by the incestuous desires of her father, who has killed himself. She makes her much the same age as herself and there is much self-presentation in the portrait. But Matilda, who like Justine avoids suicide though she contemplates it a great deal, is also the age of the dead Fanny, and again there seems some resonance from the sad incidents of 1816.

Much later, when the widowed Mary Shelley reached the age of her mother on her death, she wrote a book in which she actually used the name of Fanny for the first time. *Lodore* was the usual Mary-Shelley tale of Byronic hero and feminine heroine, his daughter. For the story of the daughter, she called on the last years of her half-sister Fanny's life, when she and Shelley were dodging creditors and bailiffs. Perhaps this recollection brought to mind the go-between of the period, for in her character of Fanny she provides a foil to the heroine, not a pretty girl but one with intellectual beauty, fair as Fanny seems to have been, with high forehead. Though talented she is unappreciated by her vulgar mother, and she is good, home-loving, kind-hearted, true and benignant, devoted to 'religion, reason, and justice'. She waits tenderly on her eccentric father while he instructs her; later in life she serves as comfort and helper to the lovers.

This Fanny, with so many of the outward circumstances of Mary Shelley's half-sister and some of her care for others, is, however, given a character and fate very different from the real Fanny. In the novel she receives the legacy Shelley apparently intended for Fanny (and which he did procure for Jane), a small fortune that would render her independent. As for her intellectual character, she is a non-sentimental benevolist, inspired by the understanding not the heart, and she seems a little quixotic because she is so unfemininely resolute and independent. She is a girl made to be loved by women more than men, says the author, complete in herself and needing no complement; she tries not to make ties that would hurt her though she feels very deeply for others, and she guards herself while yet believing in the fight for the oppressed.

In many ways, then, the fictional Fanny seems an idealization of a union of the real Fanny and her mother, the only sort of independent woman who could possibly survive in the world, as neither Fanny nor Mary Wollstonecraft succeeded in doing alone. Perhaps, how-ever, the character and fate of the real Fanny pushed too strongly on Mary Shelley for her to approach any verisimilitude in her portrait. In the end the fictional representation seems both inconsistent and implausible: on the last page of the book Fanny, not partnered off for bliss like most fictional young girls, is heading for a varied fate of 'uncontaminating' sorrow.

New Delhi, 1988

Notes

1 *Collected Letters of Mary Wollstonecraft*, ed. Ralph M. Wardle (Ithaca: Cornell University Press, 1979), p. 67.
2 *Collected Letters*, p. 262.
3 *Collected Letters*, p. 276.
4 Quoted in Emily Sunstein, *A Different Face* (New York: Harper & Row, 1975), p. 262.
5 *A Short Residence in Sweden and Memoirs of the Author of 'The Rights of Woman'*, ed. Richard Holmes (Harmondsworth: Penguin, 1987), p. 100.
6 *Collected Letters*, p. 317.
7 *Godwin and Mary: letters of William Godwin and Mary Wollstonecraft*, ed. Ralph M. Wardle (Lawrence: University of Kansas Press, 1966), p. 90.
8 *Collected Letters of Samuel Taylor Coleridge*, ed. Earl Leslie Griggs (Oxford, 1956–71), vol. I, p. 588, and C. Kegan Paul, *William Godwin: his friends and contemporaries* (London: Harry S. King, 1876).
9 For a full discussion of the Godwin finances, see William St Clair, *The Godwins and the Shelleys: the biography of a family* (London: Faber & Faber, 1989).
10 *William Godwin: his friends and contemporaries*, vol. II, pp. 213–14.
11 *The Letters of Percy Bysshe Shelley*, ed. F. L. Jones (Oxford: Oxford University Press, 1964), vol. I, p. 338.
12 For a description of this period, see Richard Holmes, *Shelley: the pursuit* (New York: E. P. Dutton, 1975), and *The Journals of Mary Shelley, 1814–1844*, ed. Paula R. Feldman and Diana Scott-Kilvert (Oxford: Clarendon Press, 1987).
13 Louise Schutz Boas, *Harriet Shelley: five long years* (London: Oxford University Press, 1962), p. 174.
14 See *Shelley and his Circle 1773–1822*, ed. Kenneth Neill Cameron and Donald H. Reiman (Cambridge: Harvard University Press, 1961–7), vol. IV, for the documents and letters concerning Fanny's final years and suicide.
15 Abinger archive, Bodleian Library, Oxford, C527.
16 Dep. b.228/8.
17 Quoted in Rosalie Glynn Grylls, *Claire Clairmont, Mother of Byron's Allegra* (London: John Murray, 1939).
18 *Shelley: poetical works*, ed. Thomas Hutchinson (Oxford: Oxford University Press, 1968), p. 546.
19 *Frankenstein*, ed. M. Hindle (Harmondsworth: Penguin, 1985), p. 130.

8 Jane Austen, politics and sensibility

I

As the mother of the patriarchal line of F. R. Leavis's Great Tradition and first gentleman of Lionel Trilling's family of liberal modern personalities, Jane Austen has been an awkward subject for feminist criticism to cope with.[1] Early in her posthumous history she was caught by Charlotte Brontë and Virginia Woolf colluding with the male desire of George Henry Lewes and the Bloomsbury men for a lady who knew her place and theirs. Charlotte Brontë found an unwomanly avoidance of the heart, while Virginia Woolf was disinclined to be left in a room alone with her.[2] After an initial reluctance, modern feminist criticism has attempted to woo Austen into the sisterhood through either downplaying or re-creating her historical context. The result has been a more feminist figure than was once imagined, but its creation has demanded a determined reading against the grain or a careful selecting from literary history.

In Sandra Gilbert and Susan Gubar's *The Madwoman in the Attic* (1979), which ranged Austen with major women who came after her, the tart Austen narrator was discovered manipulating events in stereotypically feminine fashion from behind the scenes and beneath the blotter. Her texts revealed the ubiquitous madwoman, the rebellious author's double who imaged her own desire and rage in subtle patterns on the seemingly calm surface, a woman-self who strained against the female renunciation of self encouraged by society. This Austen was uncomfortable with and alienated from her cultural inheritance and her novels became the literary version of the guns in Kipling's story of the 'Janeites' who named their First World War weapons after her characters.[3] The reading was a largely ahistorical and ungeneric one, removing Austen from her contemporary context and from the other women writers who preceded and surrounded her. It made sisterhood across time but not within it.[4]

The subversive writer of Gilbert and Gubar, who is 'just plain not saying what she means' and who through her silence rather than her formal utterances indicts a patriarchy it would otherwise be impossible to indict, has been immensely helpful for feminist criticism.[5] But it is now time to accept that not all intelligent women of the past aspired to a modern feminist view and that to assume that they did so is to silence them as thoroughly as patriarchy silenced enlightenment feminism. The desire to see covert messages may partly be a disinclination to hear the overt ones – already a feature of traditional Austen scholarship. Take the remarks about fat grief in *Persuasion*, the 'large fat sighings over the destiny of a son, whom alive nobody had cared for':

> Personal size and mental sorrow have certainly no necessary proportions. A large bulky figure has as good a right to be in deep affliction as the most graceful set of limbs in the world. But, fair or not fair, there are unbecoming conjunctions, which reason will patronize in vain, – which taste cannot tolerate, – which ridicule will seize.[6]

And the historical account:

> The real circumstances of this pathetic piece of family history were, that the Musgroves had had the ill fortune of a very troublesome, hopeless son; and the good fortune to lose him before he reached his twentieth year; that he had been sent to sea, because he was stupid and unmanageable on shore; that he had been very little cared for at any time by his family, though quite as much as he deserved; seldom heard of, and scarcely at all regretted, when the intelligence of his death abroad had worked its way to Uppercross, two years before.[7]

Some critics used to say that this harshness was clearly an error and would have been removed had *Persuasion* been thoroughly revised. But why should Austen not stand by these observations, which are common-sensical though not compassionate?

In the context of earlier women's techniques, the manoeuvre here can be viewed as a rather common female strategy under patriarchy, in many ways the reverse of the coding and concealing demanded by some feminist criticism. The aside is, for example, a sad technique in the Restoration Countess of Warwick whose harsh marital life greatly tested her puritan faith. She worked out a system of mouthing her bitterness, under her breath, and, while she repeatedly repented this activity, she simply could not give it up. So she went on moving her lips but not allowing the air to reach the open ears of her irascible spouse, although the anger was clearly expressed in her diary.[8] This is often the way of the author-narrator of Austen's novels, who comes out with statements that would be repressed in a social situation and would be impossible for the characters themselves to make. In company we all speak distress at a death, especially at the death of a child, and have been too sentimentally indoctrinated to feel at all comfortable with Austen's suggestion that some people are worthless and would be better dead. Maternal crying in such circumstances, even of the portly, is socially correct although it may remain aesthetically grotesque.

Despite many influential books following Gilbert and Gubar's lead, feminist criticism of Austen in recent years has moved decisively towards the historical in its recuperation. Again the desire has been for a protofeminist, but one who for historical reasons was associated less with Charlotte Brontë and Virginia Woolf than with Mary Wollstonecraft. Here the problem was the conservative Jane Austen delivered by Marilyn Butler's pre-feminist work *Jane Austen and the War of Ideas* (1975), which argued that Austen should be included in the conservative reaction of the late 1790s. Butler noted that the novels were less permissive, individualistic and expressive than many others by women of the time; on the evidence of her work Austen herself was, in Terry Eagleton's phrase, 'just a straight Tory'. In a later preface to this study Butler argued that Gilbert and Gubar were simply wrong in making Austen a covert radical in a man's imprisoning world because they based their views less on women writers before Austen than on a few privileged ones who came after.[9]

Using the historical method pioneered by Butler's book, several other women critics have challenged her conclusion. Margaret Kirkham in two essays in *Jane Austen: new perspectives* (1983) argued that Austen ought to be ranged with, not against the overt feminists of the 1790s such as Mary Wollstonecraft, since both desired to demystify the female character and destroy the reverential and degrading obfuscation of the real economic and social status of women. She saw Austen writing on feminist issues and considered that the authority of her fictional techniques was an aspect of her criticism of patriarchal prejudice. Fanny Price, the largest lump in the feminist throat, was relieved of her famous priggishness to become a commentary on contemporary female images. In her weakness and sexually arousing religiosity she resembled the heroines of the sort of conduct-books Mr Collins failed to read to the bored Bennet sisters in *Pride and*

Prejudice. At the same time, Fanny was also intractable and rational, close to the radical woman. In the first case, Kirkham argued, irony was turned on the character; in the second, on the reader who might approve the wrong aspects. *Mansfield Park* became a great comic novel regulated by the sane laughter of a rational feminist.[10]

The problem with such an attractive reading was the exclusion of many contemporary conservative novelists from the debate, in whose pages most of the approved but ambivalent notions of the early feminist rationalist Mary Wollstonecraft could be found, such as the need for moral autonomy and serious female education. This exclusion was to some extent rectified in Claudia Johnson's tightly argued *Jane Austen: women, politics and the novel* (1987), Mary Evans's *Jane Austen and the State* (1987) and Alison Sulloway's *Jane Austen and the Province of Womanhood* (1989), which wanted to broaden the Austen context to help answer that old damning question: where are the French Revolution in *Pride and Prejudice* and the Napoleonic Wars in *Mansfield Park?* All three wished to rescue Austen from being the gentlemen critics' provincial lady and part of Marilyn Butler's Tory faithful. Johnson set the young author in the 1790s and the adult in the Regency and showed how the change was reflected not only in what she wrote but in what she could no longer write. After Godwin had published his biography of Mary Wollstonecraft, *Memoirs of the Author of A Vindication of the Rights of Woman*, in 1798, making of his wife a public and principled whore, there was no question of any modest novelist associating with her or writing a new *Rights of Woman*. The old assumption that Austen must be conservative if she came from a conservative class was agitated by the uncertain status she actually had: the fact that Walter Scott called her middle class and Madame de Staël labelled her works *vulgaire*. Claiming that most of the political novels by women were more complicated than modern commentators made them – Fanny Burney and Jane West, arch conservatives and assumed to be guardians of home and hearth, did not portray marriage idealistically – Johnson argued that under the pressure of intense reaction women including Austen developed stylistic techniques which enabled them to use politically charged material in an exploratory and interrogative rather than hortatory manner.[11] To some extent the image delivered here, although far more historically based, was not unlike the 'coding, concealing' Austen of Gilbert and Gubar.

Another version of this image was provided by Alison Sulloway, who insisted on the grief and anger lying beneath the surface of the Austen satire; in *Jane Austen and the Province of Womanhood* (1989) she found these subtle forms of revenge against misogynist male writing which flourished throughout the eighteenth century. Sulloway's Austen is no 'mere conduit for the *status quo*' but instead mediates between traditional forces hostile to women and the opposing radical disruption. She becomes, like Kirkham's Austen, a radical woman speaking from the margins, attacking male privilege and female disenfranchisement, with a voice closer to the shocking Mary Wollstonecraft's than to the conservative Hannah More's.[12]

Mary Evans, a British writer, keener than the American Johnson or Sulloway to use the language of Marxism and the context of modern politics, pointed out that Austen endorsed values incompatible with the practices and policies of modern Toryism; she should be dissociated from conservatism since she elucidated a morality independent of the material values of the capitalist marketplace, claiming an equality of men and women and the rights of women to moral independence and autonomy.[13] Part of this argument is certainly true and Evans's view of Austen is an appealing one, but some of her points depend on obliterating the specific conservatism of the late eighteenth century, Austen's 'dear Dr Johnson' with his dislike of plebeian power and capitalist accumulation – of which Austen was heir but Mrs Thatcher not. As for women, moral independence is undoubtedly advocated and this fits with the serious concern of both radical and conservative women of the 1790s. But women's rights, as Wollstonecraft came to believe, included the right to express desire and sensibility as well as independence, and this possible right was, I believe, a more openly discussed problem than Evans and indeed Johnson or Sulloway allows.

While accepting the value of the feminist and the feminist historical figures of Austen described above, I would like to argue for another who is less comfortable because less conforming to present notions, closer to that maverick among women writers that Charlotte Brontë so famously deplored. Such a figure can be revealed through feminist literary history using empirical generic expectations and practice. This Austen uses the codes and conventions of her contemporary novel specifically to intervene in the debates about political, social and psychological issues, in the way that all the historical feminist critics have emphasized. But I want to stress two aspects of her position that they appear to have understated.

First, it is difficult to label Austen politically, because it is difficult to place single political labels on women in general, and even more difficult to distinguish a radical from a conservative line on several important issues like female education. Women called conservative or liberal, such as Hannah More, Fanny Burney and Elizabeth Hamilton, and later Jane West and Mary Brunton, all following the conservative Edmund Burke in coalescing national and familial interests, and women labelled radical or liberal, such as Mary Wollstonecraft, Mary Hays, Elizabeth Inchbald, and later Maria Edgeworth, Sidney Owenson (Lady Morgan) and Madame de Staël, all shared a desire to promote the intellectual and moral woman at the expense of the trivial lady of ornamental accomplishments which the culture appeared to endorse.

Second, political persuasion is not immediately revealed by generic literary habit in women. The promotion of the moral female occurred in novels that, while varying to some extent according to political persuasion, varied to a greater extent according to the degree of sensibility allowed into the women characters' composition and into the composition of the novels themselves. There is as much contrast between the sentimental and the unsentimental treatments as there is between the conservative and the radical, and authors can be separated from each other according to how sentimental the characters and the books were allowed to be, just as much as they can be separated by politics. An attitude to sensibility *could* imply a party political line but overwhelmingly it implied a personal political one, and here it seems to me that Austen is much easier to place then she is in the party political context.

I want to suggest that the main motivator of Austen, beyond any party political purpose, is her opposition to sensibility in all its forms, whether it be romantic fantasy in young girls, spontaneous feminine understanding or intuition, political aspirations or plot expectations. If this is true, Austen will inevitably sometimes sound more like the rationalist radical Wollstonecraft in *A Vindication of the Rights of Woman* (1792), which is virulently anti-sentimental, than like the conservative Burney, writer of the final emotional pages of *Camilla* (1796). But she will sound far less like the sentimental radical Wollstonecraft, author of *The Wrongs of Woman* (1798), than like the no-nonsense Jane West of *The Advantages of Education* (1793).

II

The eighteenth-century cult of sensibility, associating the feminine and the sentimental, brought women into the centre of culture.[14] Women's consciousness was investigated and their voice, though inevitably mediated and culturally constructed, was heard; it also brought into prominence those qualities of benevolence, tenderness, susceptibility and domesticity, thought to be quintessentially feminine. The late novel of sensibility, current when the young Jane Austen was penning her parodies, sticks to the old stock plot and characters of sentiment, suffering virtue, good daughters and bad fathers, that had done much ethical service in the past. But it was also greatly influenced by the first part of Rousseau's *La Nouvelle Héloïse* (1761), which had as its centre the story of feminine sexual and emotional desire. As a result, the later sentimental novel was more concerned with the emotive and emoting subject, with desire or self-indulgence – depending on stand-point – than with general morality. Feminine sensibility could then be purveyed in a seemingly radical novel, often in first person or letter form which could muddle the distinction of public and private. While it might suggest the importance of feminine morality, tenderness and benevolence, as all sentimental novels do, it could also preach feminine expressiveness and self-gratification – although the search for these in an anti-sentimental world would usually be disastrous. The self-expressiveness could be radically transgressive of familial pieties in its promotion of individualistic desire, as it was, for example, in Wollstonecraft's *The Wrongs of Woman*, which pleaded the right of a woman to love first and beyond marriage. On the other side, sentimental conventions could be employed solely to enhance the nuclear family and domesticity, which usually appeared the direct opposite of individual expressiveness and bolstered the status quo. Edmund Burke famously employed sentimental writing against the presumptions of impious reason in his *Reflections on the Revolution in France* (1790) and Jane West would use it again in her Burkean *A Tale of the Times* (1799). Some novels such as Mary Hays's notorious *Memoirs of Emma Courtney* (1796) managed to ask for both family and transgressive self-gratification together.

To summarize the plot from the woman-authored novel of the 1780s and early 1790s: the immaculately beautiful, pure and intelligent sentimental heroine is usually orphaned at puberty. She struggles with the desire of her father or of a male substitue, a wicked uncle perhaps who has seized her property and, in a way, her person. The story of stylized victimization becomes the fight for ownership of herself, for external marriage or friendship, creating a new nuclear family of choice. In a late radical novel the wicked male might be a husband and the freedom might become adultery, as in Wollstonecraft's *The Wrongs of Woman*; in the more conservative, the wicked uncle might be a desiring rake with Godwinian or Wollstonecraftian principles and the freedom might become chosen marriage to an ethically more reliable and certainly less mastering man. If the tale were unhappy, the heroine fell and died; if happy, she gained every good through passive suffering: property, female patronage and bliss.

The sentimental heroine was usually aristocratic, but her rank delivered not power but delicious powerlessness. Consequently the heroine had all the advantages of gentility together with a victimized status, while the hero, similarly aristocratic, was usually feminized out of patriarchal power, much of his heroic function being usurped by a female friend. As for techniques, one of the most obvious, used by conservatives and radicals alike, was the tableau, a static and ecstatic familial moment in which the response of the reader was described and demanded in the text, on the assumption that emotion through involuntary looking or hearing was spontaneous and immediately beneficial. The language delivering such scenes rather resembled the semiotic, pre-rational irruptions beloved of psycho-analytical feminists in the 1970s.[15] It was unbalanced, hyperbolic, eccentric and fragmented, suggesting suppressed thought by extra-verbal devices like the exclamation mark and dash. A short excerpt from Mary Hays's *Emma Courtney* will exemplify:

> My friend sat beside me, holding my hands in her's which she bathed with her tears. 'Thank God!' she exclaimed, in a rapturous accent, (as with a deep sigh I raised my languid eyes, and turned them mournfully towards her – 'she lives! – My Emma! – child of my affections!' – Sobs suppressed her utterance). I drew the hand, which held mine towards me – I pressed it to my bosom——'My *mother!*'——I would have said; but the tender appellation died away upon my lips, in inarticulate murmurs.[16]

In this extract there are seven dashes of differing lengths, five exclamation marks, and an italicization; these devices break up the prose to display the pre-logical character of sensibility and to convey a sense of female feeling and desire that has no easy articulation in élite literature.

Because of her implacable opposition to sensibility Jane Austen, although using the traditional feminine romantic and sentimental plot, simply does not seize the possibilities for political or psycho-logical expression, articulation of desire and protest that such a plot had opened for women writers and readers. Despite valiant efforts of commentators she was, I believe, always on the side of sense against 'feminine' sensibility and so inevitably avoiding or opposing what that sensibility articulated. When in *Jane Austen* (1986) Tony Tanner, described by Hermione Lee as 'a thoughtful feminist reader', praised Austen for dramatizing the abuse of language and, on occasion, properly preferring silence to sentimental expression, he colluded with her in silencing a specific kind of excessive female voice.[17]

Politically Austen revealed a kind of disenchantment; in Q. D. Leavis's words her values were 'not emotional but moral, critical, and rational', and she showed a scepticism about the possibility of human nature's changing or of political and social improvement through agitation and endeavour.[18] She mocked sentimental ideas and techniques in whatever party political context they appeared. In *Sense and Sensibility* the greedy shallow John Dashwoods employ the emotive language of familial sensibility to bolster their greed. They sentimentally refer to their small son as their 'poor little Harry' and through him set the selfish nuclear family, so much admired in conservative fiction, above the proper claims of the half-sisters and a promise to a dying man. Earlier the Dashwood patriarchal succession had been enforced by a spurt of the sentimental and misguided affection felt by an old man for a small, charming, but undifferentiated child. Throughout the book the conservatively supported nuclear family is the locus of boredom and nastiness. Mr Palmer, tired of politics, here simply the art of making everybody like him, runs from the impossible task into an irremediable and absurd marriage. The dependent male suffers from ennui, whether dependent on a morally admirable woman like Willoughby's aunt, Mrs Smith, or a reprehensible mother like Mrs Ferrars, and both men enter the close and cramped female Dashwood family in deep hypocrisy and guile.[19] Motherhood, so powerful a stimulus both to Burke's conservative polemics and to the effusions of assertive radical women like Hays and Wollstonecraft, becomes fond selfishness in Lady Middleton, who reveals the mother to be 'the most rapacious of human beings', rather less admirable in her maternal habits than her predatory husband.

The oppositional use is even more insistently scorned, whether sentiment is underwriting a political, psychological or generic literary notion. Austen does not allow sentimental abilities to eradicate social distinctions, as Rousseau was famous for doing when he gave equality in love to a tutor and an aristocrat in *La Nouvelle Héloïse*, and Mr Darcy has a right to be proud and overtop the charming, intimate Wickham. Lucy Steele, from inferior society, is irredeemably vulgar in spite of her frequent displays of good nature and her natural cleverness.

Despite seeming to inhabit a sentimental plot, few Austen heroines achieve the loss of both inadequate parents, so their chances of gaining bliss and their own money in tandem, as sentimental heroines frequently do, are limited. The only mysterious orphan, Harriet, fails to live up to Emma's sentimental fantasy and proves lamentably lower middle class and unendowed. Elizabeth Bennet's misery is that she is not orphaned and that her ghastly mother and father continue to embarrass her into adulthood. Women are not amazing autodidacts as in most sentimental fiction. Fanny Price achieves no learning beyond Edmund's giving, Elizabeth Bennet does not practise the piano enough and Catherine Morland rolls down the green slope in childhood and reads romances when she grows up. She might learn the dangers of patriarchy from Ann Radcliffe's *The Mysteries of Udolpho* (1794), but her marriage indicates that she does not, and it is not she but ingenious modern readers inspired by feminist sociology and psychoanalysis who modify her conclusion that such books are not great guides to life in the Midland counties of England.

Money, so embarrassingly bourgeois when fixed in amount, is much to the fore. And, unlike in liberal sentimental novels, it remains in male hands. At the end of *Mansfield Park*, where the heroine is seemingly most unremittingly patriarchal, Fanny ends up with no female patronage but is insistent instead on patronage from her uncle: 'Fanny was indeed the daughter that he wanted.' When death completes the picture of good, Fanny and Edmund remove to the parsonage of Mansfield, which grows in the last line 'as thoroughly perfect in her eyes, as every thing else, within the view and patronage of Mansfield Park'.[20] Patriarchal rule is re-established and community rests on male financial control and mutual familial selfishness, not the blissful feminine affections of sensibility.

Extra-familial friendship also gets short shrift and the possible female friend is banished to the evils of London, a sister being ensconced in her place.[21] It might be argued that patriarchy is modified in Sir Thomas's realization that he has mismanaged his daughters and followed false values, but he *is* in place and there is nothing equivalent to the humbling of the patriarch so much a feature of sentimental fiction from Rousseau's *La Nouvelle Héloïse* to Elizabeth Inchbald's *A Simple Story* (1791). Even Sir Walter Elliot, found deeply wanting, still continues to own Kellynch Hall in *Persuasion*. The female mentors of Hays or even the more conservative Edgeworth and Burney are hardly even shadowed in Mrs Gardiner, Mrs Croft or the mistaken Lady Russell, and the affective inheritance of the estate by both partners is never a feature of Austen. It is unlikely that Elizabeth Bennet will concern herself with the rents from the Pemberley farms or Emma with the accounts of Donwell Abbey. The freakish feminists with their excessive, expressive rhetoric, such as Bridgetina Botherim of Elizabeth Hamilton's *Memoirs of Modern Philosophers* (1800), Amelia Opie's eponymous heroine of *Adeline Mowbray* (1804), Harriot Freke in Maria Edgeworth's *Belinda* (1801) and Elinor Jodrell in Fanny Burney's *The Wanderer* (1814), do not appear in Austen to be mocked, but neither is their protesting rhetoric allowed room for expression.

The expressiveness of the lady as potent victim, the staple of sentimental fiction, is likewise almost entirely absent from the mature novels. When a woman falls she does so trivially like Lydia or stupidly like Maria or even down the hill like Marianne. Although the powerful fallen woman does put in an appearance, as many recent critics have noticed, pushing with odd insistence against the text of *Sense and Sensibility*, she is thoroughly silenced in the end. Despite much sentimental garrulity in the beginning about 'dear, dear Norland!' and 'ye well-known trees!', Marianne is famous now for saying nothing at certain notable points. She does so when Lucy Steele exclaims at the sweetness of the boring, selfish Lady Middleton, so that on Elinor falls the task of 'telling lies' when politeness requires it. She is also silent when she receives Willoughby's cruel letter rejecting her. Only when she agrees to marry the man twice her age in a flannel waistcoat after her earlier declaration against second love does she begin again to speak – and only when she has learnt 'to talk . . . as I ought to do'.[22] Marianne is not entirely damned – she is not completely self-deluded, since Willoughby did love her at one point – she is not made into a sentimental butt like Bridgetina Botherim, a mockery of Mary Hays and her Emma Courtney who, like Marianne, pleads her right to express her feelings openly, and she is given Cowper to read like Anne Elliot, not the Wollstonecraft and Hays served up to satirized heroines in many conservative novels. But the argument that she represents, that feminine feeling must be allowed expression because authentic, is harshly mocked in the portrait of a sensibility which is discourteous, silly, feckless and impotent. Authenticity must be compromised by discretion it seems. With all her attractions, Marianne shares her name with an early French sentimental and narcissistic heroine in Marivaux's *La Vie de Marianne* (1731–41), who also rather seductively twists her ankle at the beginning of her romance but typically gets her man, as Austen's Marianne conspicuously does not.[23]

Austen refrains from the extreme attack on permanent marriage as prostitution embedded in Wollstonecraft's *The Wrongs of Woman* and the demand for female initiative in desire of *Emma Courtney*. She also avoids the interrogation of patriarchal power involved in the conservative investigation of marriage in writers such as Fanny Burney, as well as expressions of anguish at female impotence. She does this by eschewing sentimental presentation, which allows protest through extreme depictions of misery and injustice and by limiting women's first-person expression through letters or other narrations. The letter in particular was *the* sentimental form, associated disparagingly and slightly anxiously with women and expressing desire that was assertive and might well be transgressive. It revealed the clash between public and private stances so central to the predicament of the woman of sensibility. In Austen these moments of expressiveness through letters are, ironically for the student of women's writing, given to men not women. When women like Isabella Thorpe or Mary Crawford write letters, it is usually to fool or deceive someone; other women like Elizabeth Bennet and Emma Woodhouse are heard a good deal directly without needing the device of the letter, although neither is given the sentimental heroine's latitude to express desire openly. It is men like Darcy, Colonel Brandon and the chastened Captain Wentworth who are silent or misunderstood in speech and it is they who can express their inner selves and their desire only in letters.[24] So a central technique of the earlier radical and liberal writers like Hays, Wollstonecraft and Edgeworth is taken from women and given to men who already, as Anne Elliot pointed out in *Persuasion*, had the pen quite firmly in their hands.

If, as Anne Elliot claims, books are not to be trusted since they largely record men's opinions, what has happened to the novels of the sister authors Austen had so proudly proclaimed in *Northanger Abbey?*

> Only a novel. . . . It is only *Cecilia* or *Camilla*, or *Belinda'*; or, in short, only some work in which the greatest powers of the mind are displayed, in which the most thorough knowledge of human nature, the happiest delineation of its varieties, the liveliest effusions of wit and humour, are conveyed to the world in the best chosen language.[25]

A hint of her later attitude to the writer most approved here for psychological accuracy and wit – Fanny Burney, author of *Cecilia* and

Camilla – is given in Austen's final fragment, *Sanditon*, where Charlotte Heywood rather tartly concludes after picking up a volume of *Camilla* in the local bookshop and thinking of the expense, 'She had not *Camilla's* Youth, & had no intention of having her Distress.'[26] It was Camilla's distressing debt that was most sentimentally treated in an otherwise largely unsentimental work, and such a remark suggests that, whatever may be argued for her politics, Austen's attitude to sensibility had hardened. In the end, as at the beginning, it is generic sentimental techniques that she found most irritating.

Austen had mocked the absurd literary manifestations of sensibility when still a child in pattens, insistently placing the sentimental response in a world of other people and physical results. Long before Marianne ended up with a cold from wandering mournfully where the grass was the longest and the wettest, so becoming a liability to others, the sensitive Sophia in *Love & Freindship*, who has emoted and swooned throughout the novel, finally dies from a 'cold caught by her continual fainting fits in the open air'. Before she dies she laments that her once powerful passivity has been her downfall:

> My beloved Laura (said she to me a few hours before she died) take warning from my unhappy End & avoid the imprudent conduct which has occasioned it . . . beware of fainting fits. . . . Though at the time they may be refreshing & Agreable yet believe me they will in the end, if too often repeated & at improper seasons, prove destructive to your Constitution. . . . Beware of swoons Dear Laura. . . . A frenzy fit is not one quarter so pernicious. . . . Run mad as often as you chuse; but do not faint.[27]

Laura takes the advice and lives, but she proceeds onwards in the sensitive life, making her residence in a romantic village in the Highlands in the Celtic fringe of female emotionality. There without interruption she can enjoy her own effusions of grief and indulge in her unceasing lamentations, 'in a melancholy solitude.' The characters' knowledge of the potency of fiction, the broken language and typographical eccentricity all indicate the butt of this high-spiritedness.

Jane Austen defuses the powerful plot of feminine sensibility which takes a transgressive heroine to a nasty death, sadly or properly according to political temperament. Instead of accepting it on its own terms, she tells the reader to curb her expectations and the heroines to give up their nonsense. No doubt the first readers of *Sense and Sensibility* were as surprised as Marianne, a seemingly archetypal sentimental heroine who could have existed in conservative or radical novels, to find herself not dead after many signs that she ought to be. A large number of people in the novel assume that she is dying and need her approaching death to bring out the best in themselves. Mrs Jennings and Sir John Middleton know what to expect and act properly, but none is improved beyond the moment.[28] Most incorrigible is Willoughby, who has a fine time imagining her dying, fantasizing scenarios in which she thinks of him in her last moments – though in her illness she actually raves of her mother – and finding comfort in knowing exactly what she will look like in death since his unkind action has already caused a rehearsal of the scene.

'Marianne Dashwood was born to an extraordinary fate. She was born to discover the falsehood of her own opinions, and to counteract, by her conduct, her most favourite maxims', declares the narrator smugly.[29] She was also born to break through the sentimental plot. As semi-corpse Marianne forms the second attachment into which both sentimental characters enter in contradiction to all the rules of sentiment. Only sensible Elinor gets her sentimental first love.

The most indulged character in the plot is Colonel Brandon, physically a very prosaic lover but sentimentally the most poetic. Both Elinor and the Colonel, the standards of sense, feel the soft seduction of the feminine sentimental plot and Elinor even feels pity at the self-centred sentimental scenario of feminine death Willoughby outlines for himself. It is Colonel Brandon who brings in the seduction story of the two Elizas, both seduced and abandoned – the second by Willoughby – and it is he who insists on the sentimental connection. Whatever Marianne has learnt in the novel is not replicated by Colonel Brandon, who appears to have learnt very little indeed. He shows supreme enthusiasm for Marianne in the deathly physical predicament of Eliza the first, and his emotion burgeons when he receives her pale hand, sees the hollow eye, the sickly skin and the posture of reclining weakness. Elinor, that supposed exemplar of sense, immediately assumes the shadow, the 'probable recurrence' of the first Eliza. It might be churlish to remember the Colonel's attitude at that time: that it would have been better if the girl had died quickly.[30]

In *Sense and Sensibility* there is neither radical nor conservative security. The seemingly sensible characters are implicated in a sentimental plot that has much to do with feminine suffering, and the winners, more clearly than in the other books, are the worldly: the Dashwoods, the Middletons and Lucy Steele. The good are shadowed by the bad. Willoughby is elaborately idle, but in quieter fashion so is Edward. Both trifle with women, while other women have prior claims. It would be interesting to have the story from the point of view of Lucy Steele, who allows the actual happy ending only because she refuses to wilt under a difficult engagement and knows how to manipulate men. Or even from the viewpoint of the silent Eliza the second; it might have formed a radical novel.

Despite Colonel Brandon's example, women are far more prone than men to be caught in sentimental fantasy. On the whole, Austen's men know more what they are about. In the early 'Lesley Castle' the melancholy young man recovers speedily from the loss of love and 'thinks it very good fun to be single again', while in *Love & Freindship*, as the heroines sentimentally decline or die, the elegant and sentimental young men do not follow suit but become actors, and they are last seen on the final page of the novel exhibiting their persons at Covent Garden. The gloomy Benson in *Persuasion* throws off his gloom for one lady to pay court to another, while Willoughby speaks in the rapturous language of sentiment and means not a word of it.

Women are more persistent in sentimental blunders. Fanny Price and Anne Elliot are rewarded for sentimental waiting, but the author is pretty wry about the process in both cases. In the Kotzebue play translated by Elizabeth Inchbald as *Lovers' Vows*, rehearsed to such great effect in Mansfield Park, the heroine believes in the fantasy of romantic love, sure that a peasant can have a baron in the end if she loves enough. Maria too believes that a man's physical attraction in response to female desire can bring about marriage, but the book suggests that it well may not. Even the seemingly approved Fanny Price is mocked when, exclaiming at nature and the enraptured heart as she looks out into the Mansfield night, she believes from this rapture that wickedness and sorrow have gone from the world. But the value Fanny puts on the elevation of the moment is much diminished when she turns to find that Edmund is looking at her rival and her famous harp, himself enraptured by a sentimental scene that could have come straight out of Madame de Staël's *Corinne* (1807) or Sidney Owenson's *Wild Irish Girl* (1806).

Austen comments adversely on all the writers using sentimental, romantic motifs, be they conservative, liberal or radical. She felt herself 'Stout' against anything written by Jane West (28 September 1814), the most extreme female conservative novelist of the early nineteenth century. But she was just as stout against the later expressive writers, female equivalents of the Romantic poets about whose lofty aspirations and postures she was extremely sceptical. She dismissed Byron: 'read the corsair and mended my petticoat', while she wrote to her sister of Sidney Owenson's new novel in January 1809: 'We have only read the Preface yet; but her Irish Girl does not make me expect much. – If the warmth of her Language could affect the Body it might be worth reading in this weather.'[31]

The main accoutrement of Sidney Owenson's unappreciated wild Irish girl was the harp, that romantic symbol of sentimental femininity. In this high romance the hero is drawn to scale vertical castle walls by its sounds, exclaiming after his ascent at 'the "white rising of her hands upon the harp"; the half-drawn veil, that imperfectly discovered the countenance of a seraph; the moonlight that played round her fine form, and partially touched her drapery with its silver beam – her attitude! her air!'[32] Mary Crawford might have been trying for some such electrifying effect in the parsonage of Mansfield five years later, but had little chance with such a spoilsport creator.

For by then the harp was a veritable trademark of sentimental romance, occurring most famously of all in Madame de Staël's *Corinne*, which shares many characteristics with Sidney Owenson's book. Staël's novel tells of an exotic, unconventional, witty and harp-playing young woman, who like Hays' Emma Courtney announces her love first. She is not entirely English, and proves so unconventional that her lover pays court to her conventional sister, whom he then marries. He is unhappy and after a final reunion with Corinne she dies. Shortly after *Corinne* appeared, Burney published *The Wanderer* (1814), giving her heroine Juliet some of Corinne's characteristic abilities at music. But the feminine Juliet learns that her harp-playing, though exquisite, is of no value in a world of work and duty and it will not with propriety gain her a decent living. The more radical part of *Corinne*, the plea for women's right to autonomous desire and significance, is sheered off into the masculine and eccentrically outspoken Elinor, who proposes to the hero, tries romantic suicide not as abject surrender but as a female right and is in the end routed but by no means tamed. Throughout the book her fiery rhetoric, though denounced, is given much space, and a modern reader, used now to reading against the grain, might well find *The Wanderer* in two ideological minds. These two last novels are in plot something like *Mansfield Park* if the author had decided to applaud the harp-playing Mary Crawford and had intended setting her perfections off against the narrow rigidity of the country house. It seems to me possible to see Austen's work as partly an answer to this romantic permutation of sensibility, yet another swipe at unreasonable expectations and the notion that relationships can be so romantic and valuable that they may be regarded as transcendental.

As the historical feminist studies with which I began suggest, Austen is a more specifically political figure than earlier ahistorical feminist criticism had admitted. But these historical studies have not sufficiently allowed Austen to dissent from certain views and efforts of her times with which modern feminism has broadly been in sympathy. Austen turned her harshness on all party and personal political positions when they were tinged with simplicity, and her opposition to sensibility and sentimental techniques made her an uneasy ally of the sort of Regency conservatism she seemed most of the time to profess, inevitably forcing her to avoid too fixed an agenda. At the same time this opposition separated her from the company of women writers wanting to express for women both political and personal desire. The honesty that opposed the hope of sensibility – that people are good underneath some unfortunate social patina and therefore universally educable – and the specifically feminine fantasy that desire can and should be openly avowed, was a useful refiner of that sensibility, however personally and politically effective its crude employment might be. If Austen would not on the one hand assent to the naïvety required for revolutionary change or any decided amelioration of personal and social conditions, she would not on the other settle comfortably into the pieties of home and hearth. She remained always the poker of the sceptical fire, suggesting that change might make things worse but that things might already be deplorable, that children were not always loved or deserving of love, and that oppressed women might be as bitter or bad as dominating men and might do well for themselves and society by keeping their honest feelings under control.

Cambridge, 1989

Notes

1 F. R. Leavis, *The Great Tradition* (London: Chatto & Windus, 1948), and Lionel Trilling, 'Mansfield Park', in *The Opposing Self* (New York: Viking, 1959).
2 See G. H. Lewes, 'The novels of Jane Austen', repr. in B. C. Southam (ed.), *Jane Austen: the critical heritage* (London: Routledge, 1968), p. 160, and 'Personalities', in *Collected Essays of Virginia Woolf* (London: Hogarth

Press), II, p. 276. For a discussion of Woolf's complex attitude to Jane Austen, see chapter 9.

3 Sandra Gilbert and Susan Gubar, *The Madwoman in the Attic: the woman writer and the nineteenth-century literary imagination* (New Haven: Yale University Press, 1979), p. 112.

4 In this context, see also Tony Tanner's *Jane Austen* (London: Macmillan, 1986) which argued that what mattered in Austen was not 'content' but her 'moral relation to language'. He made no reference to the major women political writers of her time and asserted that 'Jane Austen's fiction just does not include or examine a hero or heroine whose "individual fate" becomes "bound up" with matters and movements of wide public and historical significance' (p. 6).

5 See, for example, Mary Poovey's *The Proper Lady and the Woman Writer: ideology and style in the works of Mary Wollstonecraft, Mary Shelley, and Jane Austen* (Chicago: University of Chicago Press, 1984).

6 *Persuasion* (London: Oxford University Press, 1965), p. 68.

7 *Persuasion*, pp. 50–1.

8 *Memoir of Lady Warwick: also her diary from AD 1666 to 1667* (London: Religious Tracts Society, 1847).

9 Marilyn Butler, *Jane Austen and the War of Ideas* (Oxford: Oxford University Press, 1975). This book was the first to insist on the systematic discussion of the *female* literary and political context of Austen

10 Margaret Kirkham, 'The Austen portraits and the received biography', and 'Feminist irony and the priceless heroine of *Mansfield Park*', in *Jane Austen: new perspectives*.

11 *Jane Austen: women, politics and the novel* (Chicago: University of Chicago Press, 1987), p. xxi.

12 Alison Sulloway, *Jane Austen and the Province of Womanhood* (Philadelphia: University of Pennsylvania Press, 1989), p. xix.

13 Mary Evans, *Jane Austen and the State* (London: Tavistock, 1987), pp. ix–x.

14 I have argued this case more fully in *Sensibility* (London: Methuen, 1986) and *The Sign of Angellica: women, writing and fiction* (London: Virago, 1989).

15 See, for example, Hélène Cixous in 'The laugh of the Medusa,' *Signs* I (summer 1976), pp. 875–93, and Lucy Irigaray in *Le Speculum de l'autre femme* (Paris: Minuit, 1974).

16 Mary Hays, *Memoirs of Emma Courtney* (New York: Garland, 1974), II, p. 123.

17 Tanner, *Jane Austen*, p. 6.

18 Q. D. Leavis, 'Jane Austen and a changing society', *Collected Essays*, p. 59.

19 For a full discussion of the stern depiction of the family in *Sense and Sensibility*, see Johnson's *Jane Austen: women, politics and the novel*, pp. 50–5.

20 *Mansfield Park* (London: Oxford University Press, 1966), pp. 472 and 473.

21 I have argued this case more fully in *Women's Friendship in Literature* (New York: Columbia University Press, 1980).

22 *Sense and Sensibility* (Oxford: Oxford University Press, 1987),pp. 27 and 344. See Angela Leighton, 'Sense and silences: reading Jane Austen again', in *Jane Austen: new perspectives*, pp. 128–41.

23 An interesting discussion of the relationship of Austen's novels to Marivaux's work occurs in Evelyn Farr's M.Phil. thesis on Jane Austen, London University, 1989.

24 Marilyn Butler made this point more fully in a lecture on women writers given at Cambridge University in Michaelmas Term 1989.

25 *Northanger Abbey* (London: Oxford University Press, 1965), p. 38.

26 *Minor Works* (Oxford: Oxford University Press, 1982), p. 390.

27 *Minor Works*, p. 102.

28 See Johnson, *Jane Austen: women, politics and the novel*, pp. 64–5.

29 *Sense and Sensibility*, p. 378.

30 Alison Sulloway argues that Colonel Brandon's rhetoric differs from that of Austen's other secular males in being close to the unctuous tones of the disapproved sentimental conduct-book writer, James Fordyce, *Jane Austen and the Province of Womanhood*, p. 44.

31 *Jane Austen's Letters to her Sister Cassandra and Others* (London: Oxford University Press, 1969), 28 September 1814; January 1809.

32 *The Wild Irish Girl* (London: Pandora, 1986), p. 43.

9 Who's afraid of Jane Austen?

In her essay on George Eliot, Virginia Woolf wrote of the heroines that 'the ancient consciousness of woman, charged with suffering and sensibility, and for so many ages dumb, seems in them to have brimmed and overflowed and uttered a demand for something – they scarcely know what – for something that is perhaps incompatible with the facts of human existence.'[1] Suffering and sensibility characterize women for Virginia Woolf, and her reading of their literature is marked by the expectation. In *A Room of One's Own*, her longest description of her female precursors, sensitive women writers are carried relentlessly through suffering to death. Witches evoke the woman poet 'who dashed her brains out on the moor or moped and mowed about the highways crazed with the torture that her gift had put her to'. When Virginia Woolf fabricates her own female artists, they are similarly doomed. Judith Shakespeare, the 'wonderfully gifted sister' of William, passes archetypally through seduction to suicide.[2]

In other essays Virginia Woolf treats individual women extensively, and her choice is often of the odd and unconventional, those thought mad, like the 'fantastic and fastidious' Duchess of Newcastle, or bad, like Aphra Behn. Caught in the rush and gush of her prose, the women sob, rage and suffer, now heroic and vital, now silenced by the needs and sounds of patriarchy. They usually write, but they are not primarily writers and their written work forms a kind of preliterature to the art of woman which Virginia Woolf is presumed now to be creating, a pre-text for her text.

The biographical sketches, written over many years and mostly reprinted in the two *Common Readers*, are partly idiosyncratic, partly typical of the critical and journalistic writing of her period. They are entertaining, readable, impressionistic, sure in judgment, like the portraits of her friend Lytton Strachey, and memorable in metaphor and phrase. Reading several, one is struck by the prose, not the personalities, the phrase that catches, not the woman caught.

Indeed the women seem to merge into each other. Virginia Woolf isolates them from their times, leaving out a history of kings and culture, which she regards as male, and the female subculture of particular women. Her characters exist in their own small tableaux, suddenly and individually illuminated. They are not connected, nor are they consecutive; neither spatial nor temporal relations are allowed them. They live similarly and apart in the Woolfian present tense.

In her sketches Woolf aims to discover a moment, an image or a stance which exhibits and exposes the life and personality of her character. So Madame de Sévigné is caught in a central relationship: she loved her daughter, comments Virginia Woolf, 'as an elderly man loves a young mistress who tortures him' (III: 67). For Harriette Wilson, the discovery is of a moment – when at fifteen she crossed from respectability to freedom and ineradicable impropriety. In Woolf's words, 'at once, the instant her foot touched those shifting sands, everything wobbled; her character, her principles, the world itself – all suffered a sea change' (III: 228).[3]

In 'The Art of Biography' and 'The New Biography' Virginia Woolf wrestles with the problems of the genre, with fact, fiction and fictionalized fact, and with the presence of the author. In 'The Art of Biography' she ties her biographers to fact and sees them opposing the fiction-writers, but in 'The New Biography' she admits the distinction is unclear. The light of personality is the biographer's business, and to catch it 'facts must be manipulated'. Although she stresses their integrity and is uneasy at Harold Nicolson's mixing of fact and fiction in his biographies, she is yet fascinated by the ability of this mixture to transmit personality effectively. 'He does not cumber himself with a single fact about them,' she writes of his subjects. 'He waits till they have said or done something characteristic and then he pounces on it with glee' (IV: 233). And the method has other implications, for, if it can deliver its subject's personality, it can also catch its author's; it is this aspect of the new biography that strikes Virginia Woolf most strongly: 'By the end of the book', she says, again of Nicolson, 'we realize that the figure which has been most completely and most subtly displayed is that of the author.' Fact and fiction mingle to create character and author – both become 'at once real and imaginary' (IV: 233).

Virginia Woolf writes evaluatively, as though Harold Nicolson's method were external to her, but in fact it is very close to her own. In her sketches fact is manipulated to expose personality of a particular kind. The women become what Virginia Woolf needs them to be, female heroes or distressed ladies of sensibility, and they write at her dictation. With this method, they do not express themselves so much as they express their author; they become excuses for the reader to watch the musing of Virginia Woolf's mind and see her inspiriting herself with images.

An example is Mary Wollstonecraft. It is difficult to judge exactly what Virginia Woolf knew of her subject, but she had read William Godwin's *Memoirs* of his wife and some of Wollstonecraft's works. Other biographies and papers were available, but she chose to ignore them, and the woman she creates is often freed from fact. Wollstone-craft appears first as hero, forced into the fight through childhood injustice. So Virginia Woolf takes on trust the formative incident of the young girl lying on the landing to guard the mother from the father's wrath, an incident rather close to a famous one in Rousseau, whom Wollstonecraft much admired. One sister in the narrative does duty for another, and, because her subject is for Virginia Woolf essentially alone, it matters not a whit whether it is Eliza or Everina who bites at her wedding ring, or whether she is miserable when being married or afterwards. Mary Wollstonecraft's own misery is supported by Virginia Woolf's exaggeration: so she travels from home to the humiliation of governessing with no stop for her own school, and her father, once a gentleman, becomes simply a farmer, and the red face and dirty hair of his dishonoured old age mark his earlier manhood as well. Wollstonecraft becomes the creature of injustice, the fighting feminist who asserts ringingly, 'I never yet resolved to do anything of consequence that I did not adhere readily to it', not the wavering woman who lamented that she would remain a fool to the end of her days. Then the female hero goes to France and grows all suffering and sensibility, too much so, and the artist Virginia Woolf reduces her two suicide attempts to one. The rather prickly woman who unsettled her lover's vulgar dinner table with her criticisms of his guests becomes a passionate lady in distress, and the problematic relationship with Imlay is caught by one of those memorable images with which Virginia Woolf fixes and simplifies her material and imposes herself all at once: 'Tickling minnows, he had hooked a dolphin, and the creature rushed him through the waters till he was dizzy' (III: 193–9).

Mary Wollstonecraft, the complex, self-pitying, insensitive, brave, and thinking woman, becomes the Virginia Woolf hero, now fighting, now suffering. It is an inspiring and noble portrait, made possible for Woolf mainly by her own artistic superiority to her subject and her readers' assumed ignorance of the facts.

Mary Wollstonecraft and Madame de Sévigné write, but they are not artists in Virginia Woolf's sense; they are unconcerned with their craft and with form and they need not be judged by standards of art. Indeed, their thrusting and vital personalities, so much praised by Virginia Woolf, are not for the artist and, when she writes of the craft of writing, it is usually to male artists that she looks. Her views on art, which resemble those of her Bloomsbury contemporaries Clive Bell and Roger Fry, are reiterated throughout her criticism. Briefly, she follows Coleridge, Pater, and Henry James in stressing the aesthetic value of art and the closeness of critic and artist – 'Indeed, it seems impossible for anyone who is not actually dealing with the problems of art to know the nature of them' – although she does not go as far as Pater in seeing criticism itself as an art.[4] Like Henry James, she regards the work as a living, coherent unit. 'A novel', wrote James in *The Art of Fiction*, 'is a living thing, all one and continuous, like any other organism, and in proportion as it lives will it be found . . . that in each of the parts there is something of each of the other parts.'[5] With such a concept, polemics, preaching and personality must all be pushed aside. A writer, Virginia Woolf stresses in an essay on Gissing, should not use personal suffering to rivet the reader's sympathy and curiosity; imagination loses its sweep and power and becomes petty and personal when limited to considering a particular case demanding sympathy.[6]

Yet in one respect the writer's situation must (sadly) intrude on the writing. In 'The Niece of an Earl' Virginia Woolf writes that 'the English novelist in particular suffers from a disability which affects no other artist to the same extent. His work is influenced by his birth. He is fated to know intimately, and so to describe with understanding, only those who are of his own social rank' (I: 221). Class inevitably signs art, then, but other externals should be rigidly controlled.

The women writers Virginia Woolf discusses were chosen for the pain and personality they expressed, for not sticking to what they knew, and for demanding something 'perhaps incompatible with the facts of human existence'. Women who wrote in the past, then, seem excluded from the group, writers as artists.

Across this antithesis falls Jane Austen, who refuses to be a fighting hero or a distressed heroine, whose small amount of public life is

publicly known, and who, ignoring the Woolfian categories, composed *Sense and Sensibility* instead of 'Suffering and Sensibility'. Jane
Austen is the first indubitably great woman writer in English,
whether one looks back through F. R. Leavis's great moral tradition
or through Virginia Woolf's and Henry James's great aesthetic one.
It was inevitable, then, that Virginia Woolf as a woman and an artist
should tangle with her great precursor. In *The Anxiety of Influence*,
Harold Bloom has described the struggle in literary history as 'a
battle between strong equals, father and son as mighty opposites,
Laius and Oedipus at the crossroads'.[7] Ignoring the strident masculinity and simplification of this formula, one can find it relevant to
the relationship of Virginia Woolf and Jane Austen. If, to write at all,
Woolf had to nullify her eminent Victorian father, Leslie Stephen –
'His life would have entirely ended mine', she wrote, speculating
what would have happened had he lived – to write as a woman she
had to come to terms with the mother of writers, Jane Austen.
'Revision – the act of . . . seeing with fresh eyes, of entering an old
text from a new critical direction' – Adrienne Rich calls 'an act of
survival'.[8]

II

Like King Charles's head, Jane Austen is always intruding. She
functions in Woolf's essays as a talisman or counter, separated from
the scrutiny she suffers elsewhere. For although Virginia Woolf
reacts against the Arnoldian touchstone system, modified and
adopted by her father in his criticism, she herself is rather apt to hit
writers – especially the much despised Edwardian trio of Wells,
Galsworthy and Bennett – with the names of the sacred dead.[9] Of
these Jane Austen is usually the only woman, coming with Dickens,
Carlyle and Macaulay to belittle the moderns and provide 'that
solace, that security, that sense that the human heart does not
change. . . .' (II: 263). Elizabeth Bennet will always defeat Arnold
Bennett.

Elsewhere Austen represents with Trollope 'sober reality' or with
Peacock comic genius. When gender is at issue, she is always one of
the big four, with George Eliot and Charlotte and Emily Brontë. She
even enters sometimes with Stendhal and Chekhov as a creator of
real characters or with Turgenev as the pure artist. But usually she is
not ranged with foreigners; in her essay 'The Russian Point of View',
Virginia Woolf distinguishes British from Russian novelists, and her

summary of the former could read as a description of Jane Austen.
Where Russians worry over souls and greath truths, notes Virginia
Woolf, the British discourse on class and forms, and incline to satire,
looking not at the individual but at society.

On her own, Jane Austen most commonly signifies perfection – a
hard, forbidding quality beside the touchstone wit of Meredith, the
range of Thackeray or the 'intellectual power' of Tolstoy. Perhaps
Woolf comes closest to catching it when she speaks of an Austen
successor and mediator for herself, Henry James. 'All great writers',
she remarks of him, 'have . . . an atmosphere in which they seem
most at their ease and at their best, a mood of the great general mind
which they interpret and indeed almost discover, so that we come to
read them rather for that than for any story or character or scene of
separate excellence' (I: 270).

Jane Austen fulfils all Virginia Woolf's requirements for the great
artist. First, she does not preach. In *A Room of One's Own*, commenting on women writers, Woolf exclaims: 'What genius in the midst of
that purely patriarchal society to hold fast to the thing as they saw it
without shrinking. Only Jane Austen did it and Emily Brontë. It is
another feather, perhaps the finest, in their caps. . . . Of all the
thousand women who wrote novels then, they alone entirely ignored
the perpetual admonition of the eternal pedagogue – write this, think
that.'[10] She reiterated the point in 'Women and Fiction': 'The genius
of Jane Austen and Emily Brontë is never more convincing than in
their power to ignore . . . claims and solicitations and to hold on
their way unperturbed by scorn or censure. But it needed a very
serene or a very powerful mind to resist the temptation to anger'
(II: 144).

Secondly, Jane Austen has no personal life in her novels. She does
not insist on self. Like the Greeks and Shakespeare, she comes with
little baggage. We do not know her as we know Keats in letters or
poetry, and our judgement cannot be clouded by our response to the
woman. In a review of an anecdotal book on Jane Austen, Virginia
Woolf attacks those critics who escape a proper responsibility by
delving into biographical irrelevancies: 'Only to hear Jane Austen
saying nothing in her natural voice when the critics have been
debating whether she was a lady, whether she told the truth,
whether she could read, whether she had personal experience of
hunting a fox is positively upsetting. We remember that Jane Austen
wrote novels. It might be worthwhile for their critics to read them.'[11]

Virginia Woolf's slightly priggish tone here cannot disguise that
she is being disingenuous, for to her it certainly mattered, as to 'the

critics', what status Jane Austen had. Indeed if there is one judgement that is repeated, it is that Jane Austen is a lady. In a piece on
Miss Mitford, Virginia Woolf muses on what a lady is and settles the
matter neatly by affirming: 'Jane Austen was a lady and . . . Charlotte
Brontë was not one' (IV: 105). In the essay 'On George Eliot', the
novelist is firmly put in her place as 'the granddaughter of a
carpenter', and Charlotte Brontë is frequently exposed to assure Jane
Austen's privilege, her lower-middle-class roots sticking uncouthly
through the soil of her genius (I: 198). We do not, Virginia Woolf tells
us, read Charlotte Brontë 'for a philosophic view of life – hers is that
of a country parson's daughter.' There is a hierarchy of parsonages,
it seems, and breeding will out, certainly in fiction. Jane Austen's
Emma knows exactly when she has said enough; Mrs Casauban
would have talked for an hour and bored her well-bred listener. 'One
hesitates to call Jane Eyre a lady', writes Virginia Woolf in 'The Niece
of an Earl', 'the Elizabeths and the Emmas of Miss Austen could not
possibly be taken for anything else' (I: 221). This class sureness of
Jane Austen leads to her third characteristic as an artist, a sureness
of tone and subject matter. A lady is never seduced out of her subject:
'The writer of perfect judgement and taste, like Jane Austen, does no
more than glance across the gulf' into the working classes (I: 220).

Although Austen is no artist-critic like Henry James and Virginia
Woolf herself, she is a woman aware of her craft. In 'The Anatomy
of Fiction', where Virginia Woolf describes ways by which a novelist
speaks of art, she finds Jane Austen teaching 'how exquisitely one
incident relieves another; how definitely, by not saying something,
she says it; how surprising, therefore, her expressive phrases when
they come. Between the sentences, apart from the story, a little shape
of some kind builds itself up' (II: 138).

Of such an artist as Jane Austen, impersonal, non-polemical,
properly classbound, classic and critically aware, one would expect
minute probing, but it is largely missing. Virginia Woolf's most
extended description of Jane Austen occurs in 'Phases of Fiction', but
her art is not really investigated and indeed it seems, like Topsy of
Uncle Tom's Cabin, to have just 'grow'd'. Austen is filed here with
Dickens among the character-mongers and comedians and praised
highly for her sense of organic form, so prized by Virginia Woolf,
and her brilliant use of dialogue; she works 'by means of perfectly
natural question and answer' (II: 75). Other mentions are even
vaguer. She is said to have written a female sentence, and to have
created a universal, perfect prose, but there is no analysis. Instead
there are images; an Austen book is like a shell, a gem, a crystal. Of

all great writers, Jane Austen is 'the most difficult to catch in the act
of greatness'. Austen herself exists in the essays without a tradition
that would give her meaning and without the novelists of sensibility
from Richardson to Fanny Burney who would give her satire point.
Indeed, while Virginia Woolf lavishes time on Defoe and Sterne
among eighteenth-century writers and on the Duchess of Newcastle
and Laetitia Pilkington among women, she is strangely silent on
Austen's major predecessors. Fanny Burney, it is true, does appear
but mainly in the light, charming piece about her flighty half-sister.

Virginia Woolf is uneasy in the presence of Jane Austen. She
renders her lack of ease by modifying those very characteristics
which made Austen the great artist, not merely the woman writer.
So her impersonality becomes aggravating, her non-polemical stance
passionless, her ladylikeness a limitation, and her artistic perfection
negation. And, like any minor woman writer, she is made to submit
to the Woolfian personality and sit in silence for her portrait while
the author sketches herself.

Impersonal art is reverenced in Shakespeare, but in Jane Austen it
seems almost impertinent. 'There is Jane Austen', writes Virginia
Woolf in her essay 'Personalities', 'thumbed, scored, annotated,
magnified, living almost within the memory of man, and yet as
inscrutable in her small way as Shakespeare in his vast one. She
flatters and cajoles you with the promise of intimacy and then, at the
last moment, there is the same blankness. Are those Jane Austen's
eyes or is it a glass, or mirror, a silver spoon held up in the sun? The
people whom one admires most as writers, then, have something
elusive, enigmatic, impersonal about them. . . . All has been distilled
into their books. The life is thin, modest, colourless, like blue
skimmed milk at the bottom of the jar. It is the imperfect artists who
never manage to say the whole thing in their books who wield the
power of personality over us' (II: 275). How can the 'small' Jane
Austen dare to be so reticent, she seems to ask.

Virginia Woolf's hostility at this control and reticence spills over
into belittling images. In the essay 'Reviewing', she had asked, 'Who
would not spout the family teapot in order to talk with Keats for an
hour about poetry, or with Jane Austen about the art of fiction?'
(II: 213). But in 'Personalities' she writes almost with a sneer, 'Here
is Jane Austen, a great writer as we all agree, but, for my own part, I
would rather not find myself alone in the room with her. A sense of
meaning withheld, a smile at something unseen, an atmosphere of
perfect control and courtesy mixed with something finely satirical,
which, were it not directed against things in general rather than

against individuals, would be almost malicious, would, so I feel, make it alarming to find at home' (II: 276). Here one feels the shudder as if the room of one's own were already uncomfortably and uncompromisingly occupied.

Virginia Woolf is eager to find Jane Austen at tea. Although she deplores critics who make Austen domestic and ladylike – in a 1936 letter to R. W. Chapman she stresses Austen's coarseness and her own annoyance at 'people who talk of her as if she were a niminy piminy spinster' – she frequently puts her behind the cups. She is watched sitting by the pot or picking out roses from the china. Woolf is never tempted, as she is with another artist, Christina Rossetti, to smash the teacup to reach her. In *Night and Day* Katherine Hilbury, pouring tea, reckons her activity occupies about a fifth of her consciousness.[12]

Henry James saw Austen as 'the brown thrush who tells his story from the garden bough'. Woolf makes the twittering image domestic: 'Humbly and gaily she collected the twigs and straws out of which the nest was to be made and placed them neatly together' (I: 148–9). But the motherly housewife metaphor will not stick and, referring to a contemporary comment, Woolf exclaims in her predecessor's accent, 'A wit, a delineator of character, who does not talk is terrific indeed!' (I: 144). And she comments, 'Sometimes it seems as if her creatures were born merely to give Jane Austen the supreme delight of slicing their heads off' (I: 149). The motherly domestic image fades before Medea in Hampshire.

When Woolf reads Jane Austen's letters, she decides that the reticence, the refusal to 'talk' mars the fiction. Considering why Austen failed to be 'much better than she was', she answers in her diary, 'Something to do with sex, I expect; the letters are full of hints that she suppressed half of her in her novels.'[13] We view her cosily at tea, then, because she refuses to let us see upstairs.

Virginia Woolf's irritation does not always take so open a form. Elsewhere she simply refuses to accept Jane Austen's secrecy. In her character sketches of women, she sought the typical moment or gesture that opened up the life and let in the critic. With Jane Austen she tries the same method, sometimes almost approaching success. In *A Room of One's Own*, she enters Jane Austen's circumscribed life: 'If Jane Austen suffered in any way from her circumstances it was in the narrowness of life that was imposed upon her. It was impossible for a woman to go about alone. She never travelled; she never drove through London on an omnibus or had luncheon in a shop by herself. But perhaps it was the nature of Jane Austen not to want what she had not. Her gift and her circumstances matched each other completely.'[14] Here Virginia Woolf veers off from her assessment and questions whether Jane Austen really belongs at all to the group of aspiring women – of Charlotte Brontë and herself, for instance – and empathy is lessened. Something in addition disturbs, for one is conscious that this need to break off, to swerve from empathy, may be due to Virginia Woolf's realization of her own smugness. For surely it is Virginia Woolf who travelled through London on an omnibus and had luncheon in a shop by herself.

A similar focus on the critic, not the criticized, comes from Woolf's decision to concentrate on Austen's juvenilia. Quoted in Virginia Woolf's prose, a passage renders Jane Austen a precocious child and her critic a kindly aunt reporting on her progress. ' "I die a martyr to my grief for the loss of Augustus. One fatal swoon has cost me my life. Beware of Swoons, Dear Laura . . . Run mad as often as you chuse, but do not faint. . . ." And on she rushed, as fast as she could write and quicker than she could spell to tell the incredible adventures of Laura & Sophia . . . ' (I: 145). Here the Austen quotation from *Love & Freindship*, one of the very few slightly extended examples, is distanced and made girlish by Virginia Woolf's own powerfully idiosyncratic prose.

Only in one respect does Virginia Woolf try for an extended time to make an Austen personality as woman. Significantly, it is not with the aid of the book always held up as the masterpiece – *Pride and Prejudice* – but through the last of Jane Austen's completed works, *Persuasion*, the one Virginia Woolf declared her favourite in a letter to David Cecil, and the only one not thoroughly revised by the author. Here, ignoring the irony that might reasonably connect this novel with Austen's other works and forgetting her own practice described by one critic as the rewriting of the same book 'of which she has given us nine different versions',[15] she insists on seeing the comment on Anne Elliot as entirely untinged with irony: 'She had been forced into prudence in her youth, she learned romance as she grew older.' The famous speech on female constancy, 'All the privilege I claim for my own sex . . . is that of loving longest, when existence or when hope is gone', is likewise given a single tone and made to prove the biographical fact that Jane Austen had loved – and presumably lost (I: 152).

So if the poker spinster Austen repulses, a more sympathetic lovelorn lady, created by Woolf, can attract. The same tendency to make a sympathetic image to which the critic can respond is present in Woolf's efforts to turn Jane Austen, who died at forty-two, into a

Keatsian tragic artist. For this image *Persuasion* becomes a kind of *Fall of Hyperion*, an unfinished transitional masterpiece, pointing towards radical change, and its author a nineteenth-century caterpillar about to emerge as a modernist butterfly. *Persuasion* turns into a new departure, with no links to its fictional predecessors. In this novel the sweet, sad influence of autumn, of suffering and sensibilbity, overwhelms the Austen fictional presence, and the sentimental leaves and dirty bottoms of *Sense and Sensibility* are forgotten.

Consideration of *Persuasion* leads Virginia Woolf to muse on what Jane Austen would have been had she lived, speculation employed also for Charlotte Brontë. In a letter of December 1932 she says confidently of Jane Austen, 'she died at 42: the best to come.' The 'best', not surprisingly, is rather close to the fiction of Virginia Woolf herself. Jane Austen's admitted great strengths – her sure syntax and her concise dialogue – give way to reflections in the Woolfian manner. 'Those marvellous little speeches which sum up, in a few minutes' chatter, all that we need to know of an Admiral Croft or a Mrs Musgrove for ever, that shorthand, hit-or-miss method, which contains chapters of analysis and psychology, would have become too crude to hold all that she now perceived of the complexity of human nature. She would have devised a method, clear and composed as ever, but deeper and more suggestive, for conveying not only what people say, but what they leave unsaid; not only what they are, but what life is' (I: 153). In other words, she would have become a kind of ur-Woolf.

The method of translation is employed not only in books Jane Austen did not write but also in those she did. Woolf, who professes organic form and savours works in their total integrity, rarely looks at an Austen book as a whole, trying instead in her criticism the method she used so bewitchingly in biography – the fictional investigation of a characteristic event. So *Mansfield Park*, that most hard-grained of novels, suddenly displays a Woolfian moment, and the critic insists that the reader follow her own code of female sensibility and ignore the comic:

it is midday in Northamptonshire; a dull young man is talking to rather a weakly young woman on the stairs as they go up to dress for dinner, with housemaids passing. But, from triviality, from commonplace, their words become suddenly full of meaning, and the moment for both one of the most memorable in their lives. It fills itself; it shines; it glows; it hangs before us, deep, trembling, serene for a second, next, the housemaid passes, and this drop, in which all the happiness of life has collected, gently subsides again to become part of the ebb and flow of ordinary existence. (I: 150)

This is far from the effect of the Austen passage to which Woolf must be referring. The elements are certainly the same. Fanny Price, jealous of Mary Crawford's hold over her much beloved cousin Edmund, is walking upstairs when she is hailed by him. The cousins speak of Fanny's tiredness and Edmund's relationship with Mary, and he admits his misgivings about her character. They are interrupted by a housemaid. Yet the tone and treatment of the incident are profoundly at odds with the Woolf rendition. In Austen, conversation is rarely trivial without being comic, and the sentences are precise and full of surface significance. Silences are motivated; Fanny either struggles for conventional utterance against her deep emotions or she is silent while considering what to say and breaks off when embarrassed at the clarity of her own warning: 'Excuse the liberty – but take care *how* you talk to me. Do not tell me any thing now, which hereafter you may be sorry for.' Edmund, replying as precisely, assesses the two women and adequately conveys his dual emotion: 'I can never be ashamed of my scruples; and if they are removed, it must be by changes that will only raise her [Mary's] character the more by the recollection of the faults she once had. You are the only being upon earth to whom I should say what I have said.'

The interruption by the housemaid is not arbitrary, as in Woolf, but indicated by both Fanny and her comic novelist:

They were now on the second floor, and the appearance of a housemaid prevented any further conversation. For Fanny's present comfort it was concluded perhaps at the happiest moment; had he been able to talk another five minutes, there is no saying that he might not have talked away all Miss Crawford's faults and his own despondence. But as it was, they parted with looks on his side of grateful affection, and with some very precious sensations on her's.[16]

Virginia Woolf's Jane Austen is dreamy and word-obsessed, and the encounter of the cousins becomes a kind of epiphany, but its effect is strangely insincere, with the moment taking more symbolic weight than it needs or can bear. At the end of *The Waves*, Bernard remembers when he and his friend first heard of the death of Percival and how they had compared him to a lily: 'So the sincerity of the moment passed; so it became symbolical. . . . Let us commit any blasphemy of laughter and criticism rather than exude this lily-sweet glue.'[17]

The co-opting of Jane Austen is only partial, and she can never enter the Woolfian prose completely. Most of the time the critic seems mildly irritated at the subject she cannot quite control. For example, she grumbles at Jane Austen's impersonality: 'Her absence has', writes Virginia Woolf, 'the effect of making us detached from her work and of giving it, for all its sparkle and animation, a certain aloofness and incompleteness' (II.76). The text, inhuman and inhumane, is standoffish. It is an interesting judgement, when one considers not only Virginia Woolf's critical bias towards the impersonal in art but also the overwhelming presence of Jane Austen as narrator in all her books, including the much misused *Persuasion*. Other women Woolf chooses to probe do express themselves – Mary Wollstonecraft or Dorothy Wordsworth, for example. In an essay on 'Aurora Leigh', she writes with a mixture of condescension and admiration: 'Mrs Browning could no more conceal herself than she could control herself' (I: 212).

Irritation is even clearer when Woolf contemplates Austen's lack of the polemics and passion which mark female texts from Charlotte Brontë to Virginia Woolf herself. Even the gothic novelist Ann Radcliffe, much mocked by male critics who venerate Austen, surpasses her great contemporary in feeling. 'Jane Austen might have done worse than take a leaf from Radcliffe's book', Virginia Woolf considers and, concluding that Austen travelled too far from feeling, wrote, 'I'm not sure I shan't lead a Radcliffe relief party.'[18]

Although Ann Radcliffe and other writers are sometimes cited to counter the passionless Austen presence, the usual opposite is Charlotte Brontë, blamed, in *A Room of One's Own*, for disturbing the text with her intrusive pain. When only art is in question, Charlotte Brontë is rebuked for her crudeness by a Jane Austen made subtle and multifaceted, but when, as Charlotte Brontë herself might have said, it is 'a question of the heart', then Jane Austen lacks the vehemence, the indignation and the genius of Brontë. Interestingly, Virginia Woolf blames Charlotte Brontë for her famous blindness to her great predecessor, while echoing it herself: 'Vice, adventure, passion were left outside.' By elevating suffering and sensibility, Charlotte Brontë's characteristics, Virginia Woolf makes Jane Austen seem tame and limited. In 'On Re-reading Novels', Charlotte Brontë lodges with the intoxicating novelists who surpass the cool Jane Austen in genius; only, Woolf admits, they can't quite express it all. Jane Austen 'with less genius for writing than Charlotte Brontë . . .

got infinitely more said.' Her lack of passion and preaching is predicated on her tame, inscrutable life. 'If Jane Austen had lain as a child on the landing to prevent her father from thrashing her mother, her soul might have burst with such a passion against tyranny that all her novels might have been consumed in one cry for justice' (III: 194).

Even in class stability, seemingly so much approved by Virginia Woolf, where Austen clearly overtops the ambiguous Brontë, she is sometimes disparaged. Virginia Woolf praises Jane Austen as a lady, and yet the praise is edged. Artistic judgements grow tinged with class and become trivialized. For example, Austen's values, like her social credentials, are termed 'impeccable', and her discretion, although praised, is a matter of fictional care and social correctness. Morality becomes not feeling and judgement but upper-middle-class good breeding. Class limits her subjects and confines her plots: 'There was the big house and the little house; a tea party, a dinner party, and an occasional picnic; life was hedged in by valuable connections and adequate incomes; by muddy roads, wet feet, and a tendency on the part of the ladies to get tired' (I: 149). Even her purity of form, a usual value in Woolf criticism, seems to concern class as much as artistry. Most of all, however, her class position connects with her lack of female feeling. 'In 'Outlines', the Jane Austen type of lady is described as reticent and avoiding open passion. Ladylikeness comes to preclude womanliness.

In fact Jane Austen seems thoroughly unwomanly, despite her position in Virginia Woolf's pantheon of women, and her activity mocks the generalizations. In *A Room of One's Own*, Woolf judged the possession of a room essential for a woman artist, and yet she notes almost testily that Austen 'had no separate study to repair to' and she quotes the remark of Austen's nephew, that 'most of the work must have been done in the general sitting-room, subject to all kinds of casual interruption.'[19] The female novel of the early nineteenth century is autobiographical, Virginia Woolf announces; yet Jane Austen, its greatest exponent, hides away her love life so resolutely that not even Virginia Woolf can find it out. The sentence, once delcared female in Jane Austen's hands, is forgotten when Virginia Woolf generalizes that writing is male and that women's use of it must be marked and marred by struggle and domination. Values, too, are patriarchal, inimical to a woman who must alter them and make new ones, which will, however, seem trivial and sentimental-ized. But Jane Austen is not sentimental and she shows no embar-rassment or discomfort at conventional values. About her art she is not vastly ladylike and she could not echo her admired Mary Brunton, who wrote of her horror of 'being suspected of literary aims', 'my dear, I would sooner exhibit as a ropedancer.'[20] At the same time she does not tout her art or kick against the limits, accepting with proper pride her own 'little bits . . . of Ivory'. In short, Jane Austen seems hardly a woman writer. If Virginia Woolf has an androgynous vision, as Carolyn Heilbrun and Nancy Bazin believe, the sexes must be for her in some sense polarized, initially at least.[21] Jane Austen seems, annoyingly, quite oblivious of this scheme. She is not androgynous, merely devoid of gender. Her artistic novels prove it, for otherwise she would, like Mary Wollstonecraft, have subsumed them into one passionate cry.

Virginia Woolf praises Jane Austen as an artist and stresses her perfection. Yet the praise is often strangely negative and the perfection a matter of limits. Even in the review of the anecdotal book, all laudatory of Austen, Woolf admires her for saying nothing. So, in the criticism of Brontë, Jane Austen succeeds by not having anger and, in the criticism of Gissing, by not expressing personal suffering. Even in the most extended and appreciative passage in 'Phases of Fiction' there is the tendency towards negation:

> The talk is not mere talk; it has an emotional intensity which gives it more than brilliance. Light, landscape – everything that lies outside the drawing room is arranged to illumine it. Distances are made exact; arrangements accurate. It is one mile from Meryton; it is Sunday and not Monday. We want all suspicions and questions laid at rest. It is necessary that the characters should lie before us in as clear and quiet a light as possible since every flicker and tremor is to be observed. Nothing happens, as things so often happen in Dickens, for its own oddity or curiosity, but with relation to something else. No avenues of suggestion are opened up, no doors are suddenly flung wider; the ropes which tighten the structure, since they are all rooted in the heart, are so held firmly and tightly. For, in order to develop personal relations to the utmost, it is important to keep out of the range of the abstract, the impersonal; and to suggest that there is anything that lies outside men and women would be to cast the shadow of doubt upon the comedy of their relationships and its sufficiency. . . . But personal relations have limits, as Jane Austen seems to realize by stressing their comedy. Everything, she seems to say, has, if we could discover it, a reasonable summing up. (II: 75–6)

The phrases here are lined with dissatisfaction. Perfection, always allowed, is becoming a gloss for meanness and, as the passage goes on, the great sureness, Jane Austen's chief merit, is undercut by the tentativeness she inspires in the critic-respondent. Her emphatic 'is' turns into 'seems' in two adjacent sentences. The dissonant final comment with its double embedding, 'she seems to say' and 'if we could discover it', renders its subject limited, misled and misleading, above all prosaic. For, when the Austen smoothness is reduced to this roughness, nothing, Virginia Woolf 'seems to say', is left.

Perfection is dull. In the essay 'How It Strikes a Contemporary', Virginia Woolf laments the 'unabashed tranquillity' of great books, found 'in page after page of Wordsworth and Scott and Miss Austen which is sedative to the verge of somnolence' (II: 158). An example of the limits of perfection, which seems to preclude doubting subtlety and awareness, comes from Jane Austen's unfinished novel, *The Watsons*:

> From what, then, arises that sense of security which gradually and delightfully and completely overcomes us? It is the power of their belief – their conviction, that imposes itself upon us. . . . They know the relations of human beings towards each other and towards the universe. Only believe . . . that a nice girl will instinctively try to soothe the feelings of a boy who has been snubbed at a dance, and then, if you believe it implicitly and unquestioningly, you will not only make people a hundred years later feel the same thing, but you will make them feel it as literature. For certainty of that kind is the condition which makes it possible to write. (II: 159)

Jane Austen's artistic limitations are partly her own fault and partly the result of her position in history, for Virginia Woolf saw the novel as a progressive form taking in more and more of life. The limitations are expressed in metaphor, and the books are trapped in those same domestic and ordered images which Woolf used for Austen the woman and which the detractors have always employed for the prose. Sir Walter Scott, a partial admirer, started the tradition with his impression of Jane Austen's cottages and meadows, and Charlotte Brontë added hostility, making the Austen fictional world a 'carefully-fenced, highly-cultivated garden, with neat borders and delicate flowers; but . . . no open country, no fresh air, no blue hill, no bonny beck'.[22] Emerson irascibly saw Austen's novels in terms of an 'English boarding house', pinched, narrow, sterile, and he judged suicide 'more respectable'.[23]

For Virginia Woolf, Austen's art is one of enclosure. It is a domestic garden beside the lighthouse of her own art. In *Between the Acts* there is a blue that never touched a garden, a vision that an Austen could never catch. A passage in *To the Lighthouse* expresses something of the geographical effect: 'It was all familiar; this turning, that stile, that cut across the fields. Hours he would spend thus, with his pipe, of an evening, thinking up and down and in and out of the old familiar lanes and commons . . . but at length the lane, the field, the common, the fruitful nut-tree and the flowering hedge led him on to that further turn of the road where he dismounted always, tied his horse to a tree, and proceeded on foot alone. He reached the edge of the lawn and looked out on the bay beneath.'[24] Jane Austen knows the land but not the bay. Remove the hedges from Austen's world, Woolf writes, and how much remains?

Even in small touches, Jane Austen's effect seems synonymous with domesticity and limit. Her life is the residue of skimmed milk and, in a letter of 1936, Virginia Woolf sees her lecture on Jane Austen as a new fold to that so often neatly folded. Austen is clean linen and neatnes, a sorry fate for a writer who in *Northanger Abbey* mocked us all with her laundry list.

III

So why is Virginia Woolf so ambivalent and uneasy? There are, no doubt, many reasons, some to do with her own art, some with her life, and a few, very few, to do with Jane Austen herself, who as the author of the six novels largely disappears from Virginia Woolf's pages.

As noted, Jane Austen fails to fit in with Woolf's views on women writers: women are marked by suffering and sensibility, and yet *Pride and Prejudice* shows no signs that her circumstances have harmed Austen's work in the slightest. Indeed she seems annoyingly comfortable within the patriarchy that gives Virginia Woolf and her sister authors so much trouble.

Austen fails in particular to accord with Virginia Woolf herself, and the criticism throws the reader back not only to Virginia Woolf's essay personality but also to her own life and fiction. Virginia Woolf rebukes Jane Austen as woman and writer; so Jane Austen seems to rebuke Virginia Woolf.

First is the matter of class. Here there is some ambiguity in Virginia Woolf. Although securely upper middle class from her parents, and related through them to major administrators and writers of her time, she would have to move only a generation or two backwards to remove the 'upper'. In addition, her husband, being Jewish, was always slightly outside the British class system, however intellectually aristocratic he might have seemed.[25] In the matter of class, Virginia Woolf wished to have her cake and eat it. Despite being found unladylike by Henry James, she felt herself a lady and of high class through intellect and social standing.[26] In an embarrassing letter, published as 'Middlebrow', she tries to define class in intellectual terms, although the concept is shot through with social consideration. Insisting on the term 'highbrow' for herself, she makes a personality of a woman who breakfasts in bed, derives from drunken, good-living forebears, and boasts an aunt who resides in India. She mocks the middlebrow and middle class who, like Jane Austen but without her breeding, pour tea and who reside in inferior parts of London: 'If your reviewer, or any other reviewer, dares hint that I live in South Kensington, I will sue him for libel' (II: 203).

Woolf escaped into Bloomsbury, where hierarchy was to be based on merit and art, but she took along her social rank. So she can both fulminate against snobbishness and show all its marks. Her pronouncements are imbued with class, and her famous statement that 'in or about December, 1910, human character changed' is entirely interpreted through social status: the Victorian cook in the depths of the house gives way to the Georgian servant, democratically in and out of the drawing room (I: 320). Jane Austen is as class-bound as her successor, but she knows nothing of it, and Virginia Woolf almost envies her this ignorance.

Jane Austen and Virginia Woolf share gender and childlessness; Jane Austen – Miss Austen, as Woolf tends to name her – went further by failing even to marry, so affronting D. H. Lawrence among others with her spinsterhood. Virginia Woolf was, it appears, happily married, and she seems both proud of and uneasy at her state. She admires married women like Mrs Ramsay and is often merciless to single ones like Doris Kilman; yet she asks the question in *Orlando*: 'If one still wished, more than anything in the whole world, to write poetry, was it marriage?'[27]

In addition, her relationship with Leonard was more or less sexless. According to her biographer Quentin Bell, she felt no physical attraction for him, and he was cold. Her choice of women for discussion may reflect a deep need to probe a companionable, not a sexual relationship: she writes on Swift and Stella, on Cowper and Lady Austen, and on William and Dorothy Wordsworth. In each there is the giftedness and subordination of the woman, and in each there is sexual refusal. In each of these relationships one of the partners went mad, as did Virginia Woolf herself beside Leonard in her companionable marriage.

Madness in women is a form of silencing. Other female writers Virginia Woolf chose to describe were silenced or overwhelmed, not by madness, but by fatherly images or marriages, rather as Virginia Woolf feared she might have been had her father lived: Dorothy Osborne, subsumed in Temple; Maria Allen, tamed by an exacting husband; and Sara Coleridge, endlessly editing her father. Jane Austen is not silenced, mad or married. She is overwhelmed by no man.

But she did love her sister, although Virginia Woolf is strangely silent about this. Indeed Woolf tends, with the exception of the piece on Jane Carlyle and Geraldine Jewsbury, to underplay female ties, as she does in the essay on Mary Wollstonecraft, or concentrate on unequal ones like that of Selina Trimmer and her pupil. Yet her niece Angelica Garnett noted her desire to be loved by her sister Vanessa and her demand for 'various kinds of kisses', and she describes the 'very intimate, complicated and somewhat jealous relationship with Vanessa who was a second mother to her and whom she worshipped'.[28] By what Jane Austen failed to do, then, and by what she did, Virginia Woolf seems strangely shadowed.

Jane Austen intrudes into Virginia Woolf's own writing. A review of Jane Austen's letters in the *Times Literary Supplement* of 1932 was thought by some to be by Virginia Woolf, for E. M. Forster, its author, had appropriated her style. A friend called the review her 'very best', though Virginia Woolf testily pronounced it 'feeble in the extreme'.

More important, Austen invades the novels. An artist should be unpolemical, according to Woolf; yet she herself cannot be judged so if one considers the *Three Guineas*, the psychiatrists Holmes and Bradshaw of *Mrs Dalloway*, or Lily Briscoe crying out about her painting, 'And it would never be seen; never be hung even, and there was Mr Tansley whispering in her ear, "Women can't paint, women can't write. . . ."'[29] In her diary Woolf worried over the intrusion of the ego into her fiction; in 1920 she wrote: 'Whether I'm sufficiently mistress of things – that's the doubt . . . I suppose the danger is the damned egotistical self.' And she expresses her fear: 'Have I the power of conveying the true reality? Or do I write essays about myself?'[30] Her novels were labelled works of sensibility; excessive sensibility was the butt of Jane Austen's six novels. Woolf distrusted the quality in theory – as her discussion of Sterne shows –

yet the women she praises display excess of it and her diary and novels prove her fear of falling victim herself.

Virginia Woolf was conscious of writing modern fiction, but the elements of the traditional novel, however crude – precise plot, detail, character and dialogue – pressed on her achievement. She was criticized for inattention to detail and she snapped back that one expects accuracy from Jane Austen – and, one might add, the precise biographer Leslie Stephen – but not from a writer like herself who was 'trying to do something else'. The traditional novel had to be fought; she called her books an elegy (*To the Lighthouse*), a play-poem (*The Waves*), and an essay-novel (*The Years*). She avoided plot and character – 'little snapshot pictures of people', she wrote contemptuously – where Jane Austen was supreme. By so doing she invited criticism, and E. M. Forster obliged: 'She dreams, designs, jokes, invokes, observes details, but she does not tell a story or weave a plot, and – can she create character? That is her problem's centre'; and again with the inevitable Austen slap, 'She could seldom so portray a character that it was remembered afterwards in its own account, as Emma is remembered.'[31]

The Austen image threatened the younger Virginia Woolf, who was mortified to find critics yoking them together. In 1919 she confided to her diary about Katherine Mansfield's review of *Night and Day* that she found the comparison with Jane Austen spiteful. 'A decorous elderly dullard she describes me', Woolf complains, 'Jane Austen up to date. Leonard supposes that she let her wish for my failure have its way with her pen.'[32]

The comparison with Jane Austen seems to deliver failure, then. Unfortunately it is repeated. H. W. Massingham, writing on *Night and Day*, mocks its author's preoccupation with taxis and tea-drinking rather in the manner of Woolf on Austen, and he calls the four main characters 'Four Impassioned Snails'. Another reviewer answered Massingham's 'cutting paragraph', as Virginia Woolf called it, by supporting the Austen comparison. And yet clearly it is one Virginia Woolf feared. 'I had rather write in my own way of "Four Passionate Snails" than be, as Katherine Mansfield maintains, Jane Austen over again.'[33]

Certainly Woolf struggled to avoid the repetition, moving from the early Austen-invoking novels to the experiments of *To the Lighthouse* and *The Waves*. Yet Austen is always somehow there to mock; her perfection, so ambiguously appreciated in the criticism, rebukes the fiction, and ner nineteenth-century sense sobers the twentieth-century sensibility.

one must (we, in our generation must) renounce finally the achievement of the greater beauty; the beauty which comes from completeness, in such books as War and Peace, and Stendhal I suppose, and some of Jane Austen . . . Only now that I have written this, I doubt its truth. Are we not always hoping? . . . I was wondering to myself why it is that though I try sometimes to limit myself to the thing I do well, I am always drawn on and on, by human beings, I think, out of the little circle of safety, on and on, to the whirlpools; when I go under.[34]

Austen is to Woolf's text the context that limits and proves limits. Embraced imperfection is still simply imperfection, and the sensitive something Woolf seeks may indeed be 'incompatible with the facts of human existence'.

'Whatever "Bloomsbury" may think of JA., she is not by any means one of my favourites', Woolf admitted. 'I'd give all she ever wrote for half of what the Brontë's wrote – if my reason did not compel me to see that she is a magnificent artist.'[35] A diary entry is more plaintive; topics for discussion read: 'Jane Austen, novels, pessimism'.

New Brunswick, NJ, 1979

Notes

1 Virginia Woolf, *Collected Essays* (London: Hogarth Press, 1966), I: 204. References in the text are to these volumes.
2 Virginia Woolf, *A Room of One's Own* (London: Hogarth Press, 1929), p. 70.
3 For a discussion of this aspect of Virginia Woolf's biographies, see Josephine O'Brien Schaefer, 'Moments of vision in Virginia Woolf's biographies', *Virginia Woolf Quarterly*, 2, pp. 294–303
4 *Times Literary Supplement*, 21 December 1916, p. 623.
5 Henry James, *Essays in Modern Literary Criticism* (New York: Holt, Rinehart, 1961), p. 15.
6 For a description of Woolf's critical premises, see Mark Golman's *The Reader's Art: Virginia Woolf as literary critic* (The Hague: Mouton, 1976).
7 Harold Bloom, *The Anxiety of Influence* (New York: Oxford University Press, 1973), p. 26.
8 'When we dead awaken: writing as re-vision', *Adrienne Rich's Poetry* (New York: Norton, 1975), p. 90.
9 See Noel Annon, *Leslie Stephen: his thought and character in relation to his time* (Cambridge, MA.: Harvard University Press, 1952), pp. 249–55.
10 *A Room of One's Own*, p. 112.
11 *Times Literary Supplement*, 29 October 1920, p. 699.

12 *The Letters of Virginia Woolf* (London: Hogarth Press, 1946), VI: 87; Virginia Woolf, *Night and Day* (London: Duckworth, 1919), p. 1.
13 *Diary of Virginia Woolf*, ed. Anne Olivier Bell (London: Hogarth Press, 1977), V: 127.
14 *A Room of One's Own*, p. 102.
15 Jean Guiguet, *Virginia Woolf and Her Works* (New York: Harcourt, Brace & World, 1965), p. 196.
16 Jane Austen, *Mansfield Park* (Harmondsworth: Penguin, 1966), pp. 275–6.
17 Viriginia Woolf, *The Waves* (London: Hogarth Press, 1946), p. 188.
18 *The Letters*, III: 418.
19 *A Room of One's Own*, p. 100.
20 Anne K. Elwood, *Memoirs of the Literary Ladies of England* (London, 1843), II: 216.
21 See Carolyn Heilbrun, *Toward a Recognition of Androgyny* (New York: Knopf, 1973); Nancy Bazin, *Virginia Woolf and the Androgynous Vision* (New Brunswick: Rutgers University Press, 1973).
22 G. H. Lewes, 'The novels of Jane Austen', repr. in B. C. Southam, ed., *Jane Austen: the critical heritage* (London: Routledge & Kegan Paul, 1968), p. 160.
23 *Journals of Ralph Waldo Emerson: 1856–1863* (1913), ed. E. W. Emerson and W. E. Forbes, IX: 336–7.
24 Virginia Woolf, *To the Lighthouse* (Harmondsworth: Penguin), p. 51.
25 Claire Sprague, Introduction to *Virginia Woolf: a collection of critical essays* (Englewood Cliffs: Prentice-Hall, 1971), p. 3.
26 Leonard Woolf, *Sowing* (London: Hogarth Press, 1960), p. 107.
27 Virginia Woolf, *Orlando* (London: Hogarth Press, 1964), p. 238.
28 Quoted by Peter Lewis, *Sunday Telegraph*, 24 January 1982, pp. 6–7.
29 *To the Lighthouse*, p. 57.
30 *Diary*, II: 14.
31 E. M. Forster, 'Virginia Woolf', *Virginia Woolf: a collection of critical essays*, p. 19.
32 *Diary*, I: 314.
33 *Diary*, I: 316.
34 *Letters*, II: 599–600.
35 *Letters*, V: 127.

Index